DISTINCTION

OF

FICTION

DORRIT COHN

THE DISTINCTION OF FICTION

THE JOHNS HOPKINS

UNIVERSITY

PRESS

Baltimore and London

Johns Hopkins Paperbacks edition, 2000

2 4 6 8 9 7 5 3 1

The Johns Hopkins University Press

2715 North Charles Street

Baltimore, Maryland 21218-4363

www.press.jhu.edu

Library of Congress

Cataloging-in-Publication Data

will be found at the end of this book.

A catalog record for this book

is available from the British Library.

ISBN 0-8018-6522-0 (pbk.)

Contents

Preface   vii

1. Focus on Fiction   1

2. Fictional versus Historical Lives:
    Borderlines and Borderline Cases   18

3. Freud's Case Histories
    and the Question of Fictionality   38

4. Proust's Generic Ambiguity   58

5. Breaking the Code of Fictional Biography:
    Wolfgang Hildesheimer's *Marbot*   79

6. "I Doze and Wake":
    The Deviance of Simultaneous Narration   96

7. Signposts of Fictionality:
    A Narratological Perspective   109

8. The "Second Author"
    of *Death in Venice*   132

9. Pierre and Napoleon at Borodinó:
    Reflections on the Historical Novel   150

10. Optics and Power in the Novel   163

References   181

Index   193

Preface

The "distinction" that my title attributes to fiction is to be understood in two senses of the word: *uniqueness* and *differentiation*. This study aims to show that fictional narrative is unique in its potential for crafting a self-enclosed universe ruled by formal patterns that are ruled out in all other orders of discourse. This singularity, as I will try to show, depends on differences that can be precisely identified and systematically examined. First rehearsed on a far more limited scale in a Christian Gauss Seminar delivered at Princeton University, my argument advances by alternately opening theoretical perspectives and closing in on individual texts, both with a view to tracing borderlines between fictional and nonfictional—notably historiographic—narrative domains.

The critical climate of recent decades has tended to disregard these distinctive differences, successively leaning toward deconstructive attributions of fictionality to all manners of discourse and toward ideological emphases of overriding thematic issues. But if, as Paul Ricoeur says (after devoting some six-hundred pages to this subject in *Time and Narrative*), "the relation between fiction and history is assuredly more complex than we will ever be able to put into words," such disregard cannot make this problem disappear. One of my purposes in undertaking this study is to show that it remains with us even (and perhaps especially) in the face of certain postmodern practices that have pretended to efface generic borderlines.

My own words on this subject, even when they seek to articulate an encompassing theoretical vision, largely deal with the words that make up the texts we read. Building on the insights of narratology, the rigorous and systematic analysis of narrative language, they take this discipline in directions it has barely explored.

Though a number of its chapters are revised versions of articles published in professional journals and collective volumes, my book is unified by its abiding focus on the issue of fictionality. Its occasional reiterations are not merely aimed at emphasis but also designed to allow for the separate understanding of each chapter. Thus chapters that deal with individual works can be read without prior knowledge of the theoretically oriented chapter that underlies them and that they are (also) meant to illustrate. These reiterations often concern the ideas of the theorists who have—even when I disagree with them—nourished my own thinking, prime among them Käte Hamburger, Gérard Genette, and Philippe Lejeune.

The following preview of my book's sequential content will orient the reader toward the areas that correspond to his or her dominant interests: The opening chapter surveys the unsettling semantic multiplicity of the term *fiction* and explains why and how its literary-critical meaning needs to be limited to the genre of nonreferential narrative—a meaning to which the present study adheres throughout.

In Chapter 2 I propose a set of theoretical norms for segregating historical from fictional narratives that center on individual lives. I specify different criteria for separating biographies from their counterparts in third-person fiction and autobiographies from their counterparts in first-person fiction, while insisting that these borderlines are highlighted rather than effaced by borderline cases.

The four following chapters apply these criteria to works that have appeared to problematize and/or subvert them. Chapter 3 examines Freud's most famous case histories with a view to demonstrating their historical status in the face of the currently pervasive attribution of fiction-likeness to these texts. Chapter 4 confronts the unique equivocality of literature's most extensive narrative in the first-person singular, *A la Recherche du temps perdu,* whose critical reception has left it generically suspended between novel and autobiography. Chapter 5 takes up the curious case of Wolfgang Hildesheimer's *Marbot,* a work that applies a purely historical code to tell the life of a fictional participant in the English Romantic movement. Chapter 6 investigates the "abnormal" novelty of self-narrated novels that cast their text from first to last in the present tense, with J. M. Coetzee's *Waiting for the Barbarians* serving as the principal illustration.

Returning to a theoretical perspective, Chapter 7 addresses an essential issue not previously approached on narratological grounds: the overridingly distinctive nature of fictionality. It identifies three signposts that allow one to delimit fictional narrative from historiography: adherence to a bi-level story/discourse model that assumes emancipation from the enforcement of a referential data base; employment of narrative situations that open to inside views of the characters' minds; and articulation of narrative voices that can be detached from their authorial origin.

These signposts point the way to the readings that follow: of *Death in Venice* in Chapter 8 and of an episode from *War and Peace* in Chapter 9. The first of these takes Mann's novella as a paradigm for fictional works narrated by an unreliably biased voice that the reader is encouraged to disengage from its author's. The second takes Tolstoy's presentation of the Battle of Borodinó in *War and Peace* as a paradigm for the historical novel, a genre unmistakably distanced from historiography by being focalized on and by the characters present on the scene.

The concluding chapter projects the concerns of this study onto the contemporary critical scene. Focusing on the widespread tendency to ignore the formal complexity of the novel as a genre by applying to it the (Foucault-inspired) model of panoptic vision, it points up the misapprehensions that result from an oversimplifying correlation of discursive patterns and ideological interpretations.

Various moments of my book were substantially improved by suggestions from the anonymous scholar who read my manuscript for the Johns Hopkins University Press. The Proust chapter benefited greatly from discussion with my student Charitini Douvaldzi. My friends Thomas Pavel and Shlomith Rimmon-Kenan gave valuable advice and encouragement at crucial times. My son Stephen Cohn provided a professional publisher's wise counsel, my son Richard Cohn a fellow-academic's supportive understanding. I thank them all.

Chapters 2, 4, 7, and 10 correspond to articles first printed in *The Journal of Narrative Technique, Genre, Poetics Today,* and *New Literary History.* Chapter 3 initially appeared in *Telling Facts: History and Narration in Psychoanalysis,* edited by Joseph H. Smith and Humphrey Morris; Chapter 5, in *Traditions of Experiment from the Enlightenment to the Present,* edited by Nancy Kaiser and David E. Wellbery; Chapter 6, in *Tales and "their telling difference,"* edited by Herbert Foltinek, Wolfgang Riehle, and Waldemar Zacharasiewicz; and Chapter 8, in *Probleme der Moderne: Studien zur deutschen Literatur von Nietzsche bis Brecht,* edited by Benjamin Bennett, Anton Kaes, and William J. Lillyman.

I

Focus on Fiction

As the philosopher Hans Vaihinger remarked almost a century ago, "The word 'fiction' is subject to chaotic and perverse linguistic usage; even logicians employ it in different meanings, without taking the pains to define the term or to distinguish among its different meanings."[1] Divergences in the significance of the term are plainly visible from dictionary entries under fiction. Their only common denominator, it appears, is that they all designate "something invented"—a notion no less vaguely denotative than (though not exactly identical to) the word's Latin root, *fingere*, "to make or form." This divergence of meaning may also be sensed from a sampling of the many sometimes expressly paradoxical titles that feature the word in nominal or adjectival form: *The Art of Fiction* (Henry James); *Freud, Proust, and Lacan: Theory as Fiction* (Malcolm Bowie); *Fictional Truth* (Michael Riffaterre); "Notes toward a Supreme Fiction" (Wallace Stevens); *When Is Something Fiction?* (Thomas J. Roberts); *Factual Fictions* (Lennard J. Davis); *The Fictive and the Imaginary* (Wolfgang Iser); "The Writer's Audience Is Always a Fiction" (Walter Ong); *Fictions in Autobiography* (Paul John Eakin); *Fiction and Diction* (Gérard Genette); *The Fiction of Reality* (Zulfikar Ghose).

To come to terms with this term seems to me the first order of business for a book that once again uses the word *fiction* in its title, especially since a careful sorting of its semantic ambiguities is essential to bringing into focus the "distinction" that my title affixes to it, foreshadowing segregating qualities that apply to the term only when it is understood in its specific generic meaning as a literary nonreferential narrative text. This use of the word is not unusual: in English critical language, *fiction* as the designation for an invented narrative—novel, novella, short story—has been current for more than a century and is, of course, a standard term for publishers, book reviewers, and librarians. In contemporary literary scholarship, however, this sense of the word is often compounded with

---

1. Hans Vaihinger, *Die Philosophie des Als Ob,* 140; my translation. The passage containing this sentence is omitted in the English translation of this work to which I refer below.

its other meanings, creating confusions that easily surpass those Vaihinger attributed to the logicians of his time. With the scope and slipperiness of its referential field favoring imperceptible glides, the homonymic plurality of the word *fiction* has notably eased the erasure of boundaries between different types of discourse. Since the present study aims to counteract this tendency, the separation of the generic significance of *fiction* from competing other meanings is its logical starting point.[2]

Four such other meanings will be distinguished below: fiction as untruth, fiction as conceptual abstraction, fiction as (all) literature, and fiction as (all) narrative. Though primarily systematic, my discussion on occasion glances at moments of historical change, particularly in, and after, the eighteenth century. Following this survey of the word's semantic multiplicity and of the ensuing instability in critical discourse, this introductory chapter explains in greater detail how I conceive of fiction in the particular significance I give it throughout this study.

THE PLURI-SIGNIFICANCE OF "FICTION"

When, in our daily lives, we charge journalists or rumor mongers with having written or told "a fiction," we use the term in its derogatory meaning of a doubtful or untrue statement—alternately attributing it to deliberate deception, faulty memory, or misinformation. This meaning is, on occasion, specifically signified in works of literary criticism as well: thus a scholar, examining Mary McCarthy's autobiographical writings for the intentional and unintentional "lies" she tells, informs us that, as we enter the private world of the self, we inevitably "meet the grinning face of fiction at the door"; another asks word-playfully whether "the distinction between fiction and nonfiction [is] fiction or nonfiction."[3]

Though this reproachful sense of the word has been noted lexically,[4] little attention has been given to its potential consequence: that it may

2. The only work I have found that explicitly segregates the generic meaning of *fiction* from the various other meanings I discuss below is Peter Lamarque and Stein Haugom Olsen, *Truth, Fiction and Literature: A Philosophical Perspective*. As their title indicates, the authors of this work are primarily concerned with "fictional truth," a problem of considerable importance for philosophers but not immediately relevant to my own study. I will nonetheless refer to their argument at moments when it overlaps with my own.

3. Paul John Eakin, *Fictions in Autobiography: Studies in the Art of Self-Invention*, 25; Berel Lang, *The Anatomy of Philosophical Style*, 169.

4. See meaning 3 under "fiction" in the *Oxford English Dictionary*: "The action of 'feigning' or inventing imaginary incidents, existences, states of things etc., whether for the purpose of deception or otherwise." Raymond Williams notes in *Key Words: A Vocabulary of Culture and Society* that the word has "the interesting double sense of a kind of *imaginative literature* and of a pure (sometimes deliberately deceptive) invention" (134).

imbue the word *fiction* with a degree of covert negativity and frivolity even when the term is overtly targeted to a quite different meaning. One may even suspect that *fiction* is at times chosen over other available terms when denigration is (more or less consciously) implied. This may, for example, have prompted Jeremy Bentham to call the legal abstractions to which he so strenuously objected "fictitious entities"; it may likewise have induced Hayden White to climax his critique of historical texts by tagging them "verbal fictions."

We may also conjecture that it was its pejorative meaning of untruth that delayed the lexical move of calling novels "fiction" to a time when this genre had become a well-established, highly respected literary form. In the early eighteenth century at any rate—at a time when Hume was still calling poets "liars by profession"[5]—the pretense of factuality in the prefaces to first-person novels like *Robinson Crusoe* was clearly an attempt to escape the charge of falsity by escaping the charge of fiction, or vice versa, or both at once. Historians of the novel have shown that, as the century advanced and as readers learned to accept the norms of literary realism, novelists tended to drop claims to reality or factuality.[6]

In our own age, of course, the negative meaning of *fiction* as "untrue statement" has melted away from its use as a generic term, and with it the danger of these two meanings interfering with each other. It is noteworthy, however, that several critics have recently felt the need to differentiate them in adjectival form, proposing that *fictional* be reserved for matters related to literature, *fictitious* for matters related to life. Thus Michael Riffaterre glosses the title of his book as follows: "The only reason that the phrase 'fictional truth' is not an oxymoron, as 'fictitious truth' would be, is that fiction is a genre whereas lies are not."[7] It would be tempting to use the concluding dictum of this sentence as a basis for eliminating at least one of the meanings of our homonymous word. But this would ignore the regrettable fact that lexical matters are not subject to legislation.

Whereas fiction in its mendacious meaning has been and needs to be a matter of some concern for theorists no less than for historians of literature, its meaning as a philosophical term—to the degree that it comes to

---

5. David Hume, *A Treatise on Human Nature* (1739), bk. I, pt. III, sect. 10.
6. See Lennard J. Davis, *Factual Fictions: The Origins of the English Novel*; Geoffrey Day, *From Fiction to Novel*; Philip Stewart, *Imitation and Illusion in the French Memoir Novel, 1700–1750*.
7. Michael Riffaterre, *Fictional Truth*, 1. Thomas Pavel likewise differentiates between the two adjectives, with *fictional* signifying "contained in a work of fiction" and *fictitious* signifying "inaccurate"; see "Between History and Fiction," in Ann Fehn, Ingeborg Hoesterey, and Maria Tatar, eds., *Neverending Stories: Toward a Critical Narratology*, 18.

the attention of literary scholars—tends to throw critical discourse into considerable disarray. The reason is that, oddly, hardly anyone has noticed that *fiction* means something entirely different in philosophical discourse than in the discourse concerned with literature.[8]

The principal difference is that when philosophers employ the word, far from its designating anything related to literature or narrative, it refers to a concept or idea. Thus Bentham calls the juridical term *right* "a fiction,"[9] Kant explains that the products of our intellectual intuition (notions like time and space) are "heuristic fictions,"[10] and Nietzsche tells us that an individual's sense of existing as a unified subject (of having a unified self) is "the fiction that many similar states in us are the effect of one substratum."[11] In commentaries on science, social thought, and psychology, one finds *fiction* designating a wide variety of explanatory notions—Newton's gravitational force (which he himself called "a fiction"), Rousseau's state of nature, Goethe's original plant (*Urpflanze*), Freud's unconscious. Whether this designation has positive or negative implications can usually only be gathered from the context.[12]

The work that gave this meaning of the word its greatest prominence and scope, as well as its most positive assessment, is Hans Vaihinger's *The Philosophy of "As if": A System of the Theoretical, Practical and Religious Fictions of Mankind*, originally published in 1911. The phrase "As if" (*Als Ob*) in Vaihinger's title pinpoints his principal thesis: that we persistently, and sometimes quite purposively, make use of contrary-to-fact notions to make sense of our world, and that notions of this kind are essential to human thought. As his subtitle indicates, Vaihinger presents an entire system of the different types of "fictions" (mathematical, ethical, symbolic,

8. A welcome exception in this respect is the book by Lamarque and Olsen (see note 2 above), where the philosopher-authors draw the distinction as follows: "The level at which philosophers speak of objects as 'constructs' or 'fictions' or 'mind-dependent' is quite different from that at which readers of stories notice that characters and events are 'made up,' 'fictional,' or 'unreal.' . . . Indeed the kind of 'making' involved in 'making up a story' turns out, on examination, to have little or nothing in common with the 'making' that, for example, constructivists in epistemology see as basic in cognition" (15; see also 19 and 191).

9. "The word 'right' is the name of a fictitious entity; one of those objects the existence of which is feigned for the purpose of discourse—by a fiction so necessary that without it discourse could not be carried on" (C. R. Ogden, ed., *Bentham's Theory of Fiction*, 118).

10. Immanuel Kant, *Critique of Pure Reason*, quoted in Hans Vaihinger, *The Philosophy of "As if*," 283.

11. Friedrich Nietzsche, *The Will to Power*, 269.

12. See the account—which moves from authors who cast a negative light on fictionality (Bacon, Bentham) to those who cast a positive light on it (Vaihinger, Nelson Goodman)—in chapter 3 ("Fiction Thematized in Philosophical Discourse") of Wolfgang Iser, *The Fictive and the Imaginary*.

utopian, etc.) that inform and shape different disciplines and world-views.[13] It is not my purpose here to survey Vaihinger's captivating (if controversial) ideas and subtle distinctions.[14] But there is one aspect of his work that is important for my present concerns: the fact that fiction, in the *literary* sense of the word, is conspicuous for its absence. In fact, Vaihinger devotes no more than a single paragraph to what he calls "aesthetic fictions," which he regards largely as adaptations of such mythological images as Pegasus or the Sphinx. He even proposes in a note that, strictly speaking, imaginary entities of this sort should be designated as "figments," not "fictions," reserving the latter term exclusively for scientific and theoretical discourse.[15]

A number of critics have tried to co-opt or adopt this philosophic-theoretical meaning of *fiction* for literary scholarship. One scholar, for example, in support of his claim that there is a collateral relationship between Bentham's conception of legal fictions and the emergence of the realist novel in the eighteenth century, casts a negative light on these novels by way of a strikingly deflating phrase the early Bentham applied to legal fictions: "the pestilential breath of fiction."[16] What this scholar fails to note is that Bentham himself explicitly draws attention to the difference between the potentially misleading "Fictions of the Logician" and the harmlessly entertaining "Fictions of the Poet."[17] Bentham accordingly proposes at one point (as Vaihinger was to do later on) a different term for the products of a poet's imagination: *fabulous*.[18] More far-reaching confusions are induced by some moments of Frank Kermode's influential book, *The Sense of an Ending*. Here we read that "it is pretty surprising . . . that nobody . . . has ever tried to relate the theory of literary fictions to the theory of fiction in general. . . . But that there *is* a simple relation between literary and other fictions seems, if one attends to it, more obvious than has appeared."[19] When, in the following pages, Kermode specifically proposes the application of Vaihinger's theory to liter-

13. Only one of Vaihinger's fictional types develops into a narrative form of sorts: juristic fictions (see *The Philosophy of "As if,"* 33–35). But since their peculiarity (and the reason they can be subsumed under the "as if" heading) is that they are cast in the conditional tense, their structure differs in an essential way from the normal (indicative) telling of literary narratives.
14. For recent discussions of Vaihinger's work, see Iser, *The Fictive and the Imaginary,* 130–52; and Lamarque and Olsen, *Truth, Fiction and Literature,* 186–88.
15. Vaihinger, *The Philosophy of "As if,"* 81.
16. John Bender, *Imagining the Penitentiary: Fiction and the Architecture of the Mind in Eighteenth-Century England,* 213. For the Bentham quote, see Ross Harrison, *Bentham,* 24.
17. C. R. Ogden, ed., *Bentham's Theory of Fiction,* 18.
18. Ibid., xxxv–xxxvi.
19. *The Sense of an Ending: Studies in the Theory of Fiction,* 36.

ary fiction,[20] it becomes clear that the "simple relationship" he envisions here is nothing less than the global running-together of fiction as a theoretical construct and as a generic term—a wishful proposal, no doubt prompted by Kermode's overall (and rather doubtful) thesis that a basic analogy exists between the eschatological or millennial visions of religious thinkers and the modern novel.[21]

The critic who has spoken most forcefully against the confounding of theoretical fictions, in Vaihinger's sense of the word, and literary fictions is Käte Hamburger in *The Logic of Literature*. Hamburger suggests that when we perceive literary characters "as fictive, this is not based on an as-if-structure, but rather, so we might say, on an *as-structure*."[22] Novels present us with a semblance or illusion (*Schein*) of reality that we don't take in a conditional sense, but that we accept *as* a reality so long as we remain absorbed in it. More will be said below about the theory that inspires Hamburger's rejection of the "as-if" structure of fiction.

It is not always easy to separate *fiction* in the sense just discussed—its meaning as abstract concept—from its meaning as verbal or literary expression generally. This induces me to glance in transit at a work that seems to involve both of these meanings at once: Wallace Stevens' cycle of poems, "Notes toward a Supreme Fiction." Approaching the ultimate vision imprinted in its title by way of such notions as verbal control, abstraction, absolute order, and ultimate mastery, "supreme fiction" is here evoked as the ideal goal of spiritual creativity. These associations can be gathered from the few moments of this highly diversified poetic sequence that take the form of more or less doctrinal pronouncements.[23] Even though these are largely cast as negative formulations and—as always in Stevens—depreciatingly hedged with qualifications of all sorts, they are pronouncements nonetheless, adumbrating an elusive "it" that may be understood as the aim of literary creation and perhaps specifically of the poet's craft.[24] Understood in this fashion, Stevens's "supreme fiction" opens to the wider meaning of

20. Ibid., 40.
21. For another critical work that argues in favor of a close analogy between Vaihinger's conception of fictions and the novel (in this case in its realist incarnation) see Harold Toliver, *Animate Illusions: Explorations of Narrative Structure*. An argument that subsumes literature as a whole under Vaihinger's "as if" structure is presented in Wolfgang Iser, "Feigning in Fiction," see esp. 215–18.
22. Hamburger, *The Logic of Literature*, 58.
23. See particularly the following poems in the three-part cycle: I/vi and III/viii, ix, and x.
24. In the much earlier poem, "A High-Toned Old Christian Woman," we in fact find the direct identification: "Poetry is the Supreme Fiction."

fiction that I am about to consider: the translation of mental experiences or visions into language.

Though the denotative field that surrounds *fiction* as a philosophical term is in itself clearer and more limited, it readily spreads into a more general and more nebulous terrain. Thus in a number of works where the term is prominently (even titularly) displayed, its meaning remains quite puzzling. One gathers with a good deal of difficulty, for example, that certain psychoanalytic studies—Maud Mannoni, *La Théorie comme fiction: Freud, Groddeck, Winnicott, Lacan*; Malcolm Bowie, *Freud, Proust, and Lacan: Theory as Fiction*—use it to hint at the fantasmatic origin of seemingly systematic oeuvres. In other instances, the word figures time and again in a vast connotative field. In the epilogue to a recent French work on the classical era, the word *fiction* in its nominal and adjectival forms appears (often more than once) on almost every one of its thirty pages in apposition to such words as *monde, univers, cosmogonie, espace,* and *distance.* On closer inspection it appears that the word functions here more or less as a synonym for *l'imaginaire* and as an antonym of *le réel,* referring to cultural phenomena that range from the dramas of Corneille to the palace of Versailles.[25]

These all-encompassing implications are somewhat restricted when the term *fiction* is applied to literature itself in its broadest conception, including historical and essayistic works as well as lyric poetry. It seems, however, that a variety of different aims are targeted when the word is used in this way. Suzanne Gearhart's argument, for example, in favor of a unified reading and understanding of certain eighteenth-century authors who wrote both expository and narrative works (Voltaire, Diderot, Montesquieu, Rousseau) calls on *fiction* to subsume all the discursive genres in which they expressed their ideas.[26] Paul de Man applies the term to underline the dichotomy between written artifacts and factual experience: "All literatures . . . have always designated themselves as existing in the mode of fiction. . . . The self-reflecting mirror-effect by means of which a work of fiction asserts, by its very existence, its separation from empirical reality . . . characterizes the work of literature in its essence."[27] Barbara Herrnstein Smith's understanding of "Poetry as Fiction" (the phrase that entitles one of her chapters) allows her to divide language into

25. Thomas Pavel, *L'Art de l'éloignement: Essai sur l'imagination classique,* 367–96. It should be noted, however, that this author has used the word *fiction* far more specifically—essentially in its meaning as nonreferential narrative—in his earlier work *Fictional Worlds.*
26. *The Open Boundary of History and Fiction.*
27. *Blindness and Insight,* 17.

two categories: "fictive discourse" (to which she assigns all literary genres—drama, lyric, epic, novel) and its antonym, "natural discourse."[28] A similar intent seems to motivate Peter McCormick in his *Fictions, Philosophy, and Poetics,* where Hume, Kant, and Hegel figure together with T. S. Eliot, Rilke, and Stevens as authors of "fictional discourse."

What all these conceptions have in common—aside from their vastness and vagueness—is an understanding of fiction that is not primarily *narrative* in nature. When (as is often the case) they do include such genres as autobiography, narrative poetry, or the novel, they tend to regard them as expressive, ideological, or visionary genres and to deemphasize their narrative structure or language. It is primarily on this basis that the application of the word *fiction* to all of literature, and sometimes even to other arts and/or systematic-theoretical works, differs from its application to all of narrative—the category of meaning I am about to consider.

No doubt the most pervasive and prominently problematic application of the word *fiction* in recent decades has been to narrative discourse in general—historical, journalistic, and autobiographical—as well as to imaginative discourse. This inclusive denotation has been forcefully, even militantly advocated by numerous voices. I quote a few random examples: "The mere selection, arrangement, and presentation of facts is a technique belonging to the field of fiction" (Arnold Toynbee); "All accounts of our experience, all versions of 'reality,' are of the nature of fiction" (Ronald Sukenick); "There is no fiction or nonfiction as we commonly understand it: there is only narrative" (E. L. Doctorow); "If it is true that narratives give us no reliable knowledge of what they purport to relate, they are all fictions, including those of history" (Wlad Godzich). It is important to realize that, unlike the meanings of the term previously surveyed, this identification of narrative and fiction is weighted with considerable ideological freight. The motive force behind it is nothing less than the contemporary critique of the entire intellectual foundation of traditional historical practice—of the entire practice that is based on belief in the factuality of past events.

This thesis has found its most eloquent and influential protagonist in Hayden White, for whom historical narratives are no less "verbal fictions" than their purely imaginative counterparts in literature.[29] Their common denominator is "emplotment": the teller's imposition of a coherent temporal order on a succession of events he perceives in the past,

28. *On the Margins of Discourse: Relations of Literature and Language,* 14–40.
29. *Tropics of Discourse,* 82.

with a view to structuring them into a unified story with beginning, middle, and end.[30] Though highly controversial and frequently contested,[31] this identification of fiction with narrative has had a far-reaching, if largely unconscious, impact on most critics who have followed the lines of thought variously labeled deconstructionist, poststructuralist, and postmodern.

One of the most probing antagonists of this thesis is Paul Ricoeur. When, early in volume 1 of *Time and Narrative,* he opts against the more encompassing meaning of the term *fiction* as narrative in general and in favor of its restricted sense of nonreferential narrative,[32] his choice—which he himself at this point attributes merely to convenience and clarity—seems to me significantly dictated by the essential distinction he attributes to verbal artistry. For it is intimately related to his perception—developed in volume 2 of this work—that literary narrative achieves something entirely alien to historical narrative: it creates for the reader "imaginary worlds" that open "an unlimited career to the manifestation of time."[33] While the projection of a plot—what Ricoeur calls "emplotment"—is common to historical and literary narrative, solely the latter can make the reader share in a character's rich and vital experience of time, as he demonstrates by his interpretations of *Mrs. Dalloway, The Magic Mountain,* and *A la Recherche du temps perdu.*

Though, unlike Ricoeur, I am not inclined to single out the temporal dimension of experience as the unique distinction of literary narrative, I share his perception that there are certain essential differences between narrative in history and in literature. It is this perception that prompts me to opt, as he does, for a definition of fiction that applies solely to nonreferential narrative.

"FICTION" AS NONREFERENTIAL NARRATIVE

Though the term *fiction* was used through the ages in all the meanings surveyed above, certain thinkers did prepare the way for its literary-generic meaning of nonreferential narrative.

According to a number of leading modern theorists, the first of these was Aristotle. This may seem surprising, in view of the fact that there is no exact Greek equivalent for the word *fiction.* Present-day interpreters of

30. Ibid., 83.
31. Lamarque and Olsen, in whose work one finds one of the most recent critiques of Hayden White, call his assimilation of narrative and fiction "illicit" (*Truth, Fiction and Literature,* 224; see also 308–10). For my own argument against White, see Chapter 7 below.
32. *Time and Narrative,* I:64.
33. Ibid., II:159.

the *Poetics,* however, believe that *mimesis,* the Aristotelian term distinctively characterizing literary artifacts, is very close, if not identical, in meaning to the word Western languages derive from the Latin *fictio.*[34] As Käte Hamburger and Gérard Genette have emphasized, Aristotle strictly limited *poiesis* and *mimesis* to dramatic and narrative modes, decisively excluding poetry.[35] Accordingly, Genette quotes from a translation that unapologetically renders *mimesis* as "fiction": "Le poète doit plutôt être artisan d'histoire que de vers, puisque c'est par la fiction qu'il est poète, et que ce qu'il feint c'est des actions" ["The poet must be a maker not of verses but of stories, since it is by virtue of his fiction that he is a poet, and that what he feigns is action"].[36] Remembering that the passage from which this quotation is taken immediately follows the one that contains the famous antithesis between poet and historian, one may readily conclude that Aristotle's *Poetics* is the work that launched the idea of fiction in the sense of nonreferential narrative.[37]

It is the authority of Aristotle that is in fact invoked in the rare instances where *fiction* is applied as a positive term in literary discussions before the late eighteenth century. That this happens primarily for the purpose of establishing the respectability of the novel is clear from one of the first treatises explicitly concerned with this genre, Pierre-Daniel Huet's *De l'Origine des romans* (1670): "Suivant cette maxime d'Aristote que le Poète est plus Poète par les fictions qu'il invente que par les vers qu'il compose, on peut mettre les faiseurs de Romans au nombre des Poètes" ["Following the maxim of Aristotle (who teaches that a Poet is more a Poet by the Fictions he invents than by the Verse which he composes), makers of Ro-

---

34. See the references to German classicists who interpret Aristotle's *mimesis* concept in this manner in Hamburger, *The Logic of Literature* (345–46, n. 7). An English precedent for rendering *mimesis* by the word *fiction* may be found in L. J. Potts, *Aristotle on the Art of Fiction.* That the identification of these two concepts is still quite controversial, however, may be gathered from Christopher Gill, "Plato on Falsehood—not Fiction," in *Lies and Fiction in the Ancient World,* 75–77.

35. See Hamburger, *The Logic of Literature,* 10–14, and Genette, *Fiction and Diction,* 6–9. Hamburger additionally advocates the identity of Aristotle's *poiesis* (his overarching term for literary artifacts) with fiction, an equation that is substantiated by the classicist Wesley Trimpi, who translates *poiesis* as "fiction" throughout his *Muses of One Mind* (e.g., 9, 25, 57).

36. *Fiction et diction,* 17; my translation. Genette does not specify the Aristotle translation from which he quotes—which may well be his own. The English translation of *Fiction et diction* loses an important step in the argument by quoting the Loeb translation of Aristotle, where *mimesis* is rendered as "representation"—the word that, in most recent translations of the *Poetics,* has taken the place of the earlier rendering of *mimesis* as "imitation."

37. For both Hamburger and Genette this holds true despite the fact that Aristotle, of course, takes tragedy, rather than fictional narrative, as the principal genre that incarnates his concept of *poiesis.*

mances may be ranked among the poets"].[38] But this dependence on Aristotle is no longer overt in the work that may well be the first to feature the word *fiction* in its title: Madame de Stael's "Essai sur les fictions" (1795). Though several types of narrative "fictions" are considered here (allegorical, historical, philosophical), the largest section of Madame de Stael's "Essai" is devoted to the type she herself favors above all others: "fictions naturelles"—the kind of narrative informed by "la connaissance intime de tous les mouvements du coeur humain" ["the intimate knowledge of all the movements of the human heart"].[39] Madame de Stael thus becomes the advocate for regarding as "fictions" (and for calling "fictions") a kind of realistic narrative approximating the novel, very much in the manner the term is routinely applied today.

But it was only quite gradually in the course of the next century that *fiction* became the standard anglophone term for literary prose narrative.[40] By the time Henry James published *The Art of Fiction* (1884), in tandem with a lecture of the same title by Walter Besant, it was no longer necessary to explain or justify this nomenclature. All dictionaries henceforth list this generic sense as one of several established meanings,[41] and it provides the *mot juste* for practicing novelists—Edith Wharton, *The Writing of Fiction* (1925)—no less than for instruction-oriented critics— Cleanth Brooks and R. P. Warren, *Understanding Fiction* (1943)—who want to designate a collective genre that includes, besides the novel, such narrative subgenres as the novella, the tale, and the short story. Though less standardized in French and German, it has become a common term for imaginative narrative in the present-day critical discourse of these languages as well.[42]

As we have seen, however, this standardization of *fiction* as a generic term has not resulted in eliminating its other meanings. And this is true despite the fact that in all four of these meanings it is used as a synonym for other, readily available words: untruth, abstraction, literature, narra-

---

38. Quoted in Genette, *Fiction et diction*, 17. The English translation quotes from the English translation of Huet's work (1672); note that the latter renders the French *Romans* by "Romances," in accordance with the prevailing critical term used in England at the time.

39. "Essai sur les fictions" in Madame de Stael, *Zulmar et trois nouvelles*, 37; my translation.

40. The most detailed account to date of this development in England is provided in Ulrich Keller, *Fiktionalität als literaturwissenschaftliche Kategorie*, 47–51.

41. The meaning numbered 4 in the *Oxford English Dictionary*, for example, reads: "The species of literature which is concerned with the narration of imaginary events and the portraiture of imaginary characters; fictitious composition. Now usually prose novels and stories collectively; the composition of works of this class."

42. For a typical example of contemporary French usage, see Genette, *Fiction et Diction*; for an example of German usage, see Keller, *Fiktionalität als literaturwissenschaftliche Kategorie*.

tive. Though it is no doubt futile to campaign for lexical reform, one may perhaps hope that a clearer awareness of the word's semantic instability will prompt literary critics to adhere to its restricted generic meaning. I intend, at any rate, to use the term *fiction* consistently throughout the present study in the exclusive sense of a literary nonreferential narrative.[43]

Nonreferential narrative: both the noun and the adjective of this definitional phrase need to be qualified before it can be meaningfully applied to matters relevant to the distinction of fiction.

Without joining the theoretical discussion of the term *narrative*,[44] I abstract from it the following fairly consensual definition: a series of statements that deal with a causally related sequence of events that concern human (or human-like) beings. Conceived in this fashion, narrative most notably excludes all general statements of "truth" that characterize theoretical, philosophical, explanatory, speculative, or critical discourse. It also excludes purely descriptive statements and expressions of emotion. In the generic sense, fiction clearly includes all the forms of discourse that this definition excludes. Numerous novels start out with statements like "Happy families are all alike; every unhappy family is unhappy in its own way"; and few narrators stay away entirely from generalizations (usually cast in the present tense) concerning the world at large, society, and human nature. Moreover, descriptive language abounds in fictional works, applying to sites (the Maison Vauquer, the house Thomas Buddenbrook built), objects (Charles Bovary's hat, the golden bowl in *The Golden Bowl*), and characters (Dorothea Brooke, Emma Woodhouse). Manifestly, the term *fiction* cannot be reserved for texts that contain no extranarrative language whatever. Still, one *can* propose that it be applied only to texts in which expository or descriptive language is *subordinated* to narrative language: texts where the principal function of generalizations is to elucidate, and of description to contextualize or symbolize, the narrated events and characters.

43. In *The Fictive and the Imaginary,* Wolfgang Iser reverts to a different strategy for separating fictionality as a concept central to literature from its other (notably its philosophical) associations: he proposes replacing *fiction* in its literary meaning by "the imaginary." It seems to me, however, that the English term *fiction* has become too solidly established as the designation for a literary genre to allow one to opt for the rejection of this meaning once and for all. What is more, Iser's "imaginary" can hardly be considered to be a term with clarifyingly univalent meaning. Another critic reacts to the ubiquity of the term *fiction* with the even more radical proposal of applying the term *antifiction* to aesthetic works; see Odo Marquand, "Kunst als Antifiktion," 35–54.
44. See Philip M. Sturgess, *Narrativity: Theory and Practice,* esp. the opening chapters; Marie-Laure Ryan, "The Modes of Narrativity and Their Visual Metaphors"; Monika Fludernik, *Toward a "Natural" Narratology,* 26ff. and 318ff.

We must be aware, however, that subordination is not a purely quantitative matter; readers may disagree about which language is subordinated to which in a text. Though it is hard to imagine someone who would maintain that *Anna Karenina* is not a narrative work but merely an illustration of the generalization that launches it, some critics of *A la Recherche du temps perdu* have in fact argued that its narrative is merely an illustration of ideas Proust developed in the essayistic passages of his work.[45] Though this question—which arises most forcefully for genres that call on what Marie-Laure Ryan names "Instrumental Narrativity" (fables, parables, anecdotes)[46]—is not central for my concerns in the present study, I did not want to pass it in silence.

The adjective *nonreferential* in the definitional phrase "nonreferential narrative" needs to be qualified at somewhat greater length. First and foremost it signifies that a work of fiction itself creates the world to which it refers by referring to it.[47] This self-referentiality is particularly striking when a novel plunges us from the outset into the spatial perceptions of a fictional figure, as in *The Castle:*

> It was late in the evening when K. arrived. The village was deep in
> snow. The Castle hill was hidden, veiled in mist and darkness, nor was
> there a glimmer of light to show that a castle was there. On the
> wooden bridge leading from the main road to the village, K. stood for
> a long time gazing into the illusory emptiness above him.
> Then he went on to find quarters for the night.[48]

Here, as in what follows in Kafka's novel, we know and see only what K. knows and sees, including the empty space that may (or may not) contain "a castle." The unnamed village in which K. arrives remains nameless as the novel proceeds and is never situated in any country, and the time of the happenings is never historically specified. The world of *The Castle,* in short, remains to its end severed from the actual world, creating in its purest form what Benjamin Harshaw calls "an internal frame of refer-

45. See, for example, Roland Barthes, "Longtemps je me suis couché de bonne heure . . . " in *The Rustle of Language,* 277–90.
46. Ryan, "The Modes of Narrativity," 380–81.
47. Statements to this effect can be found in most theories that insist on a firm borderline between fictional and nonfictional texts. See for example Benjamin Harshaw, "Fictionality and Fields of Reference," 232; Uri Margolin, "Reference, Coreference, Referring, and the Dual Structure of Literary Narrative," 520. The first to formulate this idea may have been Margaret MacDonald in an article of 1954, "The Language of Fiction," 176.
48. Franz Kafka, *The Castle,* 3.

ence."[49] We might note in passing, however, that internal frames of reference are by no means entirely independent of the actual world we know. If we are able to relate to Kafka's beginning despite its un- or other-worldliness, it is because its references point to things we know: snow, darkness, a village, a bridge, nocturnal arrival in an unknown place.

But purely internal frames of reference are rather exceptional in fiction. If the adjective *nonreferential* is to be meaningful, it must not be understood to signify that fiction never refers to the real world outside the text. Many realist novels begin in the manner of *A Sentimental Education:*

> On the morning of 15 September 1840 the Ville de Montereau was lying alongside the quai Saint Bernard belching clouds of smoke, all ready to sail. . . .
>
> Finally the vessel cast off and the two banks of the river, packed with warehouses, yards and factories, began to unwind like two broad lengths of ribbon.
>
> Standing motionless beside the helm was a long-haired youth of eighteen holding a sketchbook under his arm. . . .
>
> Frédéric Moreau had recently matriculated and was on his way to Nogent-sur-Seine where he'd be kicking his heels for the next couple of months before returning to embark on his legal studies. . . .
>
> Frédéric was thinking of the room he'd be living in in Paris, of an idea for a play, of a subject for a painting, of future passionate affairs of the heart. He felt that the happiness owed to such a pre-eminently sensitive soul as himself was slow in coming.[50]

Flaubert starts out with precise specifications of historic time and geographic space: the narrator names a real steamship that in 1840 departs from a real Parisian quai and heads for a real provincial town. However, with the introduction of Frédéric, the life of an invented person is embedded in this actual world: first by explaining his circumstances, soon after by rendering his perceptions, thoughts, and feelings. Here then we have what Harshaw calls a "double-decker" model of reference: an internal frame nested within an external frame.[51]

---

49. "Fictionality and Fields of Reference," 232.
50. Gustave Flaubert, *A Sentimental Education,* 3–4.
51. Harshaw, "Fictionality and Fields of Reference," 249. Some theorists distinguish further types of referents beyond the two labeled by Harshaw, e.g., "intertextual referents," and "autorepresentational referents"; see Margolin, "Reference, Coreference, Referring," 521; and Linda Hutcheon, "Metafictional Implications for Novelistic Reference," 9.

As these typical beginnings indicate, when we speak of the nonreferentiality of fiction, we do not mean that it *can* not refer to the real world outside the text, but that it *need* not refer to it. But beyond this, the adjective of my definitional phrase also signifies that fiction is subject to two closely interrelated distinguishing features: (1) its references to the world outside the text are not bound to accuracy; and (2) it does not refer *exclusively* to the real world outside the text.

The potential of fiction to refer to the actual world inaccurately is most obvious when unreal localities are placed in real surroundings: when Proust's narrator vacations at a Normandy resort called Balbec, when Emma Bovary takes a postal coach from Yonville to Rouen, when Mann's Adrian Leverkühn moves from his school in the fictional Kaisersaschern to the real university of Halle. It is equally evident (i.e., readily revealed by consulting historical sources) that no man named Willie Stark was ever the governor of Louisiana, that the entire post-Napoleonic government of the dukedom of Parma is one that Stendhal fabricated out of full cloth, and that the stepson whose death Dostoevsky mourns in J. M. Coetzee's *The Master of Petersburg* in fact survived the writer (and plagued him financially throughout his life). These imaginative manipulations of more or less well-known facts highlight the peculiar way external references do not remain truly external when they enter a fictional world. They are, as it were, contaminated from within, subjected to what Hamburger calls "the process of fictionalization."[52]

Understood in this manner, the definitional adjective *nonreferential* allows one to discriminate between two different *kinds* of narrative, according to whether they deal with real or imaginary events and persons. Only narratives of the first kind, which include historical works, journalistic reports, biographies, and autobiographies, are subject to judgments of truth and falsity. Narratives of the second kind, which include novels, short stories, ballads, and epics, are immune to such judgments. As one theorist puts this binary opposition, with particular regard to historiography: "History is a narrative discourse with different rules than those that govern fiction. The producer of a historical text affirms that the events entextualized did indeed occur before entextualization. Thus it is quite proper to bring extratextual information to bear on those events when interpreting and evaluating a historical narrative. . . . It is certainly otherwise with fiction, for in fiction the events may be said to be created by and with the text. They have no prior tem-

---

52. Hamburger, *The Logic of Literature*, 113.

poral existence."[53] Another way of expressing this opposition is to say that referential narratives are verifiable and incomplete, whereas non-referential narratives are unverifiable and complete. We can check on the accuracy of a Thomas Mann biography, point out factual errors, and write a new one based on newly discovered evidence; but no competent novel reader would be inclined to check on the accuracy of Hans Castorp's life as told in *The Magic Mountain* or consult the archives to find out whether he was killed on the World War I battlefield where his fictional life ends.

As the two beginnings of novels quoted above also suggest, the principal process by which fiction alters the actual world, even when it strictly adheres to the latter's geographical and historical data, is by augmenting its population: by implanting within it the imaginary beings we customarily call characters. This brings me to the second of the special features mentioned above, for it is by its unique potential for presenting characters that fiction most consistently and most radically severs its connections with the real world outside the text.

In fiction cast in the third person, this presentation involves a distinctive epistemology that allows a narrator to know what cannot be known in the real world and in narratives that target representations of the real world: the inner life of his figures. This penetrative optic calls on devices—among others free indirect style—that remain unavailable to narrators who aim for referential (nonfictional) presentation.[54] These textual markers can be shown to stamp fictional characters as citizens of an artfully created world, a world that, no matter how close the resemblance in other respects, is never identical to the one inhabited by the author who has invented it or by his readers. And this fictional stamp, as one theorist proposes, makes such a text "epistemologically illegitimate" to the point where its speaker must appear as "insane" to someone who mistook it for a historical text.[55]

---

53. Robert Scholes, "Language, Narrative and Anti-Narrative," 211.
54. These devices are detailed in Dorrit Cohn, *Transparent Minds: Narrative Modes for Presenting Consciousness in Fiction*. The strongest argument for presentation of the inner life as the essential differentiation of fiction from nonfiction is found in Hamburger, *The Logic of Literature*; however, she applies this thesis exclusively to fiction in the third person, which alone constitutes what she calls "epic fiction." Though I agree with much of her argumentation, I disagree with her on this point. When fiction is cast in first-person form, although introspection takes the place of the unnatural presentation of the inner life found in third-person fiction, the narrator herself or himself is nonetheless an unnaturally presented imaginary being, whose distinction from the author marks his or her fictionality; see Chapter 2 below.
55. Félix Martínez-Bonati, "The Act of Writing Fiction," 426. It is surprising to find how rarely

The foregoing indications of what the word *nonreferential* signifies in my definitional phrase are meant to be introductory rather than conclusive. At this stage they may well raise more problems than they resolve. But these problems will come closer to clarification when they are taken up again by way of the more specific issues considered in the chapters that follow.

---

theorists of fictionality acknowledge the marked textual deviance of fiction in this respect. Many, in fact, deny or overlook that any kind of semantic or stylistic indicators draw attention to a narrative's fictionality. This includes theorists who stress on principle that the emancipation from referentiality is the be-all and end-all of fiction. The following passage from Lamarque and Olsen, *Truth, Fiction and Literature,* is quite representative in this respect: "We can eliminate fairly swiftly some potential candidates for the constitutive feature (or features) of fictionality. . . . There is no 'language of fiction' as such. . . . The search for necessary and sufficient conditions among stylistic and formal features of language is doomed from the start" (30). This negation is also current among speech-act theorists, even though they are widely known for their insistence on the different communicative conventions that prevail in the writing and reading of fiction.

2

Fictional versus Historical Lives

Borderlines and Borderline Cases

Though this chapter will address a quite limited area of the two vast domains of fictional and historical narratives, my assumption is that this area can act as a focus for the larger complex—not only in the sense of a significant center of attention, but also in the sense of a clarifying image, perhaps even of an irradiating source of light.

This restrictive optic is clearly more limiting on the side of history than on the side of fiction. History is more often concerned with humanity in the plural than in the singular, with events and changes affecting entire societies, than those affecting the lives of individual beings. For this reason biography is often regarded as a minor historical genre, and by some even as "a simple form of historiography."[1] Within fiction, by contrast, plots that center on the lives of single, more or less singular individuals shape the dominant generic modes known in French by the term *roman de l'individu,* in German by the term *Figurenroman.* Not all novels of this type follow what Bakhtin calls the chronotope of biographical time. Indeed one of the distinctions of fictional as compared to historical narrative is that the former is able to make an entire life come to life as a unified whole in a short span of story time, as short as a single day in novels like *Ulysses* and *Mrs. Dalloway.*

Granting their unequal relative scope within the two narrative domains, I nonetheless see historical and novelistic narratives that center on a life plot as the generic region where factual and fictional narratives come into closest proximity, the territory that presents the greatest potential for overlap. By the same token, the telling of lives also constitutes a peculiarly privileged site within the system of genres for drawing theoretical borderlines and investigating critical borderline cases.[2]

1. See Karlheinz Stierle, "Erfahrung und narrative Form: Bemerkungen zu ihrem Zusammenhang in Fiktion und Historiographie," 104.
2. I have found surprisingly little awareness of the privileged status of narrated lives in recentattempts to differentiate between historical and fictional narratives on modern theoretical grounds; Paul Ricoeur's *Time and Narrative* is no exception: its index contains no entry for biography.

I have found, however, that a survey of this region can yield theoretical and critical light only if it is carried on separately in the two regimes of person, by which I mean the two principal ways a life can be told: by the self or by the other. This distinction of person seems to me the enabling move for obtaining a clear vision of the interface between historical and fictional life stories. My approach accordingly postulates a two-dimensional schema, crossing the opposition between the historical and the fictional domains with the opposition between the third- and the first-person narrative forms. The result is the four-partite division diagrammed below and exemplified with a random quartet of familiar works:

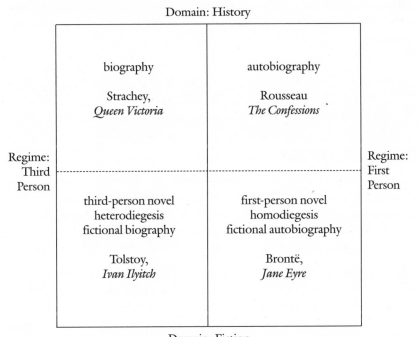

In framing these genres, I have deliberately inscribed the two horizontal boundaries by broken lines to suggest that they can be straddled, even traversed. Their symmetric appearance, however, is a crude shorthand: they are regulated by substantially different parameters in the two narrative regimes, each of which I take up separately in the two parts of this chapter.

THE THIRD-PERSON REGIME

I will begin by demonstrating how a poetics that compounds the regimes of person looks right past the most visible distinctions between historical and fictional biography. Many contemporary theorists could provide exhibits, but I will spotlight the blind spot in one who plays directly into my hands.

In an essay entitled "Poetry as Fiction," Barbara Herrnstein Smith develops the thesis that literary works of all genres are "representations" of what she calls "natural discourse."[3] In respect to novels, in particular, she maintains that they "have typically been representations of chronicles, journals, letters, memoirs, and biographies." Her most extensive demonstration, as it happens, concerns novels that "represent" biographies. She works it by juxtaposing two narrative passages, one that introduces the personage of John Hambden in Clarendon's *History of the Rebellion,* and another that introduces Ivan Ilyitch in Tolstoy's novella:

> He [John Hambden] was a gentleman of good family in Buckinghamshire, and born to a fair fortune, and of most civil and affable deportment. In his entrance into the world, he indulged himself all the license in sports and exercises and company which was used by men of the most jolly conversation; afterwards he retired to a more reserved and melancholy society.

> He [Ivan Ilyitch] had been a member of the Court of Justice, and died at the age of forty-five. His father had been an official who, after serving in various ministries and departments in Petersburg, had made the sort of career which brings men to positions from which by reason of long service they cannot be dismissed.

Smith explains: "I am suggesting here that the relation between the two passages is that the second is a representation of the sort of thing the first really is, namely a biography. *The Death of Ivan Ilyitch* is not a biography of a fictional character, but rather a fictive biography. . . . Tolstoy is, if you like, pretending to be *writing* a biography while actually *fabricating* one."[4]

---

3. In *On the Margins of Discourse,* 14–40. This thesis is commonly held by speech-act theorists, who likewise agree with Smith's corollary notion that fictional and factual narratives are lookalikes. John Searle writes, for example: "There is no textual property, syntactic or semantic, that will identify a text as a work of fiction" ("The Logical Status of Fictional Discourse," 325). But similar statements are also made by theorists of different persuasions. We read, for example, in a work that proposes to differentiate between historical and fictional narratives on Marxist grounds: "There is no specifically linguistic essence of fictionality that is immediately perceptible in the particulars of a text" (Barbara Foley, *Telling the Truth: The Theory and Practice of Documentary Fiction,* 40).
4. Smith, *On the Margins of Discourse,* 29–30.

Smith has picked her passages adroitly: the quote from Tolstoy does indeed sound like the inception of a biography. But this effect is purely local—limited to the summary exposition of the protagonist's life in the second of the twelve chapters. The story proper, in accordance with its title, begins only when Ivan Ilyitch begins to die. And here we get a text that sounds nothing like a biography—certainly nothing like Clarendon's report of this same John Hambden's death (which takes up all of one subordinate clause). What we do get, for pages on end, is this kind of thing:

> For three whole days, during which time did not exist for him, he [Ivan Ilyitch] struggled in that black sack into which he was being thrust by an invisible, restless force. He struggled as a man condemned to death struggles in the hands of the executioner, knowing that he cannot save himself. And every moment he felt that despite all his efforts he was drawing nearer and nearer to what terrified him. He felt that his agony was due to his being thrust into that black hole and still more to his not being able to get right into it. . . .
>
> Suddenly some force struck him in the chest and side, making it still harder to breathe, and he fell through the hole and there at the bottom was a light. . . .
>
> "Yes, it was all not the right thing," he said to himself, "but that's no matter. It can be done. But what *is* the right thing?" he asked himself, and suddenly grew quiet.[5]

Clearly, the last thing Tolstoy is doing here is "pretending to be writing a biography." A competent reader of fiction, I would maintain, understands the author to be communicating to his reader a fictional narrative about the death of an imaginary person. Ivan Ilyitch's struggle "in that black sack," his terror, his fall and ultimate illumination, and his directly quoted question—"'But what *is* the right thing?' he asked himself"—are purely inner experiences that no biographer can know about a real person's death, and none would dare to invent.

Death scenes are actually among the most predictable, most standard moments in biographies. They normally include medical diagnoses and testimonials of witnesses, all more or less tastefully arranged, and (for the luckier biographer) the quotation of poignantly significant last words. There are, to be sure, certain biographers who allow themselves to *specu-*

5. Leo Tolstoy, *The Death of Ivan Ilyitch and Other Stories*, 154–55.

late on what goes on in their subject's mind at the point of death. None, perhaps, does this more artfully than Lytton Strachey, when he ends Queen Victoria's life by telling us: "She herself, as she lay blind and silent, seemed to those who watched her to be divested of all thinking. . . . Yet, perhaps, in the secret chambers of her consciousness . . . " And now follows a passage too long to quote that evokes, in reverse chronological order, the high points of Victoria's life.[6]

No instant of life (if one can call it that) highlights more dramatically than death and dying the difference in kind between biography and fiction, between the biographer's constraint and the novelist's freedom. For here fiction is able to represent an experience that cannot be conveyed by "natural" discourse in *any* manner or form. This may well be why novelists—great realists no less than great antirealists—perennially give us the mimesis of a dying consciousness. Besides the many instances in Tolstoy, think of the extensively focalized death scenes in *A Simple Heart, Death in Venice, The Death of Artemio Cruz,* and *The Death of Virgil.* The last of these is an especially relevant case in point, since the protagonist of Hermann Broch's novel is no less historical than Strachey's Victoria. This work of over five hundred pages deals in its entirety with the last twenty-four hours of the Roman poet's life, presented by way of what is probably the most sustained exercise in free indirect discourse in world literature. No reader could ever mistake a single one of its pages for a historical biography, despite the appended list of historical sources.

Nor is *The Death of Virgil* the only fictional text that experiments daringly with the presentation of a historical figure's inner life. Büchner's *Lenz* (1831), a novella that tells of the Storm and Stress dramatist's bout with insanity, is known as a pioneering venture in focalized narration; Mann's *The Beloved Returns,* in its seventh chapter, treats us to an interior monologue of Goethe in person as he awakens from sleep. A few notches below on the quality scale, but still quite adventuresome stylistically, we have Anthony Burgess's *Nothing Like the Sun: A Story of Shakespeare's Love Life,* which follows Will's stream-of-consciousness in and out of familiar quotations. And lower still, the multitude of formally less ambitious and more predictable novels of this type by such best-selling authors of their and our day as Bulwer-Lytton, Mereshkowski, Feuchtwanger, and Irving Stone.[7] Turn to any of the individual turning points you can inti-

6. Lytton Strachey, *Queen Victoria,* 269.
7. Some of the more recent works of this type are examined in Ina Schabert, *In Quest of the Other Person: Fiction as Biography.*

mate from historical data, and you will find fireworks of internally voyeuristic techniques. Open Stone's *Passions of the Mind,* for a sample, to the chapter that deals with the crucial days in October 1897 when Freud discovered the Oedipus complex; you will be treated to childhood memories surfacing in the mind, inner voices resisting the awful truth (in direct quotation), and eventually to Freud in bed, dreaming the *mater nuda* dream. Stone knows his trade, knows that there would be no point writing a Freud novel without fearlessly treading where the Ernest Joneses fear to tread.

My detour into textual practice has pointed up, I think, the impaired vision of theorists like Barbara Herrnstein Smith who look upon fiction *in toto* as a representation of "natural" speech acts. They literally disregard the moments in third-person fiction that cannot be accommodated in their model, notably those moments—in some instances extended over the entire length of a long novel—that narrate life as experienced in the privacy of a character's consciousness. Clearly there is a crying need for a different model, one that is better suited to account for our pervasive mind-reading experience in third-person novels, that awakens our sense of wonder at this singular experience, and that raises our theoretical awareness of its uniqueness.

A model of this kind was, in fact, proposed some forty years ago by the German theorist Käte Hamburger in *Die Logik der Dichtung* (*The Logic of Literature*), a work that—though available in English since 1973—has failed to enter the mainstream of anglophone narrative poetics.[8] One reason for this exclusion is no doubt the exclusiveness of Hamburger's theory of fictionality: for even as this theory delimits fiction from nonfiction more sharply than any other before or after, it is also designed to apply solely to fiction cast in third-person form. Since roughly half of the works we customarily regard as fiction are cast in *first*-person form, this amputation may well appear as an unacceptable price to pay for clarity. As I will propose below, however, there is a way of avoiding this expense. For the moment I shall outline Hamburger's model without attending to this problem, merely asking my reader to keep in mind that for Hamburger the term *fiction* means third-person fiction exclusively.

As I have already mentioned, Hamburger approaches fictionality from a direction diametrically opposed to that of speech-act theorists. Her starting point is not sameness but difference, the quiddity or quintessence

8. The English translation by Marilynn J. Rose is based on the second—strongly revised—German edition published in 1968; the original German edition was published in 1957.

of fiction that sets it apart from all other linguistic performances, including, above all, historical narrative. In the section where she develops her main thesis—significantly entitled "Fictional Narration and its Characteristic Features"—she locates the crux of fictionality precisely in those textual moments of third-person novels that we found so disturbingly disregarded by Smith: moments, that is, where fiction conveys the intimate subjective experiences of its characters, the here and now of their lives to which no real observer could ever accede in real life—such moments, in short, as the death of Ivan Ilyitch. It is this phenomenal phenomenological "otherness" of fiction that Hamburger pinpoints in the following dictum: "Epic fiction is the sole epistemological instance where the I-originarity (or subjectivity) of a third person *qua* third person can be portrayed."[9]

"I-originarity of a third person," though not a catchy phrase, one that attempts to frame a complex phenomenon with utmost precision. A brief excursion into linguistics will help to explain it. Hamburger derives "I-originarity" from the key concept "Ich-Origo" coined by the philosopher of language Karl Bühler. What he means by it is the zero point (or center of orientation) in space and time determined by the here-and-now of the speaking subject. The idea—if not the term—will be familiar to readers of Emile Benveniste, one of the linguists most closely affiliated with modern French narrative poetics. For Benveniste, as for Bühler, every linguistic utterance defines, and is defined by, the subjectivity of the speaker. Thus the first-person pronoun in Benveniste's familiar tautology refers to "the individual who utters the present instance of discourse containing the linguistic instance I"; and it is also this speaking subject who actualizes the floating meaning of the spatial and temporal adverbs he uses: here, there, now, tomorrow.[10] But neither Bühler nor Benveniste considers the fundamental disruption of this systematic subjectivity of ordinary language that can (and often does) occur in fictional narrative. As Hamburger shows, the paradoxical distinction, the utterly *extra*-ordinary artifice of fictional discourse is precisely that the subjectivity of its language *can* be situated, not in the self-referential "I" who utters the discourse, but in the "she" or "he" to whom the discourse refers.

This dislocation of the "I-origin" from speaking self to silent other results in literally unheard-of departures from standard grammatical norms, most strikingly in a sentence like this: Now was his last chance to see her; his plane left tomorrow. Conjoining as it does verbs in the past

9. Hamburger, *The Logic of Literature*, 83.
10. Emile Benveniste, *Problems in General Linguistics*, 218–19.

tense with adverbs signifying the present and future, a sentence of this type epitomizes for Hamburger the deviance of a language that creates the reality of unreal, imaginary beings — its deviance and its logic. When we read such sentences in a novel, they strike us as perfectly logical — or better, they don't strike us at all. Here language is ruled by different norms: norms indicating that the epistemological limitations of everyday life have been suspended. We are in a linguistic domain in which the past tense no longer needs to refer to the speaker's own past, where it *can* refer to the "now" of an individual whose plane "left tomorrow"; a world where a speaker *can* tell exactly what another person feels and perceives and remembers and plans without that person ever having told anyone; a world, in a word, "where the I-originarity of a third person can be portrayed."

Now Hamburger, of course, is neither the first nor the last to have pointed up that a novel can adopt the perspectives of its characters. From James's central intelligence to Genette's internal focalization, this narrative mode has been identified and provided with a variety, if not a surfeit, of tags. And its principal stylistic devices, notably free indirect style, have been discussed in numerous studies, including my own *Transparent Minds*. But where Hamburger's theory differs from all of these typologies is that for her, psychic omniscience is not a narrative type or mode or device or technique, but *the* pivotal structural norm that rules the realm of third-person fiction and that is logically ruled out in all other discursive realms. In this respect her theory has had no precedent and — with one possible exception[11] — no progeny.

Having used such authoritarian terms as *dictum, norm,* and *rule* to describe Hamburger's theory of fictionality, it is time to add some moderating remarks. First, this theory should not be taken to mean that every sentence of every third-person novel takes the form of "his plane left tomorrow." It merely holds that it is in the nature of fiction to *enable* this type of unnatural discourse; or, to put it another way, that fiction is recognizable as fiction only if and when it actualizes its focalizing potential. This qualification has special relevance for textual beginnings. Few novels written before 1900 start *in mediam mentem* — in the manner, say, of Joyce's *Portrait of the Artist*. More traditional novels are more apt, at the outset, to read like various types of nonfictional discourse, including biography, of course,

---

11. In *Unspeakable Sentences,* Ann Banfield radicalizes Hamburger's conception of fictionality on the basis of generative linguistics and extends it to first-person fiction. For a judicious critique of this work, see Brian McHale, "Unspeakable Sentences, Unnatural Acts: Linguistics and Poetics Revisited."

so that their move *in* and *into* the subjectivity of the protagonist is variously deferred. Nor do they necessarily stay inside once they are in. There are
notable cases where the open mind of a character is suddenly closed off at
critical junctures of his life. Dostoevsky, for example, in striking contrast to
Tolstoy, never depicts his characters' deaths from within. And the fact that
Bakhtin singles out this practice as a striking singularity of Dostoevsky's
fictional world—sufficiently striking to call for interpretive explanation—
is entirely in keeping with Hamburger's *Logic*.[12] It goes to show that in a
novel, it is the reversion to quasifactual discourse, rather than the adherence to arti-factual discourse, that draws attention to itself—especially
where moments of radical privacy are concerned.

This instance also makes it clear that Hamburger's ruling norms are not
well served when they are taken as normative rules. They do not rule out
exceptions, but they make them visible, illuminating both the practice of
novelists and the expectations of their readers. They explain in particular
why biographies that regale us with inside views of their subjects strike
us as somehow illegitimate; and, conversely, why a novel that remained
from start to finish in the mode of external focalization on its protagonist
would strike us as something of an anomaly.

Before looking at some of these border-crossing cases, the borderline
itself deserves a closer look. Needless to say, this line does not run simply
between a realm that includes, and another that excludes, psychological
discourse per se. Any biographer who goes beyond the mere compilation
of vital facts will be more or less concerned with his subject's mental actions and reactions. The question is not *whether* but *how* he will express
these concerns. The line that separates historiographically legitimate
from "illicit" (fictionlike) practices accordingly hinges on subtle technical differentiations.

Of the various techniques for presenting the mental life of third persons, the one that prevails in biography is *psycho-narration:* a technique
where the narrator's voice is clearly set off from the language that runs
through his subject's head.[13] But even this most distanced of the fictional modes of psychic presentation takes on quite special forms that mark a
biographer's epistemological constraints when he deals with the inner life
of a historical figure.

12. Bakhtin's discussion of Dostoevsky's death scenes is detailed in Caryl Emerson, "The Tolstoy
Connection in Bakhtin."
13. For a definition of the term *psycho-narration* and a discussion of this technique in works of
fiction, see Cohn, *Transparent Minds,* 21–57.

The most common marker of biographical psycho-narration is its con-jectural and inferential syntax. We have already seen the former displayed in Strachey's speculations on Victoria's dying thoughts—"perhaps, in the secret chambers of her consciousness . . ." When a biographer can, or thinks he can, speak with a greater degree of authority, he will pass from conjecture to inference, becoming—in a term once applied by John Up-dike in the *New Yorker* to the author of a book on Kafka—"a dues-paying member of the 'must-have' school of biography." The popularity of the must-have construction with life-historians is no doubt due to its allow-ing them to look inside their subject's mind without thereby transform-ing him or her into an imaginary being. It gives their views an air of log-ic, of inevitability, without giving them the air of omniscience. When, in the biography reviewed by Updike, we are told that Kafka "must have been wildly resentful" of the birth of two younger brothers who died in infancy, that he "must have wished them out of his life, done away with them in primitive fantasies,"[14] we may be justified in accusing the author of dime-store psychology, but not of having made Kafka's life into a fiction. No matter how fanciful its content, the *form* of an inferential state-ment puts a stamp of historicity on the text that contains it.

Where verbs of inner happenings are concerned, a punctilious biogra-pher will abandon the inferential past for the past indicative only under special circumstances: when he can base his statements on autobio-graphical documents. Whence the typical chapters in life histories where lengthy quotations from memoirs, letters, or diaries are woven together by inductions concerning what a person "thought" or "felt." These in-ductions themselves can range from dissonant critique to consonant "reenactment."[15] At one extreme, we have the severely analytic discourse of the psychobiographer bent on motivating his subject's behavior by un-conscious drives—drives that, by definition, escape self-awareness; at the other extreme, we have the harmonizing discourse of the empathic biog-rapher who espouses his subject's self-perception on the model Dilthey called for with such terms as *Einfühlung* (empathy) and *Sichhineinverset-zen* (to put oneself in someone's place). [16] But even the most sympathet-ic biographer will, so long as he remains historiographically scrupulous, clearly mark off his subject's discourse from his own and resist, above all, lapsing into free indirect style. The result is usually a highly heteroge-

14. Ernst Pawel, *The Nightmare of Reason: A Life of Franz Kafka*, 16.
15. The term is R. G. Collingwood's; see *The Idea of History*, 214.
16. For an examination of the contrastive relationship between Freud's and Dilthey's approach-es to biography, see Jürgen Habermas, *Erkenntnis und Interesse*, 262–67.

neous textual surface that cannot readily be mistaken for the homogeneously omniscient inside views ruling third-person novels.

Now as we all know, there are biographers whose priority is less to im-
press their public by their scrupulousness and more to attract it by their
readability. And the single most effective way of producing a "good read"
in a life history is quite simply to integrate autobiographical source materials seamlessly into the psycho-narrative text, with explicit quotation
yielding to implicit paraphrase. At the hypothetical limit, this process
would result in a biography that transvocalized an *auto*biography from
start to finish, transposed it literally from first- to third-person form. I
doubt that this limit has ever been reached in actual practice. But many
biographies approach it off and on, perhaps quite inadvertently—at
which points they momentarily read like novels, even if their notes continue to provide archival references.[17]

Still, such occasional skids are qualitatively different from the deliberate steps over the border by biographers who, casting away all historiographic inhibitions, write what has been called hybrid biographies.[18]
Characterized by their unlimited irradiation of the minds of their historical subjects, such works were particularly popular in the nineteen-twen-
ties, when they appeared under the name New Biography. Emil Ludwig's
Napoleon (1925) is a good example. Assuring his readers that "in this book,
all the data are recorded facts," the author adds with disarming candor "except the soliloquies [*Selbstgespräche*]" (681). But rather than quote the latter directly, Ludwig renders them by the more insidious device of free indirect style, melting them into his narrative language in such a way that
the reader can't tell where the documented fact stops and the invention
starts. The voyeuristic illusion this creates no doubt accounts for the immense popularity of this genre in its own day. But serious readers recognized the sleight of hand, even though they may not have identified the
technical trick that produced it. Virginia Woolf, for one, reacted with pre-
scriptive severity: "Let it be fact, one feels, or let it be fiction. The imagination will not serve under two masters simultaneously."[19]

The New Journalists of the seventies may, I think, be regarded as a
postmodern reincarnation of the New Biographical trend, though they

17. Prominent illustrations of this practice are found in Jean Delay, *The Youth of André Gide,* and
Celia Bertin, *Marie Bonaparte: A Life.*
18. This term is employed in Ina Schabert, "Fictional Biography, Factual Biography, and their
Contaminations," where this trend in modern biographical practice is examined.
19. "The New Biography," in *Collected Essays,* IV:234. For a later reaction of a historian, see
Siegfried Kracauer, "Die Biographie als neubürgerliche Kunstform," in *Das Ornament der
Masse,* 75–80.

are far more self-conscious of their purpose. Some have actually laid claim to the creation of a new literary form that wipes out for good and all the antiquated distinction between factual and fictional writing.[20] But a look at the oxymoronic subtitles featured on the title pages of these newer crossbreeds—True Life Novel, Novel Biography, Nonfiction Novel— makes it clear that they were largely written and read for their transgressive shock value. Closer study would confirm that their fictionalizing devices boil down principally to the consistent application of focalizing technique—sometimes in stream-of-consciousness form—to real-life sports heroes, rock stars, and convicted murderers.[21] In this perspective, biographies that act like novels, far from erasing the borderline between the two genres, actually bring the line that separates them more clearly into view.

The same is true when, approaching this line from its nether side, we look at the case of a novel that acts like a biography. I use the singular advisedly, since I know only a single case of this kind: Wolfgang Hildesheimer's *Marbot,* which I examine in Chapter 5 below. Typologically, as we will see, *Marbot* may be described as the inverse of such works as *The Death of Virgil* or Stone's Freud novel. In lieu of applying fictional discourse to bring a historical figure to life, it applies historical discourse to bring a fictional figure to life. But this relationship between matter and manner, deviant as it is within the third-person regime, is precisely the standard relationship that pertains in the first-person regime, as we shall see.

At this point of passage between the two regimes of person, mention must be made of a special type of historical biography that has a strong component of autobiography. Boswell's *Life of Johnson* is no doubt the most famous example, but Max Brod's *Franz Kafka* and Stanislav Joyce's *My Brother's Keeper* are two other well-known instances. (As I will show in Chapter 3 below, Freud's case histories can also be assigned to this category.) These "witness biographies," as we might call them, have their fictional counterparts in such novels as Thomas Mann's *Doctor Faustus*— subtitled *The Life of the German Composer Adrian Leverkühn as Told by a Friend*—Butler's *The Way of all Flesh,* Balzac's *Louis Lambert,* Conrad's

20. See Mas'ud Zavarzadeh, *The Mythopoetic Reality: The Postwar American Non-fiction Novel* and Tom Wolfe, "The New Journalism," in *The New Journalism*. Here Wolfe, who was at the time a leading spokesman for the New Journalism movement, goes so far as to claim that reportive writing based on interviews can "penetrate the thoughts of another person" and thereby supplant, and even surpass, the novel as the privileged medium for the representation of life (32).

21. Wolfe gives a surprisingly well-informed technical account of the focalizing devices he employed in his New Journalistic writings (*The New Journalism,* 17–21).

Marlow novels, Nabokov's *The Real Life of Sebastian Knight,* and many more. Unlike the standard third-person novels considered above, novels that adopt this structure—like the first-person novels about to be considered below—simulate a natural (referential) discourse and accordingly a realistically motivated narrative situation. This severely precludes inside views of the biographical subject, a cognitive constraint often thematized in novels of this type by the narrator's laments concerning his nonomniscience in the face of an opaque Other.[22]

THE FIRST-PERSON REGIME

In the first-person regime, a number of theorists besides Käte Hamburger provide guide wires for drawing a borderline between historical and fictional lives: notably Michál Glowínski, Elizabeth Bruss, and Philippe Lejeune.[23] These theorists share two basic assumptions: first, that autobiography—no less than biography—is a *referential* genre, a discourse that refers to the past of a *real* speaker; and second, that the first-person novel, at least in its classical guise of fictional autobiography, is the deliberate artificial simulation of this referential genre.[24] The pervasive homology between these two types of text is thus not to be understood as a sign of consanguinity: they are not related in the manner of identical twins, but as a facsimile relates to its original. Various terms have been proposed for this relationship: Glowínski calls it "formal mimetics";[25] Hamburger, "feigned reality statement."[26] As the likeness of these terms to Barbara Herrnstein Smith's "representations of natural discourse" suggests, the model here proposed for first-person fiction corresponds to the

22. For a brief account of this fictional type, see Franz Stanzel, *A Theory of Narrative,* 205–9. See also a lengthier study—more existential than technical in orientation—of this novelistic form by Bruce H. Kawin, *The Mind of the Novel.*

23. Glowínski, "On the First-Person Novel"; Bruss, *Autobiographical Acts: The Changing Situation of a Literary Genre*; Lejeune, "The Autobiographical Pact," in *On Autobiography,* 3–30.

24. To avoid confusion, I should specify that what I mean by "fictional autobiography" is a novel where a fictional narrator gives a retrospective account of his life, and not one thought to be based on the *author's* life. My criterion, in short, is narrative form, not narrative content. I would maintain that autobiographically inspired works are more appropriately labeled by the inversely compounded term "autobiographical fiction"—the advantage being that the adjective can be more readily qualified than the noun. Most of us would probably agree that all fiction is autobiographical—some more, some less—whereas not all novels are cast in the form of an autobiography—some are, some aren't. *Tonio Kröger* is, on the basis of what we know about Mann's early life, an autobiographical fiction; *Death in Venice* is, on the same basis, less autobiographical. Both these third-person novellas are more autobiographical than the first-person novel *The Confessions of Felix Krull*; however, in my terms, the latter is decidedly a fictional autobiography.

25. Glowínski, "On the First-Person Novel," 106.

26. Hamburger, *The Logic of Literature,* 313.

one speech-act theorists apply to fiction across the board, without distinction of person.

The intentional and receptional norms that govern real autobiography have in fact been most clearly defined in speech-actional terms. In her book *Autobiographical Acts,* Bruss formulates a number of interrelated "rules" that create the illocutionary force of her titular concept, all of which relate to the author's need to assert and the reader's need to accept the "truth value" of the narrated events, more precisely their "purported truth value." The rule that applies to this communication process on the author's side reads: "Whether or not what is reported can be discredited, . . . the autobiographer *purports* to believe in what he asserts." On the reader's side, the rule-abiding expectation that the report is true implies the freedom to "check up" on its accuracy by way of appropriate verification procedures.[27] In this perspective, the truth claim of autobiography in no sense implies the *actual* truth of an autobiographer's statement. Going Bruss one better, Lejeune in "The Autobiographical Pact" even proposes that the referentiality of the genre, far from being undermined, is much rather confirmed by the reader's customary expectation that self-representation always involves a measure of misrepresentation.[28]

It now becomes clear that the referential nature of autobiography can only be theoretically secured by a shift of emphasis from its content to its speaker. For if the genre is defined by way of the reality of its speaking subject, then it remains no less real when the subject lies or fantasizes about his past than when he utters verifiable truths. This conception of autobiography provides a much needed vindication for those of us who have resisted the idea—rampant ever since Northrop Frye first proposed it in *The Anatomy of Criticism*—that autobiography is a (form of) fiction. It allows us to justify this resistance even if we share—as who does not these days—the skeptical perspective of modern thinkers on the notions of stable identity, truthful introspection, unified selfhood, authentic memory, the translatability of experience into language, and the narratability of life.

When autobiography is understood as a referential genre in the sense just defined, the principal criterion for differentiating between real and fictional self-narration jumps into view. It hinges quite simply on the ontological status of its speaker—by which I mean his identity or noniden-

27. Bruss, *Autobiographical Acts,* 11. Bruss's approach to autobiography is developed further by H. Porter Abbott in "Autobiography, Autography, Fiction: Groundwork for a Taxonomy of Textual Categories."
28. Lejeune, *On Autobiography,* 23.

tity with the author in whose name the narrative has been published.[29] This status is, in the majority of cases, plainly in evidence. When a title page reads: Thomas Mann, *The Confessions of Felix Krull, Confidence Man*, we know this book is a novel. Mann's title—like any number of analogous ones from the canon—features what I take to be the essential token of fictionality in the first-person regime: the creation of an imaginary speaker. As long as this speaker is named, on or within the text, and named differently from the author, the reader knows that one is not meant to take the discourse as a (referential) reality statement.[30]

On this basis it would appear that fictional autobiography shares one essential feature with fictional biography: both tell the life of an *imaginary* person. This commonality secures firm ground on which to restore a unified domain of fiction, from which (as we must now recall) Hamburger had severed the first-person form. It allows us, moreover, to restore this domain without thereby effacing Hamburger's crucial division between the two regimes of person.[31] For even though the imaginary existence of the biographee is signaled in both regimes, it is signaled quite differently in each. In contrast to the distinctive fictional discourse that creates the mind of an imaginary "he" or "she," there is nothing distinctively fictional about the discourse of an imaginary "I." The only mark of its fictionality is the nonreferential identity tag affixed to the person, the mind, the voice of its speaker.

It is by way of this nominal signpost that the author of a fictional autobiography contracts with his reader what Lejeune, as a counterpart to his "autobiographical pact," calls the "fictional pact."[32] But it seems to me

29. This formulation can readily accommodate fictional biographies whose speakers are historical figures, as in Marguerite Yourcenar, *Hadrian's Memoirs*, or William Styron, *The Confessions of Nat Turner*.

30. This onomastic criterion has been intensively investigated by Lejeune in "The Autobiographical Pact"; see also his "Autobiographie, roman et nom propre," in *Moi aussi*. Lejeune's reaction to the curious case of a work deliberately written to disprove his onomastic criterion—Serge Doubrovsky's *Fils*—is discussed in Paul John Eakin, *Touching the World: Reference in Autobiography*, 25–27.

31. In her discussion of first-person fiction (*The Logic of Literature*, 311–41), Hamburger fails to perceive that fictionality in this regime, though its "symptoms" are entirely different from those she discovers for fiction in the third-person regime, can nonetheless be *qualitatively* defined on the basis of the speaker's marked fictionality. Her argument that there is a merely quantitative difference between real and fictional autobiography—a variable "degree of feint" corresponding to the degree of realism in an autobiographical text's *content* (328–29)—seems to me fallacious and out of keeping with her theory as a whole.

32. Lejeune, *On Autobiography*, 14–15. Strictly speaking, a narrator's nominal differentiation from the author is not the only way his imaginary nature can be marked in the text. Lejeune allows for the theoretical possibility of an autobiographical narrative that would declare itself a novel on its title page and whose narrator would remain a nameless "I"; but in practice he finds no work that conforms to this virtuality (16).

important to point up the essential dissymmetry that pertains between these symmetrically labeled pacts. In effect, all fictional autobiographies offer a telescoped *double* pact: an autobiographical pact impacted within a fictional pact. I see in this literally equivocal origin of its discourse *the* decisive factor that (not always consciously) shapes our reading experience of a novel cast in first-person form and that sets it apart from the experience of reading a real autobiography.

The difference between these two reading processes comes into view when we consider the ways we react to signs of impaired vision in confessional texts. To take a notorious pair: the real Rousseau's *Confessions* and the fictional Michel's confessions in Gide's *The Immoralist*. The critical reader of *The Confessions* has no choice but to refer all the telltale evidence of self-deception to Rousseau himself, thereby subverting his explicit authorial intentions, his authority as self-narrator. We see this process at work in every penetrating Rousseau reader. Paul de Man's reading of the stolen ribbon episode is exemplary in this respect.[33] By scanning the narrative language for signs of inauthenticity, he finds Rousseau's exhibitionism transparently displayed. Needless to say, this can hardly be the transparency Rousseau himself had in mind when he declared: "Je voudrais pouvoir . . . rendre mon âme transparente aux yeux du lecteur" ["I would like to be able . . . to render my soul transparent to the eyes of the reader"] (275; my translation).

In the confessional discourse of Gide's Michel, likewise, various incongruities, gaps, over- and under-emphases reveal the speaker's self-delusion, in particular his ignorance of his true sexual orientation. But the reader who detects these symptoms has every right to assume they are clues intentionally planted there by the author. Gide's *récit*, in other words, tells a different story from the one his narrator tells. And it is only when we discover Michel's unconscious homosexuality that the authorially intended meaning passes from author to reader—behind the narrator's back. This makes Michel a classic case of what Wayne Booth calls an "unreliable narrator," one who (to quote his definition) "does not speak in accordance with . . . the implied author's norms."[34] But we know that this disaccord of norms is not always easy to recognize, and once recognized, not easy to demonstrate without relying on extratextual evidence. Albert Guerard, who was one of the first to discover it in the case of Michel (some fifty years after the publication of Gide's work), attributes the delay to "the inveterate tendency of critics to take a narrative told in the first

33. Paul de Man, "Excuses (Confessions)," in *Allegories of Reading,* 285.
34. *The Rhetoric of Fiction,* 158–59.

person at its face value and to confuse the narrator's consciousness with the author's."[35] This inclination must, I think, be acknowledged, even if it is nowadays severely frowned upon. What it shows is that the distance separating author and narrator in any given first-person novel is not a given and fixed quantity but a variable, subject to the reader's evaluation. And this perennial unknown is one of the factors that makes the reading of a fictional autobiography *in principle* such a different kind of experience from the reading of a real autobiography, where the parameter of unreliability (in Booth's sense of the word) is *by definition* reduced to zero.

The reader's interpretive freedom to maximize or minimize the distance between authors and narrators sharpens to the horns of a dilemma when he is confronted with a first-person text of the type Lejeune calls "indeterminate": when the narrator remains a nameless "I" in an autobiography that bears no other generic signals.[36] A few titles that qualify for this free-fire zone are Knut Hamsun's *Hunger*, Gérard de Nerval's *Auréla*, Jerzy Kosinski's *The Painted Bird*, and Marguerite Duras's *The Lover*. Theoretically each of these works condemns us to vacillate, or allows us to oscillate, between referential and fictional readings. To my knowledge, no one has yet systematically investigated the circumstances that attend the composition or the reception of works of this kind. In the absence of solid groundwork in this matter, I will merely refer to a couple of anecdotal episodes that give suggestive support to my separatist thesis.

One concerns *The Painted Bird*, whose story of a nameless boy's wartime experience was understood by its first readers as a direct account of Kosinski's own childhood in Nazi-occupied Poland and presumed to be factually more or less authentic. Kosinski added an epilogue, "Afterward," to later editions of the book, expressly written to dispel this reading. Here, without denying that the text may have an autobiographical basis, he explains that he had aimed to appear "purely as a story teller." He meant for the reader to identify with his child protagonist, to "enter a fictional role" rather than, as happens with autobiography, merely "to become the observer of another man's existence."[37] Though it is unlikely that the nuance of a name or even a generic subtitle would have saved

---

35. *André Gide*, 103.
36. Lejeune, *On Autobiography*, 16–17.
37. Jerzy Kosinski, *The Painted Bird*, 256 and 258. The biographical data surrounding this case—reports that Kosinski in fact encouraged his friends to believe in the autobiographical background of *The Painted Bird* and later revelations that there was no basis whatever for these claims—are not strictly relevant to the problem considered above; these data can be found in James Park Sloan, "Kosinski's War."

Kosinski from the rabid political attacks his book occasioned in the Communist Polish press, it might have helped to direct Western readers to the more universal meaning he had ostensibly intended.

An inverse case is Henry Miller's reaction to Edmund Wilson's review of *The Tropic of Cancer*, where Wilson—evidently under the impression that he had been reading a novel—describes Miller's "hero" as "the genuine American bum come to live a beautiful life in Paris." Miller riposted: "The theme [of the book] is myself, and the narrator, or the hero, as your reviewer put it, is also myself . . . ; it is me, because I have painstakingly indicated throughout the book that the hero is myself."[38] I am not as certain as Wayne Booth—whose *Rhetoric of Fiction* drew my attention to this exchange—that Miller's indignation is justified, or that Wilson's reading of *Tropic* is an example of the absurd length to which modern critics carry what Booth calls the "irony hunt" (369). All three—Wilson, Miller, and Booth—fail to note the factor that was no doubt primarily responsible for the critical *quid pro quo*. In the absence of a subtitle or nominal self-reference, how was Wilson to recognize that the ironic distance between the author and his nonheroic "I" here stood at degree zero?

What seems to me especially noteworthy in these two examples of generic misfiring is that both sides take such decisive stands in the face of such indecisive texts. If we take them at their word, neither Kosinski nor Miller aimed for ambiguity. Similarly, their reviewers apparently unhesitatingly apprehended the intended novel as an autobiography and the intended autobiography as a novel. This confirms my assumption that first-person narratives are not as a rule either written or read as semi-autobiographies or demi-novels. They are given and taken as one or the other, even when they are not taken for what they were given. In this respect I disagree with Georges May, who concludes from the existence of such indeterminate texts "that there is no essential difference between the novel and autobiography" and who proceeds on this basis to range these genres on a single continuous scale modulating by degrees from most to least fictional.[39] To me these ambiguous texts indicate quite the contrary: namely, that we cannot conceive of any given text as more or less fictional, more or less factual, but that we read it in one key or the other—that fiction, in short, is not a matter of degree but of kind, in first- no less than in third-person form.[40] I hold to this position even in the face of the work

---

38. Quoted in Edmund Wilson, *The Shores of Light*, 708–9.
39. Georges May, *L'Autobiographie*, 188–94; my translation.
40. On this point I find myself agreeing with Smith, *On the Margins of Discourse*, 47, and with Foley, *Telling the Truth*, 27.

that appears to challenge it most powerfully, a work Harry Levin called "the most extensive exercise in the first-person singular." I mean, of course, *A la Recherche du temps perdu*. The generic ambiguity of Proust's work, however, raises major and quite unique problems that I will examine in Chapter 4 below.

To this point I have adhered to the classical model of first-person fiction, the model that models itself on real autobiography, without considering the fact and the ways a first-person novel can deviate from it. But, as Głowiński observes, when a literary form imitates a real-world discourse, "the 'imitat*ing*' element does not become absolutely subordinate to the 'imitat*ed*' one."[41] Potentially a formally mimetic literary form can always emancipate itself from its mimetic matrix to take on freely innovative formal features. A process of this sort has manifestly been at work in the first-person novel over the last decades, transforming its traditional guise almost beyond recognition.

More than a century ago, Dostoevsky published a work called in English "A Gentle Creature," which he subtitled "A Fantastic Story." Here a man alone in a room with the dead body of his wife recounts the history of his sadomasochistic marriage. As the author explains in a preface, he called the story "fantastic" not on account of its content—which he regards as "eminently real"—but on account of its form. For since this tale was neither written down by the teller, nor addressed to an interlocutor, its textual existence presumes the presence in the room of an "invisible stenographer" who took down everything the man said to himself. From our present-day vantage point, this spectral stenographer takes on both an emblematic and a prophetic meaning: he stands for the effect of irreality created by first-person fiction as soon as it departs from its mimetic matrix.

The most important new fictional genre that sprang from this emancipation was the so-called interior monologue novel.[42] No one was clearer than Joyce about its radical nature, its discontinuity with the narrative tradition. Speaking of Dujardin's novel, *Les Lauriers sont coupés* (which he regarded as the model for the "Penelope" section of *Ulysses*), he declared: "In that book . . . the uninterrupted unrolling of that [the protagonist's] thought, replac[es] the usual form of narrative."[43] A text of this type, as

---

41. Głowiński, "On the First-Person Novel," 106.
42. The final chapter of my *Transparent Minds* is devoted to a study of this form under the title "The Autonomous Monologue."
43. Quoted in Richard Ellmann, *James Joyce*, 534.

Joyce realized, is based on new conventions, a new code: in lieu of the simulation of a real language, written or oral, we now get the simulation of an unwritten, inaudible language—one that was never meant to reach a reader's eye or a listener's ear. No matter how great the psychological verisimilitude created by this language, it can only exist in a fictional work.

Well-known as this modern form is, I will illustrate it with a passage that highlights its fictionality with particular poignancy:

> The cars have gone from the road farewell bus what's this the siren of a ship like the wail of a little cat hearing nothing seeing nothing farewell street enough street and suddenly a little bell a whistle oh the telephone is ringing like a little lamb beside me someone is calling wants me weaker and weaker not a bell but the whistle of a dying wind I know but do not hear too bad too bad about me too bad for I am dead too bad, for I am not[44]

In this passage from *The Lover* by the Israeli novelist A. B. Yehoshua, we hear the silent voice of an old woman at the point of death (from a section of a novel entirely filled by figural voices). Note that she does not *narrate* her death in the manner of a ghost, after the fact, but that the text conveys it by way of the words that pass through her mind instantaneously at the moment she dies. There is no way such a moment could have been rendered in a traditional first-person novel that followed the autobiographical model, but only in a traditional third-person novel like *Ivan Ilyitch*, by way of a narrator's mediation.

As I will show in Chapter 6 below, contemporary fiction has tended to sever first-person narration from autobiographical mimetics in even more radical ways by using the present as a narrative tense. In works of this kind, as in autonomous monologues, fictional self-narration evolves in directions where none of the essential differences between the two regimes of person that I have stressed in the present chapter continue to apply. These changes open the way to absolutely unreal narrative situations, enabling characters to live and tell—and even to die and tell—simultaneously. But this (post)modernist development in no sense invalidates the differential distinctions I have drawn in what precedes between fictional and historical lives that adhere to traditional norms.

44. A. B. Yehoshua, *The Lover,* 346.

3

Freud's Case Histories and
the Question of Fictionality

Among literary critics and their readers, Freud's stature as a novelist is growing rapidly. Already he has been compared with Dickens, Dostoevsky, Henry James, Conan Doyle, Joseph Conrad, Proust, Mann, Joyce, Faulkner, Virginia Woolf, Nabokov, Borges, and several other masters of fictional Realism and Modernism. This reputation rests largely on the three texts nicknamed "Dora," "Wolf Man," and "Rat Man," notwithstanding the rather less literary sound of their full names: "Fragment of an Analysis of a Case of Hysteria" ["Bruchstück einer Hysterie-Analyse"], "From the History of an Infantile Neurosis" ["Aus der Geschichte einer infantilen Neurose"], and "Notes upon a Case of Obsessional Neurosis" ["Bemerkungen über einen Fall von Zwangsneurose"]. By now it no longer surprises us to find these works featured in critical, historical, and theoretical studies on fiction. In *Reading for the Plot* (1984), Peter Brooks sandwiches his "Fictions of the Wolf Man" between chapters on *Heart of Darkness* and *Absalom, Absalom!* In his volume entitled *Representations* (1975), Steven Marcus's influential essay "Freud and Dora" concludes a series of studies on assorted nineteenth- and twentieth-century novels and novelists. In *Aufschreibsysteme 1800/1900* (1987), Friedrich Kittler aligns the "psychological case novels" [*Fallromane*] of the "novelist" [*Romanschreiber*] Freud with Rilke's *Malte Laurids Brigge* and other turn-of-the-century novels, to define a literary period code. In an article entitled "The Freudian Novel" (1981), Michel de Certeau places Freud's case histories at a turning point of literary history, proposing that they dismantled the fictional norms of the nineteenth century in the manner that *Don Quixote* had deconstructed the Spanish *Hidalguia* three centuries earlier. Many further instances could be cited to show that among literary critics—regardless of their general admiration for, or hostility to, the *chose freudienne*—these texts are well on their way to becoming canonical works of modern fiction.

Remembering Freud's image of the polar bear and the whale—who don't engage in warfare because nature confines them to their respective habitats—it is perhaps natural that dissenting voices should begin to arise, not from within the professional species that treats patients and records their histories on a daily basis, but from within the one that habitually concerns itself with the nature of literature, fiction, and the novel. My own motivation, at any rate, in engaging in a critical examination of the generic assignation highlighted above is my uneasiness with the widespread trend toward ignoring distinctions between different textual categories — an uneasiness that prompts my attempt throughout the present volume to retrace the vanishing boundaries between fictional and nonfictional narrative.[1]

In the present chapter, using the generic reception accorded Freud's case histories as a case of my own, I follow four argumentative moves: first, I recapitulate the vagaries (studied more closely in Chapter 1 above) that attend the concept of fiction and look to the poetics of life histories (discussed in greater detail in Chapter 2 above) for stabilizing distinctions; second, I review Freud's own intentions in fashioning his case-historical writings; third, I examine these writings themselves for objective grounds to dispel their fictional reading; and finally, I glance at Freud's conception of historiography as it applies to the psychoanalytic narration of individual lives.

FICTION AND LIFE HISTORY

First of all, then, we must examine the concept of fiction, for it is the scope and slipperiness of this word's referential field that has enabled the ease — if not the eagerness — with which the generic borderlines between fictional and factual texts have been erased. This semantic instability, as well as the confusions and misapprehensions that ensue, can easily be detected in writings on Freud's case histories.

I can pass quickly over the derogatory everyday use of the term *fiction* to designate untrue statements; for — although Freud's case histories are known to contain untrue statements (if only because, for reasons of discretion, he variously altered the circumstances of his patients' lives) — the claim that Freud is a fiction writer is usually based on more sophisticated connotations attending the term. I would nonetheless suggest that this

1. I can only note in passing that the tendency to efface generic borderlines has affected not merely the reading of Freud's case histories but likewise the reading of his more purely theoretical texts. See, for example, Jacques Derrida, "The Purveyor of Truth," where Freud's analytic commentary on "The Emperor's New Clothes" in *The Interpretation of Dreams* is diagnosed as "belonging no more clearly to the tradition of scientific discourse than to a specific genre of fiction" (38). This and other instances of deconstructive readings of Freud's oeuvre — sometimes called "French Freud" — have begun to be seriously questioned. See in particular Stanley Corngold, "Freud as Literature?" in *The Fate of the Self*, 189–95.

meaning of the word tends to cast a negative light on Freud's case histories when they are called fictions.

In modern critical language it has become quite the norm to label as fictions all verbal accounts that superimpose a general significance, a meaningful interpretation, on events after the fact.[2] Given the quantity of conceptual abstractions Freud introduces into the telling of his patients' lives, he can easily qualify as the supreme fiction writer when the word is taken in this sense. But it is far less plausible to speak on this basis of "the fictionality of case history as a literary genre."[3] Likewise, one may readily agree with Peter Brooks when—à propos of the Wolf Man— he uses the word *fiction* in this sense: "Biography, even in the form of a case history, appears to be intimate with fiction: it is a hypothetical construction."[4] One may even want to replace "even" by "especially." But this idea by no means coincides or coheres with the principal argument of "Fictions of the Wolf Man," where fiction (as the titular ambiguity of Brooks's chapter suggests) signifies both the literary works that haunt the mind of the patient and those that supposedly haunt the psychoanalyst's narrative text (i.e., the novels of the modernist canon).

Even more pervasively in modern critical parlance, the word *fiction* is used to designate all texts that take narrative form. This turns out to be the principal meaning most Freud critics have in mind most of the time when they call his case histories "fictions." Steven Marcus, for example, quite correctly explains that in the case of "Dora," Freud wants to arrive at "a connected and coherent story, with all the details in explanatory place, and with everything . . . accounted for in its proper causal or other sequence."[5] But before long he adds: "It ["Dora"] is a story, or a fiction," explaining that this is so "not only because it has a narrative structure but also because the narrative account has been rendered in language, in conscious speech, and no longer exists in the deformed language of symptoms." His summary conclusion to this argument reads as follows: "What we end with, then, is a fictional construction which

2. This modern meaning of fiction is derived from the concept of "theoretical fiction," as used by Hans Vaihinger in *The Philosophy of "As if"* (see Chapter 1 above). The latter is clearly relevant to Freud's systematic thought. Its appearance in *The Interpretation of Dreams* has been searchingly probed by Humphrey Morris in "The Need to Connect: Representations of Freud's Psychical Apparatus," 317–27. But the more general subject still awaits investigation. That Freud knew Vaihinger's work is attested in *The Future of an Illusion*, which at one point refers to religious beliefs as "fictions" [*Fiktionen*], with a footnote to *The Philosophy of "As if."*
3. Patrick Mahony, *Cries of the Wolf Man*, 99.
4. Peter Brooks, *Reading for the Plot: Design and Intention in Narrative*, 279.
5. Steven Marcus, "Freud and Dora: Story, History, Case History," in *Representations: Essays on Literature and Society*, 277.

is at the same time satisfactory to us in the form of the truth and as the form of the truth."[6]

I have quoted at length from Marcus's essay not only because he so tellingly identifies the process of telling with the fashioning of a fiction, but also because of what happens in the paragraph that immediately follows the one I have cited. For here we can observe how easefully one can skid around the semantic field of *fiction:* how one can glide quite inadvertently from calling a narrative fiction in the sense of emplotted narrative, to calling that same text fiction in the sense we habitually identify with the novel. It is, we are told, "the great bourgeois novels of the nineteenth century" that furnish the model for Freud's case history of Dora. "Indeed we must see Freud's writings—and method—as themselves part of this culmination [of the novelistic genre], and at the same moment, along with the great modernist novels of the first half of the twentieth century, as the beginning of the end of that tradition and its authority."[7] One of the ways Marcus tries to substantiate this claim in the course of his essay is by pointing up parallels between Dora's family history (as told by Freud) and the plots and characters of "late Victorian romance" (as well as Ibsen's dramas). He apparently never asked himself whether it would not be possible (and rather more plausible) to explain these parallels by the fact that novels and dramas by Freud's contemporaries reflect the same psychologically damaging domestic situations that Freud knew at first hand from the real confessions of his real patients.[8]

Be that as it may, the fact remains that it is one thing to say that both novels and case histories are emplotted life stories, and quite another to say that case histories are novels (or, for that matter, that novels are case histories). So long as the term *fiction* clearly designates only features that all narrative texts hold in common, the attribution of fictionality to Freud's three published studies of individual patients is harmless, if rather self-evident. But when the term is semantically narrowed to the *generic* meaning of *fiction,* its association with these Freud texts becomes far more problematical.[9] For it now carries one or both of the following implications: that Freud intended his case histories as imaginative literature,

6. Ibid., 278.
7. Ibid., 278–79.
8. The same overestimation of the role literary models played for Freud also pervades "Freud and the Rat Man," in Steven Marcus, *Freud and the Culture of Psychoanalysis.* In Marcus's analysis of the "Rat Man" case, the emphasis is not on the imitation of novelistic plots, since the story line is found to be "less traditionally adequate" than in Freud's other case histories (96); instead this case history is read as a novelistic "character portrait" in the manner of Dickens and Dostoevsky (134, 146).
9. It should be noted that a number of major Freud critics have highlighted the importance of

and/or that he unintentionally lapsed into discursive modes reserved for the presentation of imaginary beings.

It is this interpretation of the case histories as "fictions" in the sense of nonreferential texts that my argument in this chapter will principally address. But before I launch it, I must remind the reader how the deviance of fiction, in this sense of the word, affects the telling of life histories.

Take the case of third-person novels first: say, *A Portrait of the Artist* or *Tonio Kröger*. The narrators of such novels have cognitive powers that are normally denied to historical biographers, notably the entirely *un*natural power to penetrate the psyches of their protagonists and to focalize the world that surrounds them through their eyes. A biographer, by contrast, is severely constrained when he comes to presenting his subject's inner life. He can do no more than speculate, conjecture, or infer what his historical subject may, might, or must have thought, felt, or perceived at certain junctures of his life. In short, where inside views are concerned, the gap between the discursive codes of historical and fictional biography is as wide as it is deep: to one side the unreal transparency of fictional characters, to the other the opacity of real persons as we know them in everyday life. This "magic" profoundly affects the structure and style of fictional, as compared to historical lives.

The case of first-person novels is clearly different. A fictional work that presents itself in the form of a self-narrated story normally imitates its nonfictional counterpart, historical autobiography, in every respect, including its introspective optics. Such fictional autobiographies (as they are often called) as *David Copperfield* look exactly like accounts that real persons bearing their narrators' names might give of their own lives. If we nonetheless know that these narrators are *not* real persons, it is because their imaginary status is signaled by the names they bear, more precisely by the fact that they don't bear the same names as their authors. An author who wants his reader to recognize a fictional autobiography for what it is will always sooner or later reveal the nonidentity between its narrator-protagonist and his own person.

One can, in addition, identify a third type of life story, a combinatory type that may be called "witness biography." Historical texts of this type, with their strong component of autobiography, have often been

---

narrative structures in his writing without ever introducing the ambiguous term "fiction." Among those particularly concerned with the narrative form of the case histories are Michael Sherwood (see *The Logic of Explanation in Psychoanalysis*, 190–91); Paul Ricoeur (see "The Question of Proof in Psychoanalysis," 843–44); Roy Schafer (see "Narration in the Psychoanalytic Dialogue," 51–52); Rainer Nägele (see *Reading after Freud*, 177–89).

imitated in fiction: in Mann's *Doctor Faustus: The Life of the German Composer Adrian Leverkühn as Told by a Friend,* in Scott Fitzgerald's *The Great Gatsby,* in Conrad's Marlow novels, and in Günther Grass's *Cat and Mouse.* Like the narrators of fictional autobiographies, the narrators of fictional witness biographies are invented characters: Zeitblom, Marlow, and Nick Carraway are, as their names indicate, every bit as imaginary as Leverkühn, Kurtz, and Jay Gatsby. And these narrating characters, unlike the omniscient tellers of third-person novels, simulate the natural (referential) discourse of their real-life counterparts, including the cognitive constraints that apply to the Other whose life they relate.

With this third narrative mode for telling lives—which, as we will see, has special relevance for Freud's case histories—my generic borderline is essentially staked out. Needless to say, much more could be said about the norms I have used to trace it, and especially about texts that infringe or ambiguate these segregating norms. In narratology, as elsewhere, norms have a way of remaining uninteresting, often even invisible, until and unless we find that they have been broken—or want to show that they have *not* been broken—which brings me to Freud's case histories.

FREUD'S NARRATIVE INTENTIONS

I take for my starting point a passage from one of Freud's earliest case histories, "Fräulein Elisabeth von R." in *Studies on Hysteria* (1895):

> I have not always been a psychotherapist. Like other neuropathologists, I was trained to employ local diagnoses and electroprognosis, and it still strikes me myself as strange that the case histories I write should read like short stories *[Novellen]* and that, as one might say, they lack the serious stamp of science. I must console myself with the reflection that the nature of the subject is evidently responsible for this, rather than any preference of my own. The fact is that local diagnosis and electrical reactions lead nowhere in the study of hysteria, whereas a detailed description of mental processes such as we are accustomed to find in the works of imaginative writers *[von Dichtern]* enables me, with the use of a few psychological formulas, to obtain at least some kind of insight into the course of that affliction. Case histories of this kind are meant to be judged like psychiatric ones: they have, however, one advantage over the latter, namely an intimate connection between the story of the patient's sufferings *[Leidensgeschichte]*

and the symptoms of his illness—a connection for which we still
search in vain in the biographies of other psychoses.[10]

This passage has been quoted time and again to legitimate a fictional reading of Freud's later case histories. Steven Marcus calls it Freud's "disarming admission" that he regards himself as a "genuine creative writer,"[11]
while Michel de Certeau comments: "This [the realization that his case
histories read like fiction] happens to him as would a sickness. His manner of treating hysteria transforms his manner of writing. It is a metamorphosis of discourse, . . . displacement toward the poetic or novelistic genre. Psychoanalytic conversion is a conversion to literature."[12] For
me this same passage opens a different, indeed a diametrically opposed
perspective: I understand it as the germinating moment of Freud's en-
during concern with the way analytic investigation of the human psyche
differs from fictional creation, as well as of his continuing effort to distance his case histories from their spurious resemblance to short stories
[Novellen].[13]

Note that Freud pinpoints the fiction-likeness of "Fräulein Elisabeth
von R." quite specifically: "a detailed description of mental processes such
as we are accustomed to find in the works of imaginative writers." He
clearly refers here to the horizon of expectation of his own contemporaries, expectations that have long since ceased to apply in our own age:
the age of psychobiography and psychohistory, when we as readers have
become fully accustomed to close-paced analytic accounts of individual
psychology outside the domain of fiction. In the pre-Freudian days of
Studies on Hysteria, however, Freud quite correctly perceived that his case
histories, on the face of it, resembled fictional narratives far more closely
than nonfictional texts of any sort. What they resembled least of all were
the case reports of contemporaneous psychopathologists. These professional works, for the most part, recorded their clinical findings in nonnarrative form: by way of static descriptions of observable symptoms and
syndromes that aimed at diagnostic classifications of the various mental
illnesses. Writings on hysteria were no exception. Freud's predecessor and

10. Standard Edition, 2:60–61; henceforth references to this edition will be made parenthetically
   in the text (S.E., followed by volume number and page number). When I quote the original
   German text, I refer to *Gesammelte Werke* (G.W.). The above quote is in G.W. 1:227.
11. Marcus, *Representations*, 273.
12. Michel de Certeau, "The Freudian Novel: History and Literature," 123.
13. Though I base it on a somewhat different understanding of its details, my reading of this passage agrees with those of Nägele in *Reading after Freud*, 14, and Yosef Hayim Yerushalmi,
   "Freud on the 'Historical Novel': From the Manuscript Draft (1934) of *Moses and Monotheism*," 388.

mentor Charcot, for example, charted the visual fields, the affected body parts, and of course the *grandes attaques* of his hysterical patients in meticulous detail without—even for his prima donna Blanche Wittman—reporting on their lives prior to hospitalization.[14] The case studies of hysterics written by Freud's principal rival, Pierre Janet, are likewise very largely synchronic: biographical data are limited to the traumatic episode (the so-called *accident initial*) that triggered the pathological crisis.

It is not at all surprising, then, that Freud himself, emerging from these clinical surroundings, should have been acutely aware that his narrative presentation of mental life broke the code of scientific discourse; nor that he should have anticipated the charge that his case histories were unserious and unscientific—"that, as one might say, they lack the serious stamp of science." In this perspective, the preemptively defensive rhetoric in the quoted passage can hardly be taken as a "disarming admission" that he was in fact infringing on the fictional preserve, much less as a symptom of his "conversion to literature." He is, much rather, asking *his readers* to convert to a different scientific code—a code in which texts that "read like short stories" are not read *as* short stories, but as bona fide scientific contributions: "Case histories of this kind are meant to be judged like psychiatric ones." And, with Freud's syntax here underlining the immediacy of the advance—an effect that is largely lost in the English translation—the same sentence now goes on to claim for narrative a unique cognitive and curative power: to understand the dynamics of a mental illness that can only be treated by tracing it back to its origin. This is as much as to say that stories—biographical stories—are Freud's medium because they are his message.

In Freud's later writings, even as he continued to point up the affinity between psychoanalytic and fictional narratives—and indeed came to regard creative writers as pioneers of his own principal discoveries—he nonetheless increasingly stressed the essential differences that separate psychoanalysts from novelists. Indeed, he tends to draw attention to these differences most insistently when the thematic analogies between their writings strikes him most deeply: in his analysis of Jensen's novel *Gradiva,* his letters to his "double" (*Doppelgänger*) Arthur Schnitzler, and in the preface to "Contributions to the Psychology of Love."

It is well known that Freud attributes a novelist's knowledge of the psyche to sources different from those he attributes to himself: whereas he acquired his knowledge by conscious, systematic study of abnormal be-

---

14. Freud himself pronounced critically on Charcot's short-circuiting of the biographical dimension as early as 1893, attributing it to an overestimation of hereditary predisposition (S.E. 3:21).

havior in his patients, novelists acquire theirs by subliminal apprehension of unconscious desires in others and in themselves. But the difference that stems from the aesthetic aim of creative writers and its effect on their productive process, as Freud conceived it, has even more immediate bearing on the case of his case histories: the belief that the writer's principal allegiance is to the pleasure principle, an allegiance he shares with—and inherits from—the child at play (S.E. 9:144, 152). In this respect it is important to note that pleasure and play in Freud's language have a common antonym: reality, as illustrated in the contrastive pair "pleasure principle/reality principle" [*Lustprinzip / Realitätsprinzip*] and in the statement "The opposite of play is not what is serious but what is real" [*der Gegensatz zu Spiel ist nicht Ernst, sondern—Wirklichkeit*] (S.E. 9:144; G.W. 7:214). On this basis it becomes clear that Freud's binary opposition between novelistic and psychoanalytic narratives is drawn along lines that essentially correspond to the criterion of referentiality. It is the nonreferentiality of fiction—"the unreality of the writer's imaginative world" [*die Unwirklichkeit der dichterischen Welt*]—that grants the creative writer his freedom to alter life as he knows it, to fashion it into appealingly persuasive stories inhabited by characters whose motivations are far more consistent than those of real persons and real patients. After describing this "poetic license," as he himself calls it, in "Contributions to the Psychology of Love," Freud adds:

> In consequence it becomes inevitable that science should concern herself with the same materials whose treatment by artists [*deren dichterische Bearbeitung*] has given enjoyment to mankind for thousands of years, though her touch must be clumsier and the yield of pleasure less. These observations will, it may be hoped, serve to justify us in extending a strictly scientific treatment to the field of human love. Science is, after all, the most complete renunciation of the pleasure principle of which our mental activity is capable. [*Die Wissenschaft ist eben die vollkommenste Lossagung vom Lustprinzip, die unserer psychischen Arbeit möglich ist.*] (S.E. 11:165; G.W. 8:66)

That Freud conceived of his case histories quite self-consciously as scientific works in the sense of "the most complete renunciation of the pleasure principle" is confirmed by his inclusion of a passage in "Dora" that addresses the same question almost a decade earlier. At the point of introducing the subject of his patient's homoerotic attachment to Frau K., her father's mistress, he tells us:

I must now turn to consider a further complication to which I should certainly give no space if I were a man of letters engaged upon the creation of a mental state like this for a short story, instead of being a medical man engaged upon its dissection [*sollte ich als Dichter einen derartigen Seelenzustand für eine Novelle erfinden, anstatt ihn als Arzt zu zergliedern*]. The element to which I must now allude . . . would rightly fall a sacrifice to the censorship of a writer [*des Dichters*]. . . . But in the world of reality [*in der Wirklichkeit*], which I am trying to depict here, a complication of motives . . . is the rule. (S.E. 7:59–60; G.W. 5:220)

One would think that this passage might have given pause to critics who argue that Freud designed the "Dora" case as a work of fiction. But this would be to underestimate the powerful effect that preconceived generic assumptions have on a reader's understanding of every textual moment. Thus Steven Marcus, after reminding us that "nothing is more literary—and more modern—than the disavowal of all literary intentions," quotes this very passage to catch Freud at "another of his crafty maneuverings with the reader," and "an elaborate obfuscation . . . truly representing how a genuine creative writer writes."[15] If one carried this reasoning to its logical conclusion, one would have to attribute "crafty maneuverings" to Freud's every claim of scientific intent, making his theoretical no less than his clinical publications into the works of a "genuine creative writer": a novelist who plays at being a psychiatrist.

A rather more plausible and responsible case can, I think, be made for Freud as a repressed novelist, who severely (perhaps over-severely, i.e., compulsively) censored his inclinations to express himself creatively. In this respect I tend to agree with Peter Gay, who writes in his Freud biography: "At times, Freud's comments on poets read like the revenge of the scientist on the artist. The tortoise maligning the hare."[16] And although Gay too believes that Freud had "certain artistic ambitions," he concludes that "with all his affection for literature Freud was all his life more interested in truth than in poetry."[17]

15. Marcus, *Representations*, 272–73.
16. Peter Gay, *Freud: A Life for Our Time,* 317–18.
17. Ibid., 323. Freud's lifelong stance of distancing his works from those of novelists is forcefully demonstrated by Yosef Yerushalmi. This author convincingly argues that the initially intended (and later discarded) subtitle "A Historical Novel" for *Moses and Monotheism* was "certainly idiosyncratic, perhaps even ironic" ("Freud on the 'Historical Novel,'" 379), a "strategy of defense" meant to "disarm potential critics" who might object to the paucity of documented evidence for his historical thesis (390). This defensive gesture—in some respects analogous to the one he made forty years earlier when he called attention to the spurious fiction-likeness of "Fräulein Elisabeth von R."—must not, in Yerushalmi's view, detract from the serious historiographic intent and meaning of the *Moses* study.

In sum, what we know of Freud's conscious intentions in no way entitles us to read his case histories as fictions on this basis. We have yet to examine whether, and by what means, Freud succeeded in implementing his intentions in practice.

FREUD'S NARRATIVE PRESENTATION

That the problems of narrative form were on Freud's mind during the composition of all three of his major case histories is documented by numerous comments, both within these works themselves and in contemporaneous letters. While preparing a first version of the "Rat Man" case for a psychoanalytic congress, he wrote to Jung: "I am having great difficulty with my paper, because a real, complete case cannot be narrated but only described."[18] And over a year later, as he was revising the same case for publication: "It [the "Rat Man" paper] is almost beyond my powers of presentation. How bungled our reproductions are, how wretchedly we dissect the great art works of psychic nature."[19] Is he implying here—in a rare show of his Romantic affinities—that nature, the supreme artist, can be emulated only by artists? Perhaps. As a scientist, at any rate, he despaired of finding a fully convincing manner to convey the matter he experienced in his consulting room. "It is well known," he tells us near the beginning of the "Wolf Man," "that no means has been found of in any way introducing into the reproduction of an analysis the sense of conviction which results from the analysis itself" (S.E. 17:13). Nonetheless, he was intent on finding a way, and the one he chose deliberately renounced from the start the principal privilege of the creative writer: to present the psyche of his subjects "omnisciently," in the manner of the narrator of a third-person novel.

In order to understand that this amounted to a genuine choice, we must remember that Freud would have been theoretically, at least on the grounds of his own theory, in a privileged position for narrating in this novelistic manner. As he said himself, toward the end of the treatment "we have before us an intelligible, consistent, and unbroken case history" [*eine in sich konsequente, verständliche und lückenlose Krankengeschichte*] (S.E. 7:18; G.W. 5:175). Had he chosen to tell his patients' lives from the vantage point of this "end," he would have known (or could have created the impression that he knew) all there was to know—could have told all, once and for all, in chronological order. What he chose to do instead was, of course, to tell not only the story he had learned from his patients in the

18. William McGuire, ed., *The Freud/Jung Letters,* 141.
19. Ibid., 238.

course of the treatment but also the story of this treatment itself, not only what he knew but also how he got to know it. Introducing the "Wolf Man" case, he describes his intention to "write a history neither of the treatment nor of the illness [*weder eine Behandlungs- noch eine Krankengeschichte*], but to combine the two methods of presentation" (S.E. 17:13). The result, as a number of critics have shown in detail,[20] is not only a text that is formidably entangled in its temporal structure, but also one that includes Freud himself, the narrator, as a figure in the past time and space of the story he tells: the therapeutic hours patient and doctor shared in the consulting room.

Now it must be granted that, by avoiding a pseudo-omniscient narrative stance, Freud's case histories do not escape fiction-likeness altogether. In fact, they correspond structurally to at least two novel types: to mystery novels by way of their anachronic temporal arrangement, with Freud himself cast in the role of detective; and to fictional witness biographies by way of their narrative situation, with Freud in the position of Marlow, Zeitblom, and other witness narrators in the works of this type mentioned earlier. But the decisive point is that neither of these novelistic genres conforms to structures that are distinctive of *fictional* narratives. The anachrony of who-done-it stories, where the body is found at the beginning and doer and deed are not revealed till the end, replicates the natural order of journalistic reports and court records. The anachronic "detective" structure of the case histories therefore in no sense lends support to the thesis that Freud wrote like a novelist.[21]

The same is true for the analogy with fictional witness biographies, a novelistic genre which, as I have previously shown, is itself characterized by its simulation of a referential, historical genre. To declare the author of the "Dora," "Wolf Man," and "Rat Man" cases to be a novelist on the grounds of this homology, one would have to find evidence that he conceived his case-historical narrator as a fictional character: a psychoanalyst whose resemblance with Dr. Sigmund Freud is purely coincidental. Meanwhile, the fact that the witness structure has been favored—for reasons that will not concern me here—by twentieth-century novelists hardly allows one to assign Freud to their ranks.[22] On this basis his status as a

20. For the anachronic structure of the "Wolf Man," see Brooks, *Reading for the Plot*, 272–73; Nägele, *Reading after Freud*, 178; and Mahony, *Cries of the Wolf Man*, 95.

21. Brooks, Marcus, and Mahony are among the critics who stress the affinities between the case histories and fiction on this basis.

22. Janet Malcolm makes this same point in an essay—the only one to date—that takes issue with readers who place the case histories in the context of literary modernism. Addressing in particular Marcus's idea that "Dora" is provided with a "Nabokovian frame," she comments as-

modernist writer would at best be reduced to a tautology: he produced biographical texts that look like novels that mimic (and therefore look like) biographical texts of the type he produced.

I will not go so far as to maintain that Freud opted for his intricate narrative presentation solely, or even mainly, to distance his case histories from novels that take on fiction-specific forms. He himself insists that an elegantly fashioned sequential story—the "smooth [*glatten*] and precise histories" he attributes to some of his colleagues—cannot begin to convey the problematics of mental illness and its analytic treatment: "If I were to begin by giving a full and consistent case history [*eine lückenlose und abgerundete Krankengeschichte*], it would place the reader in a very different situation from that of the medical observer" (S.E. 7:16; G.W. 5:173). Here Freud's didactic aim is clearly in evidence: by telling his patient's story in the incoherent, fragmented way in which it was revealed to him, he means to insure the reader's belief in the historicity of his discourse no less than to persuade him of its psychological validity.

That Freud's rejection of the pseudo-omniscient and pseudo-objective mode of telling is deeply grounded in the nature of psychoanalytic theory itself has been confirmed by Roy Schafer, who vigorously argues against the "implausibly tidy" accounts of mental illness that have become the professional norm. Recommending Freud's own case histories as formal models to his fellow therapists, he describes them as follows: "In the main each is a narrative of the analysis itself. Or perhaps, taking Freud's accompanying theoretical and methodological remarks into account as well, one should say that each case report is . . . a narrative of Freud's continuing creation of psychoanalysis."[23] Schafer's views here provide a salutary correction to those critics who identify narrativity with fictionality. Even as he acknowledges the importance and complexity of Freud's narrative practice in the case histories, including their "artful" autobiographical component, he insists on its theoretical and heuristic functionality.

We have yet to observe how, and to what degree, Freud avoided distinctively fictional techniques in presenting his patients' psychic processes, both in the history of the treatment (*Behandlungsgeschichte*) —

---

tutely: "In back of every unreliable narrator of modernist fiction stands a reliably artful author. In Dora, however, the Freud who is writing the case history and the Freud who is narrating it are one and the same person. If *Pale Fire* had been *written* by the madman Charles Kinbote as well as narrated by him, there would be an analogy between Nabokov's novel and Freud's case history" ("Reflections: J'appelle un chat un chat," 89).

23. Roy Schafer, *Narrative Action in Psychoanalysis: Narratives of Space and Narratives of Time*, 44–45.

which covers the only epoch of their lives when he actually "witnessed" them—and in the history of the illness (*Leidensgeschichte*)—which deals with a past he could only get to know indirectly, by way of the patients' own gradually emerging memories, if he could get to know it at all.

Despite the uncommon means Freud employed to get to know what was in his patients' minds as they lay in his consulting room—means that are hardly comparable to those available to the garden-variety witness biographer—he never lost sight of the categorical impossibility of looking inside another mind. The barrier that bars access is nowhere so graphically thematized as in the early "Fräulein Elisabeth von R.," the very case where Freud expressed his apprehension of novella-likeness that I quoted earlier. Since this patient refused to respond to hypnosis (which was still at this time Freud's preferred technique), he resorted to literally applying physical pressure—"the device of applying pressure to the head" (*jenen Kunstgriff des Drückens auf den Kopf*)—which he accompanied with the instruction to say the first thing that popped into her mind (S.E. 2:145; G.W. 1:208). Though less dramatic than this crude manipulation for overcoming Fräulein Elisabeth's hardheaded opacity, the technique of free association that was soon to take its place is no less clearly limited to behavioral clues for what remains forever hidden. It seems to me that Freud's awareness of his cognitive constraint also underlies a passage in "Dora" that Marcus takes as a "fantas[y] of omniscience" on his part:[24] when Freud stresses the facility he eventually acquired in interpreting what he calls "symptomatic actions" [*Symptomhandlungen*], such as Dora's suspect fiddling with her genitalia-shaped pocketbook, and adds: "He that has eyes to see and ears to hear may convince himself that no mortal can keep a secret. If his lips are silent, he chatters with his fingertips; betrayal oozes out of him at every pore. And thus the task of making conscious the most hidden recesses of the mind" [*das verborgenste Seelische bewusst zu machen*] is one which it is quite possible to accomplish [*sehr wohl lösbar*] (S.E. 7:77–78; G.W. 5:240). Freud's self-confidence here may touch on braggadocio, but it implies a world of difference between the analyst's power to interpret verbal and gestural symptoms and the novelist's power to create transparent minds. Had he wanted his readers to forget this difference, he would have had nothing to brag about.

The relationship of the narrator to his protagonist is different when the hardheaded physical presence of the patients in the story of the treatment (*Behandlungsgeschichte*) fades into the more or less distant past of the sto-

24. Marcus, *Representations,* 302.

ry of the illness (*Leidensgeschichte*), where the temptation to take on an omniscient narrative stance was potentially much greater. Freud avoids this danger precisely by the previously mentioned entwinement of the two stories. This essentially takes the form of his telling us what the patient told him about the past. Sometimes he renders this autobiographical discourse directly, as at the beginning of the "Rat Man" case, where several lengthy paragraphs quote the patient's own voice. More often these memories are presented in the form of indirect discourse or paraphrase, with their inception always clearly marked: "She [Dora] told me one day that she had met Herr K. in the street" (S.E. 7:59); "Dora told me of an earlier episode with Herr K." (S.E. 7:27); "Thus he [the Wolf Man] could recollect how he had suffered from fear" (S.E. 17:15–16); "He had preserved a memory of how, during one of these scenes . . ." (S.E. 17:28). These emphatic introductions clearly ensure that the episodes, though now cast in third-person form and freely referring to the patient's past thought and feelings, cannot be mistaken for omnisciently narrated fictional scenes in which Freud (the narrator) adopted the patient's perspective.[25]

Conversely, when Freud gives us his own, now properly biographical and interpretive account of the past, he sets it off explicitly from the patient's autobiographical discourse. His version of the scene, originally quoted in Dora's own words, where Herr K. embraces the fourteen-year-old girl—the version where her revulsion is explained by the supposition that she felt Herr K.'s erect member—is introduced as follows: "In accordance with certain rules of symptom-formation which I have come to know, and at the same time taking into account certain other of the patient's peculiarities, which were otherwise inexplicable, . . . I have formed in my own mind the following reconstruction of the scene. I believe that during the man's passionate embrace she felt not merely the kiss upon her lips . . ." (S.E. 7: 29–30). "I believe . . . she felt" (*Ich denke, sie verspürte*, G.W. 5:188): modalizing and conjectural phrases of this type abound in all three case histories, indicating that Freud, no matter how certain he was of his inferences, took care to adhere to the narrative code of historical biography.

25. That they have nonetheless been so mistaken seems to me due to a willful misreading. I cannot, at any rate, agree with critics who have sensed a fictionlike fusion, or confusion, of voices (or perspectives) between analyst and patient. See, for example, Mahony: "Freud's prose is truly one of *rapprochement*—interpersonally between author, reader, and patient" (*Freud and the Rat Man*, 206); likewise Friedrich Kittler: "Which of the two [doctor or patient] is speaking at any moment remains undecidable" (*Aufschreibsysteme 1800/1900*, 294; my translation).

In this regard it is especially instructive to observe the way Freud presents the most daring and (in)famous of all his biographical conjectures. I mean, of course, the primal scene (*Urszene*) of parental intercourse observed by the infant Wolf Man. It occurs at a point of the case history where Freud has been adhering to the story of the treatment for several pages, first quoting the Wolf Man's narration of his recurring childhood nightmare about the seven (or six, or five) wolves perched on a tree, then recounting his patient's first associations with this dream and his own first interpretive reactions. With the primal scene itself, the narration clearly changes over to the other story, the story of the illness. This is the earliest and most crucial moment of his patient's biography that Freud will attempt to recount. He introduces it as follows: "I have now reached the point at which I must abandon the support I have hitherto had from the course of the analysis. I am afraid it will also be the point at which the reader's belief will abandon me" (S.E. 17:36). After the conclusion of the primal scene, Freud once again anticipates his reader's "doubts as to its probability" [*Bedenken der Unwahrscheinlichkeit*], adding: "Later on I shall carefully examine these and other doubts [*Bedenken*]; but I can assure the reader that I am no less critically inclined than he toward the acceptance [*Annahme*] of this observation of the child's, and I will only ask him to join me in adopting a *provisional* belief in the reality of the scene" (S.E. 17:38–39; G.W. 12:65–66, Freud's emphasis). Whereupon he returns to the story of the treatment, focusing on the effects his bold interpretation had on its remaining course.

In my perspective, the reader-addressing rhetoric that brackets the primal scene is nothing more nor less than a highly emphatic version of the discursive pattern that characterizes the narration of psychic events in historical biography: the inferential "must have" construction writ large, as surely befits the enormity of the occasion. Having hedged it in this fashion, Freud allows the intervening passage—where he describes the "constructed primal scene" itself—to lapse, though only for the length of one single sentence, into the focalized mode: to show it—as its nature demands—through the eyes (though clearly not through the language) of the observing child: "When he woke up, he witnessed a coitus *a tergo* [from behind], three times repeated; he was able to see his mother's genitals and his father's organ; and he understood the process as well as its significance" (S.E. 17:37). One should perhaps grant that, read in isolation, this past indicative sentence might be mistaken for an excerpt from a rather bizarre pornographic novel. But this impression would be instantly dispelled by the framing context, which so explicitly subordinates the focalized perception of the infant Wolf Man to the self-consciously daring hypothesis of the psychoanalyst.

FREUD'S CONCEPTION OF HISTORIOGRAPHY

The nonomniscience signified by Freud's emphatically conjectural narration of the primal scene itself is further compounded in its aftermath: the addition to the case history, some four years after its original composition, of the two passages where he qualifies his *own* belief in "the reality of the scene." These insertions open to the final question I will try to clarify in this chapter: Freud's understanding of what constitutes historicity in the psychoanalytic life-narrative. It is an understanding that has, in my view, been gravely misunderstood by certain modern critics bent on attributing to Freud a vision that obliterates the distinction between fictional and nonfictional narrative. In what follows, I will address only one (highly influential) essay that moves along these lines: Peter Brooks's previously mentioned "Fictions of the Wolf Man," where, precisely, Freud's revision figures as key evidence.

The first of Freud's passages (S.E. 17:57–60), inserted at the conclusion of extensive arguments that speak *for* the "reality" of the constructed scene, in effect proposes an alternative scenario for the events that preceded and inspired the wolf dream and the infantile neurosis: the child, having watched animals copulating, fashioned a fantasy that superimposed these observations onto a "harmless" scene he had witnessed in the parental bedroom. This fantasy version, Freud concedes, is more plausible than the originally constructed primal scene, but he nonetheless defers the option between actual scene and fantasy to a later moment. That moment comes in the second insertion (S.E. 17:95–97), where Freud now provides renewed evidence for the *original* version. But ultimately he once again stops short of a final decision. We are left to share his dissatisfaction at the unanswered question in this individual case—"I should myself be glad to know whether the primal scene in my present patient's case was a phantasy or a real experience"—even as we are told that "taking other similar cases into account, . . . the answer to the question is not in fact a matter of very great importance" (*es sei eigentlich nicht sehr wichtig, dies zu entscheiden*) (S.E. 17:97, G.W. 12:131).

Peter Brooks describes the first of these revisionary additions, somewhat hyperbolically, as "one of the most daring moments in Freud's thought, and one of his most heroic moments as a writer."[26] He explains

26. Brooks, *Reading for the Plot*, 277.

that Freud here "perilously destabilizes belief in explanatory histories," that he makes biography into an "uncontrollable" genre, assigning it "to an unspecifiable network of event, fiction, and interpretation," signifying that "language itself . . . is in a state of displacement and fictionality." And to clinch the point that Freud is behaving like a modernist novelist at this juncture, we are further told that his protagonist "should perhaps be considered less a character from Mann or Proust than a Virginia Woolf-man."[27] Without doing Brooks the injustice of taking his pun too literally, I cannot pass it without recalling that Virginia Woolf's characters are invariably given life by a narrator who knows them in magically intimate ways in which no real person can ever know another; so that no greater contrast could well be imagined than the one pertaining between her hyperomniscient novelistic discourse—commonly referred to as stream-of-consciousness—and the nescient discourse of Freud at the moment when he most openly avows his uncertainties in telling his patient's mental history.

A less biased reader would, I think, be led to admire Freud's revisionary move on account of its kinship, not with modern experimental novelists, but with theoretically informed (and reformed) modern historians: those who problematize the relationship between the historical past and its representation in a historiographic account, renouncing the claim that the latter mirrors the former directly, accurately, and with absolute finality. Robert Berkhofer has described this new historiographic mode as "demystification of normal history," explaining that it "frees the historian to tell many different kinds of 'stories' from various viewpoints, with many voices, emplotted diversely, according to many principles of synthesis," without thereby in any sense spelling "the death of history doing itself."[28] In this light, Freud's self-critical supplementation to the "Wolf Man" case takes on the meaning of enlightened—demystified—historiography applied to the biographical genre: the move of a life-historian who refuses to identify referential discourse with the production of a single, irrevocable story. If anything, Freud's decision to add an alternative construction to the one he initially proposed enhances the referential status of the "Wolf Man" case rather than displacing it toward "fictionality."

Brooks, however, if I understand him correctly, imputes the fictionalizing impact of Freud's revision not solely (or mainly) to its ultimate inclusion in the case history, but also to its content: to Freud's admission that the primal scene may be a fantasy. Now it is true that Freud himself

27. Ibid., 277–79.
28. "The Challenge of Poetics to (Normal) Historical Practice," 448–50.

at times described his patients' fantasies in terms that pointedly allude to narrative fiction—as *Dichtung,* even as *Roman*[29]—and we know from such writings as "Creative Writers and Day-Dreaming" how closely he affiliated fantasies in general with literary creation. But the crucial point is, of course, that the "Wolf Man" revision casts, not the analyst, but the *patient* (the infant Wolf Man), as the creator of a "fictional" fantasy. The case historian Freud merely offers yet another biographical hypothesis to account for his patient's illness. Accordingly, when he ultimately declares that it remains undecidable whether the Wolf Man's infantile neurosis originated in a real experience or in a fantasy, this undecidability in no sense affects the generic status of his case history: the analyst's discourse is no more fictional—no less referential—when it traces the origin of the patient's neurosis back to infantile fantasies (or "fictions"), than when it traces its origin back to a potentially verifiable biographical event.

That this understanding corresponds to Freud's own is confirmed in a work published shortly before the revisionary "Wolf Man" supplements and to which he himself refers the "Wolf Man" reader (S.E. 17:97): Lecture 23 of the *Introductory Lectures on Psycho-Analysis*. Most readers seem to have understood this cross-reference to concern merely the possibility of phylogenetic causation for primal fantasies (the matter to which Freud turns next in the inserted paragraph). But there is an at least equally relevant link with an earlier passage in Lecture 23 that clarifies Freud's rationale for declaring that the choice between primal scene and primal fantasy "is not in fact a matter of very great importance." It reads as follows:

> When he [the patient in treatment] brings up the material which leads
> from behind his symptoms to the wishful situations modeled on his
> infantile experiences, we are in doubt to begin with whether we are
> dealing with reality or phantasies. . . . It will be a long time before he
> can take in our proposal that we should equate [*gleichzustellen*] phan-

---

29. At one point (though not in relation to the primal scene) Freud calls the Wolf Man's own fantasy life "imaginative composition" [*Dichtung*] (S.E. 17:20; G.W. 12:43). The phrases "tales of the individual's prehistoric past" [*Dichtungen über die Urzeit*] and "imaginative production of a positively epic character" [*episch zu nennende Dichtung*] are applied to the Rat Man's childhood fantasies (S.E. 10:207; G.W. 7:427). Another patient's fleeting fantasy is tagged "romance" [*Roman*] (S.E. 9:160; G.W. 7:193), and the latter term is of course enshrined in the special type of childhood fantasy Freud called "family romance" [*Familienroman*]. So far as I can see, the only instance—but it is a highly significant one—when Freud uses "fiction" [*Fiktion*] to refer to an imaginary past experience is the letter informing Fliess of his growing conviction that his patients' memories of sexual traumas have no basis in reality (Jeffrey M. Mason, ed., *The Complete Letters of Sigmund Freud to Wilhelm Fliess, 1887–1904,* 264).

tasy and reality. . . . Yet this is clearly the only correct attitude to adopt
toward these mental productions. They too possess a reality of a sort
[*eine Art Realität*]. It remains a fact [*eine Tatsache*] that the patient had
created these phantasies for himself, and this fact is of scarcely less importance for his neurosis than if he had really experienced what his
phantasies contain. The phantasies possess *psychical* as contrasted with
material reality, and we gradually learn to understand that *in the world
of neuroses it is psychical reality which is the decisive kind* [*dass . . . die psy-
chische Realität die massgebende ist*]. (S.E. 16:368; G.W. 11:383; Freud's
emphases)

As Paul Ricoeur has pointed out, from the vantage point of common
sense and observational science, this conception of infantile fantasies as
"a kind of reality" is paradoxical; its epistemological consequences profoundly alter the criteria of scientific truth and verification that apply to
psychoanalytic writings.[30]

I would argue that the concept of "psychical reality" has an equally profound impact on the criterion of historicity that applies to Freud's case
histories. For it imposes the idea that, in psychoanalytic telling of individual lives, a nonfactual phenomenon must be regarded as a historical
"fact" [*Tatsache*], in the sense of a biographical given, a past actuality that
predates the case-historical discourse on the same basis as all other events
in the patient's life.[31] No matter how paradoxical the notion of "psychical reality" may appear in other respects, it unequivocally reinforces the
frame of referentiality that encloses the psychoanalytic life-narrative, enabling it to accommodate "fictional" scenes without thereby transmuting
it generically into a case fiction. In this respect too, Freud's medium is his
message; and no matter what we may ultimately think of it, we misread
his message when we mistake his medium.

---

30. Paul Ricoeur, "The Question of Proof in Psychoanalysis," 839–40.
31. In this connection it is interesting to note that the distinction between psychical and material reality first appears (though in a rather more tentative formulation) in a passage that
Freud added to the concluding section of *The Interpretation of Dreams* in 1914, the year when
he began to write up the "Wolf Man" case: "Whether we are to attribute *reality* to unconscious wishes, I cannot say. . . . If we look at unconscious wishes reduced to their most fundamental and truest shape, we shall have to conclude, no doubt, that *psychical* reality is a particular form of existence not to be confused with *material* reality" (S.E. 5:620; Freud's
emphases).

4

Proust's Generic Ambiguity

When, at the end of the confessional text that concludes her recent book on Proust, Julia Kristeva contemplates writing her own autobiography, she explains: "I should only be concerned with my involuntary memory and perhaps with its formation. Yet Proust already did it, and I chose to accompany him."[1] One gathers from this that her potential work would take (or would have taken) the *Recherche* as its model. This is hardly surprising: Kristeva's autobiography would not be the first to follow Proustian mnemonic principles. What is more surprising is that, in the chapter just preceding this epilogic text, *A la Recherche du temps perdu* is declared to be, not the model autobiography, but the prototypical *novel,* in the Bakhtinian sense of the word—i.e., in the sense of a dialogic, "protean," incomparably polyvalent narrative genre: "Proust . . . offers the most complete example of the mature novel that comes of age when it is confronted with its own logic."[2] How are we to understand this successive appraisal of the *Recherche* as the ideal autobiography *and* the ideal novel? Is this double generic assignation meant to be paradoxical? Or does it follow logically from the assumption that these two genres are in fact identical? Or is this equivoque unique to Proust?

As a survey of Proust criticism makes clear, Kristeva is by no means alone in her silently posited inconsistency, though it is rarely displayed quite so blatantly. On the one hand, the problem as to whether the *Recherche* is to be read as an autobiography or as a novel tends to be discussed in a spirit of interpretive speculation uninformed by poetological reflection.[3] Scholars with firm genre-theoretical grounding, on the other hand, have considered it only in passing and have vacillated in their conclusions.

1. *Time and Sense,* 331.
2. Ibid., 324.
3. See, for example, Serge Doubrovsky, *Writing and Fantasy in Proust: La Place de la Madeleine,* 115–45. The author here successively attributes the namelessness of the *Recherche's* narrator—a textual feature intimately related to the work's generic equivoque (see below)—to Proust's striving for anonymity *and* for immortality, to his patricidal *and* his self-castratory desires, to his reach for fullness of being *and* for nonpersonhood.

What I intend in this chapter is to face the generic ambiguity of Proust's *Recherche* forthrightly, to ask how and why it has so persistently marked the reception of this work, to examine the various resolutions that have been proposed, and ultimately to open it to alternative interpretive perspectives.

THEORETICAL ASSUMPTIONS

I will begin by laying out my theoretical assumptions, which in the main follow those of Philippe Lejeune in "The Autobiographical Pact."[4] They are based on the idea that the intention behind fictional autobiographies (first-person, "autodiegetic" novels) differs on principle from the intention behind real autobiographies (self-narrated lives of real persons). Leaving aside for the moment the possibility that this differential authorial intention may be additionally and clearly stated in extratextual pronouncements (letters, interviews, etc.), it normally communicates itself to the reader by way of certain signals in (or on) the work itself, signals that tell whether a narrative in I-form is meant to be read as a fiction or as a historical document, with a view to assuring the work's "correct" reception.[5] The reason why such markers are needed hardly needs spelling out: it is quite simply that first-person novels and autobiographies are, for the most part, look-alikes.

There are two standard indicators of fictionality or nonfictionality in first-person narrative, acting separately or in concert. They are readily conceptualized in theory, and most of the time easy to spot in practice. One is to give explicit notice, paratextually (by way of title, subtitle, or prefatory statement) or textually. The other is to provide the narrator's name: its distinction from the author's name conveys fictional intentionality, its identity with the author's name autobiographical intentionality. Lejeune, who was the first to draw explicit attention to these indicators, calls their effect the "pact," or "contract," that binds the author to his reader and that informs the latter's reading experience.

One of the salient differences in this reading experience—which I mention here merely in passing but to which I will return at greater length toward the end of this chapter—is that a fictionally contracted work opens

---

4. In *On Autobiography*, 3–30. See Chapter 2 above for further discussion of Lejeune's differentiation between autobiography and the novel.

5. This differentiation—based as it is on authorial intention—avoids at least two confusions that have plagued other theoretical approaches to the problem: (1) a first-person novel is no less fictional for being "autobiographical," i.e., partly or wholly based on the author's life; (2) an autobiography is not made into a fiction when (or because) it departs from the truth, i.e., differs from the author's past as known from other sources.

to different hermeneutic options from a work that contracts autobio-graphically. This includes, notably, the understanding that its narrator may have been conceived as an ideologically unreliable speaker—an un-derstanding with far-reaching interpretive implications that do not apply to a work that presents itself as an autobiography.

Before we look at Proust's *Recherche* in this differentiating light, the concept of the pact itself must be qualified (and thereby complicated) in at least two ways. For one thing, it in no sense presumes that the drawing of its theoretical borderline rules out the existence of borderline cases. Quite the contrary is true: one of the principal aims of drawing such sim-ple distinctions between fiction and autobiography is to highlight gener-ically complex cases and to enable a clear analysis of their in-between po-sition. Thus Lejeune himself draws particular attention to self-narrative texts that, according to his system, are either "indeterminate" or "contra-dictory."[6] One motivation for the present chapter is that, surprisingly, he barely touches on the *Recherche,* the work I take to be the *most* complex in this respect.

A second qualification—disregarded by Lejeune but, in my view, quite essential—is that the two distinctive criteria posited by the pact-based classifications need not be considered as exclusive: they may be supple-mented by other, more or less clearly recognizable, relative or absolute, differential features. Content alone, for example, generally discourages an autobiographical reading of fairy tales, science fiction, or futuristic novels, even when these fictional genres are cast in first-person form. A first-person narrative likewise appears novelistic by way of its content when it includes famous persons unknown to historical sources (the com-poser Adrian Leverkühn in Mann's *Doctor Faustus*) or when it plays in ge-ographic places unmarked on the map of any country (Kaisersaschern, Leverkühn's birthplace). Autodiegetic texts may, moreover, mark their fictionality by displaying certain formal devices that break the norms of autobiographical discourse: when their narrator inexplicably manifests narrative omniscience, for example, or when he narrates throughout in a present tense that cannot be understood as a historical present. Needless to say, such fiction-specific features are occasional and by no means oblig-atory in first-person novels. Allowing for their presence in no sense in-validates the positing of the Lejeunean pact for drawing a systematic dis-tinction between fictional and real autobiography.

6. For Lejeune's discussion of indeterminate texts, see *On Autobiography,* 16; for contradictory texts, see 134–35. The latter are discussed further in "Autobiographie, roman et nom propre," in *Moi aussi*.

THE TEXTUAL DILEMMA

What light do these theoretical views cast on the *Recherche*? This question would be worth considering even if Proust himself had clearly illuminated his work's generic status by way of extratextual pronouncements. But its importance is surely compounded by the fact that he did not. Without dwelling on the inconsistency of these pronouncements, I shall merely mention that this inconsistency is amply documented by critics who have assembled the relevant quotations from Proust's correspondence.[7]

The *Recherche* does not, of course, explicitly identify itself paratextually as either an autobiography or a novel: it has no subtitle, no prefatory notice. I would suggest, however, that its main title is not entirely innocent or neutral in this regard.[8] Its featuring of the mnemonic process is actually quite typical for self-narrated life stories—Nabokov, *Speak, Memory*; Saul Friedländer, *When Memory Comes*. On this basis, *A la Recherche du temps perdu* may well sound (and mean to sound) like an autobiographical pointer of sorts, hinting that the processional activity—"A la recherche"—to which it refers, and its would-be target—"temps perdu"—are to be attributed to the author under whose name it stands. The least that can be said is that Proust's title page in no way discourages understanding it in this manner—which is not to say, however, that the graphic sequence of his name and his title *enforces* an autobiographical reading of the several thousand pages that follow.

It would be hard to deny that these pages—with the notable exception of the section entitled "Un Amour de Swann"—create the sense that they massively follow the generic norms of autobiographical narration. But is this autobiography fictional or real? Even in the absence of paratextual indications, this question could be definitively answered if the narrator gave us his name. That he leaves this name tantalizingly suspended greatly thickens the generic mystery. Its repeatedly foregrounded omission may even raise the suspicion of deliberate authorial strategy (or, alternately, the possibility of authorial indecisiveness).[9]

---

7. See especially Marcel Muller, *Les Voix narratives dans La Recherche du temps perdu*, 159–63 and Gérard Genette, *Seuils*, 348–49. It should be noted that, while Genette openly points up Proust's equivocality, Muller tends to give greater credence to the statements that support his novelistic reading of the *Recherche* than to those that contradict it. A similar bias characterizes other critics who base their generic diagnosis on extratextual evidence; see, for example, Jean-Ives Tadié, *Proust et le roman*, 17–30.

8. On Proust's initial intention to call his work "Les Intermittances du coeur"—a phrase that would have avoided the autobiographical overtones of the final title—see the "Introduction générale" to the Pléiade edition (I:lxxii–lxxiv).

9. For example: "L'huissier me demanda mon nom, je le lui dis . . . il hurla les syllabes inquiétantes . . . " ["The usher asked me my name, and I gave it to him . . . (he) roared the disqui-

This suspicion is increased by the two instances where the author's first name actually does appear in the text after more than two thousand pages, both times in *La Prisonnière* (III:583 and 663; III:69 and 153–54).[10] A note to the Pléiade edition establishes, on the basis of genetic evidence, that both these nominal entries are late additions, dispelling the view (held by earlier critics) that they are uncorrected leftovers from an early version.[11] It would seem to me that, regardless of their genetic circumstances, these two sudden appearances of the name *Marcel* so late in the text reinforce the sense that Proust was (consciously or not) of two minds regarding the naming of his narrator-protagonist.

The verbal context of the first of these Marcel-namings, moreover, is so baffling that it raises far more problems than it solves. It occurs in the scene of Albertine's matinal awakening and reads as follows: "Elle retrouvait la parole, elle disait: 'Mon' ou 'Mon chéri,' suivis l'un ou l'autre de mon nom de baptême, ce qui, en donnant au narrateur le même prénom qu'à l'auteur de ce livre, eût fait: 'Mon Marcel,' 'Mon chéri Marcel'" ["Then she would find her tongue and say: 'My—' or 'My darling—' followed by my Christian name, which, if we give the narrator the same name as the author of this book, would be 'My Marcel,' or 'My darling Marcel'"] (III:583; III:69). The wording here, for one thing, is vexingly contradictory: even as it separates author and narrator nominally, it fuses them vocally (the person whose name is Marcel and the one whose name is unknown speak with one and the same voice—or, more accurately, write with one and the same pen). But this semantic paradox is grounded in the even more startling discursive transgression of both autobiographical and fictional norms. For if the *Recherche* is read as autobi-

---

eting syllables . . . "] (III:38; II:661); "Ayant entendu ses camarades plus anciens faire suivre, quand ils me parlaient, le mot de Monsieur de mon nom, il les imita . ." ["having heard his comrades of longer standing supplement the word 'Monsieur' with my surname when they addressed me, he copied them . . . "] (III:170; II:801); "Elle [Albertine] . . . me disait . . . : 'Mais où tu vas comme cela, mon chéri?' (et en me donnant mon prénom)" ["she [Albertine] would . . . say to me . . . : 'But where are you off to, my darling—' (calling me by my Christian name)"] (III:622; III:110).

Throughout this chapter, references to the French edition of the *Recherche* (Paris: Bibliothèque de la Pléiade, 1989) precede references to the English translation; both are provided in parentheses in my text.

10. The passage in which the first mention of "Marcel" occurs will be discussed below. In the second passage, the name recurs in the quotation of a note from Albertine to the narrator: "'Mon chéri et cher Marcel, . . . Quel Marcel! Quel Marcel!'" ["'My darling dear Marcel, . . . What a Marcel! What a Marcel!'"].

11. "Ces mentions du prénom de l'auteur, loin d'être des vestiges d'un état antérieur du roman, sont des additions tardives" (III:1718) ["These mentions of the author's first name, far from being vestiges of a prior version of the novel, are late additions"; my translation].

ography, the homonymy of narrator and author is not subject to doubt, a doubt which is enforced here by the conditional tense—"en donnant... eût fait."[12] But if the *Recherche* is read as fiction, the narrator cannot (as he here does) manifest any knowledge of his author's existence, much less of his name.[13] This sentence, in fact, becomes more enigmatic the longer one focuses on it. At any rate, my brief look will have shown that here, far from resolving the generic ambiguity of his work, Proust has glaringly highlighted it.

Whereas this is the only moment of the *Recherche* that explicitly foregrounds the problematics of the narrator's name, there is a further moment, literally parenthetical, that reveals Proust's preoccupation with the author/narrator problem. Interestingly, it attributes this preoccupation to the reader himself, who is at this point heard addressing "Monsieur l'auteur." Commenting on the narrator's account of a past moment of forgetfulness (of, as it happens, a certain lady's name), the reader says: "Il est facheux que, jeune comme vous l'étiez (ou comme était votre héros s'il n'est pas vous) vous eussiez déjà si peu de mémoire" ["It is a pity that, young as you were (or as your hero was, if he be not yourself), you had already so feeble a memory"] (III:51; II:675). Hypothetically, this parenthesis posits the fleeting specter of a fictional narrator—and it does so, paradoxically, by way of addressing the author who may speak through him. This "votre héros s'il n'est pas vous" ["your hero . . . if he be not yourself"] may indeed strike a reflective reader as a tiny *mise en abyme* of the dilemma that he faces in the *Recherche* as a whole.

On the face of it, it may appear that this dilemma is at long last overtly resolved in favor of fiction when we come to the following sentence in *Le Temps retrouvé:*

> Dans ce livre où il n'y a pas un seul fait qui ne soit fictif, où il n'y a pas un seul personnage 'à clefs', où tout a été inventé par moi selon les besoins de ma démonstration, je dois dire à la louange de mon pays que seul les parents millionnaires de Françoise . . . sont des gens réels qui existent. (IV:424)

12. If, as is grammatically possible, we interpret this tense as a contrary-to-fact conditional, it even follows that the narrator here *denies* that he is called "Marcel."

13. Structural transgressions of this type are not, to be sure, entirely unprecedented in the history of the novel. The normally unbreachable boundary that separates the fictional from the real world is crossed hither and thither in E. T. A. Hoffmann's *The Golden Flowerpot,* Unamuno's *Mist,* and Fowles's *The French Lieutenant's Woman.* But this usually occurs only in heterodiegetic fictions and in those that indulge in this radical form of metalepsis not only locally but in their overall structure.

> In this book in which there is not a single incident which is not ficti-
> tious, not a single character who is a real person in disguise, in which
> everything has been invented by me in accordance with the require-
> ments of my theme, I owe it to the credit of my country to say that
> only the millionaire cousins of Françoise . . . are real people who exist.
> (III:876)

But on further consideration, this sentence too raises more questions
than it solves. Who is speaking here? Must it not be the author of this
wholly "fictitious" book? What is this real person doing in a fiction of
which he is himself the principal character? Or does he exclude himself
from "everything [that] has been invented by me in accordance to the re-
quirements of my theme"? Is the voice that speaks at this moment perhaps after all not attributed to the writer whose name appears on the title page but to an invented character? Or are they the same? Once again,
a metanarrative comment compounds the enigma that it pretends to
resolve.

We must conclude, then, that contractually (in terms of Lejeune's criteria) the *Recherche* remains suspended in a state of indeterminacy, with
every passing mention of its genre or its speaker thickening the equivoque. But these local tokens of indeterminacy must now be placed in the
context of Proust's work as a whole, where they are heavily counteracted
by signals of fictionality. A brief reminder of these signals will suffice.

As mentioned above, an autodiegetic work imposes itself as a novel
when its cast of characters includes invented "historical" figures and when
it sets its events in geographically unreal places. Educated readers of the
Recherche know without consulting an encyclopedia that the most famous
characters of Proust's Paris—the writer Bergotte, the painter Elstir, the
diplomat Norpois, the actress la Berma, the illustrious family of the Guermantes—never existed, as they know that no trains or roads lead from
Paris to Combray, Balbec, Doncières and their multiply named surroundings. Though strictly speaking this knowledge is dependent on extratextual evidence, Proust could assume it, and no doubt did; as we saw
in the passage about Françoise's family, he worried that it might lead to
the kind of "à clefs" interpretations associated with thinly disguised autobiographical fiction.

As a matter of course, Proust's invented public figures unobtrusively
interconnect with historical events, institutions, and persons (Zola, for
example, occasionally appears at the Verdurin's soirées). But there are at
least two instances where Proust carries this imbrication of his fictional

world in the real world to emphatically elaborate extremes. One of these is the passage where the narrator reads the pages from an unpublished volume of the Goncourt journal that deal with the Verdurin salon. These pages are quoted in full (IV:287–95; III:728–36), with Proust no doubt counting on the reader to recognize them as a brilliant pastiche.[14] The other is the passage where Swann is depicted in Tissot's painting of the four-member Cercle de la rue Royale (III:705; III:199), in the place that—in the actual painting—is occupied by Charles Haas (Swann's presumed real-life model).[15] Illusionist games of this sort show the length to which Proust went to anchor his fiction in reality, in a manner characteristic for realistic novels generally, but especially for historical novels or fictional memoirs—genres to which, among others, the *Recherche* conforms.

There is also a notable (and often noted) formal feature that at times perturbs the autobiographical discourse of the narrator: the cognitive liberties he takes with the minds of others. Not that he has any illusions on this score, having discovered early on (I:85; I:91) that inside views are not granted to ordinary mortals, but only to novelists. In his relation with Albertine, it is precisely the fact that her mind is a closed book that causes him the most intensive suffering. He laments at one point that it resides in "des régions plus inaccessibles pour moi que le ciel" ["regions more inaccessible to me than the sky"], "que je touchais seulement l'enveloppe close d'un être qui par l'intérieur accédait à l'infini" ["that I was touching no more than the envelope of a person who inwardly reached to infinity"] (III:887–88; III:393). Yet despite this painful knowledge, he practices mind-reading as unapologetically as any novelist when it comes to fellow beings who are less close to him: Mlle de Vinteuil, Mme de Cambremer, Charlus, and (most notoriously) the dying Bergotte.[16] In "Un Amour de Swann" this adoption of an abnormally "omniscient" stance itself becomes the norm. The would-be justification of this macroparalepsis in the

---

14. See Genette's analysis of this passage (*Figures of Literary Discourse,* 221). To my mind, Genette here overstates the scandalous "impossibility" of the Goncourt pastiche. While it is correct to describe it as "a door in the work leading to something other than the work," this opening to the historical world differs only in degree, not in kind, from other such instances that embed fiction in history—in the *Recherche* and other works: in Mann's *Doctor Faustus,* for example, one of Leverkühn's symphonies is performed by the Orchestre de la Suisse romande, under the direction of the historical conductor Ansermet.

15. The facts concerning this painting are provided in a note to the Pléiade edition (III:1742).

16. Genette discusses these principal "paraleptic" instances in *Narrative Discourse,* 207–10, noting that here "Proust manifestly forgets or neglects the fiction of the autobiographical narrator." Pointing up their implication for the generic problem, he proposes that this practice "would be impossible if the *Recherche* were—as some people still want to see it—a true autobiography."

narrator's prefatory remarks (I:186; I:203) remains unconvincing and is contradicted when he later refers to this section as one of his "romans" (III:705; III:199).[17] But motivated or not, the narrator's intimate knowledge of Swann's experience points the reader away from understanding his entire written production as a real autobiography.

In sum, the *Recherche* presents the rare and perhaps unique case of a first-person narrative where fictionality is enforced neither by a paratextual announcement nor by the name of the narrator, but by certain pervasive elements of its content and certain irregularities of its narrative form. That these elements do not, however, act on the reader with sufficient force to resolve the generic ambiguity of Proust's work once and for all is amply evidenced by the history of its reception—with which I deal in my next section.

CRITICAL APPROACHES

The scholarship on the *Recherche* strikingly, though for the most part inadvertently, displays its generic vagaries: even a summary look displays the autobiography/novel dilemma tipping to prevailing biases. More or less successively understood as camouflaged self-revelation, uniquely complex fictional masterwork, paradigmatic narrative text, writing that indifferently mutes generic distinctions, its readings reflect changes in the critical climate. Here is a four-phased sampling:

1. In the two or three decades following the dates of its publication, the biographic approach to the *Recherche* reigned supreme.[18] This is in line with the pre–New Critical habit of reading the author's life and opinions uninhibitedly into and out of literary works. As an astute critic noted in 1951, this practice was most insistent for first-person novels. Such novels (notably Gide's *L'Immoraliste*), he suggests, were often misunderstood on account of "the inveterate tendency of critics to take a narrative told in the first person at its face value and to confuse the narrator's consciousness with the author's."[19] This way of reading the *Recherche* began to give way in the years following World War II, but without ever entirely disappearing from the scene. To mention only one significant instance, the

---

17. Both of these two passages—I:186 and III:705—call for further analysis. Though they seem contradictory, I believe that the first includes a sly hint—by way of the simile of the newly invented and near-miraculous long-distance telephone—at what the second spells out: the narrator himself takes "Un Amour de Swann" as a work of fiction he has created.

18. For an overview of these unreflectively autobiographical early readings, see Muller, *Les Voix narratives,* 10–11.

19. Albert Guerard, *André Gide,* 158–59.

new novelist Claude Simon, in an interview dated 1985, grouped the *Recherche* with Rousseau's *Confessions, Les Mémoires d'Outre Tombe,* and *La Vie d'Henri Brulard,* adding that works of this type "present a thousand times more complexity, richness and fascinating subtleties than the fictional lives represented in the so-called novels of imagination."[20]

2. It is precisely as such a "novel of imagination" that the *Recherche* was classified by Louis Martin-Chauffier, who in 1943 was probably the first critic to propose a different type of reading. Comparing Proust's "I" to the first person of such novels as *Adolphe* and *L'Immoraliste*—"a false 'I', an alibi, a trompe l'oeil, a creation"—he insists that in the *Recherche,* as in all first-person novels, the events are invented, not remembered: "When 'I' . . . pretends to remember, it is the author who imagines."[21] Seconded some years later by Germaine Brée,[22] the novelistic interpretation of the *Recherche* became more firmly established on the critical scene of the nineteen-sixties, when its understanding as an autobiography became something of a scholarly taboo.[23] Unfortunately the critics who held to this position tended to disregard general poetological norms, which may also be why they never drew its full interpretive implications.

3. One can hardly agree with Paul Ricoeur when he says of this novelistic interpretation: "everyone agrees on this today."[24] Most theoretically informed critics, at any rate, have, in the course the last two decades, increasingly resisted the straightforward tagging of the *Recherche* as *either* an autobiography *or* a novel, regarding it rather as a generically hybrid creature. We will see in a moment how problematic this matter became for the master poetologist Gérard Genette. Perhaps most significantly, Lejeune himself could not decide to which of his typological categories Proust's work belongs. Having raised the question under the heading "Name of Protagonist = o," he refers to the passage in which the name *Marcel* is hypothetically proposed (see above) and concludes: "This bizarre intrusion on the part of the author functions both as a fictional pact and as an autobiographical clue, and sets the text in an ambiguous space."[25] Another critic, David Ellison—in a book devoted to Proust in its entirety—speaks of "the semi-identity of 'Marcel' and Marcel Proust,"

20. Quoted in Anthony Cheal Pugh, "Claude Simon: Fiction and the Question of Autobiography," 81; my translation.
21. "Proust et le double 'Je' de quatre personnages," 55 and 63; originally published in 1943; my translation.
22. *Marcel Proust and the Deliverance of Time*; original French publication 1950.
23. The critics who most strongly argue the case for the *Recherche* as a novel are Muller and Tadié.
24. Paul Ricoeur, *Time and Narrative,* II:132.
25. Lejeune, *On Autobiography,* 16.

proposing that the *Recherche* is neither fiction nor autobiography but "thrives on ambivalence and on the transgression of distinct boundaries."[26]

4. It is important to note, however, that its contradictory generic pointers do not lead Ellison to conclude to the singularity of Proust's work. Instead, he invalidates Lejeune's system on the grounds that it refuses to accept "the disruptions of formal or semantic multiplicity."[27] In this respect, Ellison takes a typically poststructuralist stance, a stance he shares with such critics as Roland Barthes and Paul de Man. After suggesting in *S/Z* that the Proustian "je" signifies the demise of the notion of "character" in modern writing,[28] Barthes, in his later Proust essay, describes it more generally as a "writing self," constitutionally voided of any manner of referential meaning.[29] De Man's deconstructive argument in "Autobiography as Defacement" likewise leans on Proust's generic equivocality, which he takes to support the idea "that the distinction between fiction and autobiography is not an either/or polarity but that it is undecidable."[30]

Perhaps more surprising than the changing reception Proust's generic problematics has effected in the four critical currents considered above is the vacillation it has caused in the work of Gérard Genette, a systematic theorist if ever there was one, who also happens to be a deeply probing Proust scholar. The *Recherche* not only figures as the paradigmatic center of his *Narrative Discourse* and as the subject of a number of important essays, but it also appears at crucial moments in several of Genette's subsequent poetological treatises.

Narrative Discourse touches on the problem of Proust's genre merely in passing, which may be explained by the fact that (as the title indicates) it is concerned with narrative generally, for the most part disregarding the distinctions between fiction and nonfiction. Still, Proust's "I" does come up in the chapter on "Voice." Here we are told that the speaker of the *Recherche* "is neither completely [Proust] himself nor completely someone else," that this voice reflects a slightly distanced and de-centered relationship. Referring to the "Mon Marcel" passage in a note, Genette adds

26. David Ellison, *The Reading of Proust,* 139. Ellison, however, all too quickly eludes the equivoque. Making much of the fact that the name *Marcel* appears in the mouth of Albertine rather than the narrator's own (142), he ultimately proposes a Lacanian and/or deconstructive analysis of the name problem (183–85) that I find largely unconvincing.

27. Ibid., 141.

28. Roland Barthes, *S/Z: An Essay,* 95.

29. Barthes, "Longtemps je me suis couché de bonne heure . . . ," in *The Rustle of Language,* 282.

30. Paul de Man, "Autobiography as Defacement," 921.

that this relationship is "wonderfully symbolized by that barely suggested, seemingly accidental semihomonymy of the narrator-hero and the signatory."[31] This semi-demi position—clearly in line with the third critical approach identified above—is reinforced in a note to the essay "Métonymie chez Proust," where his imagery is said to open at every point "an unending debate between a reading of the *Recherche* as fiction and a reading of the *Recherche* as autobiography." This note's final sentence reads: "It may well be that one has to remain *within* this whirligig"[32]— an advice Genette (like most other critics) has found it difficult to follow consistently. He only apparently adheres to it when he calls the *Recherche* a "semiautobiographic text" in *Narrative Discourse Revisited*; for here— momentarily adopting the deconstructive position (see section 4 above)—he declares that its "mixture . . . forms the standard fare of our narratives, literary or not."[33]

In two of his subsequent works, however, one finds Genette—now drawing largely on extratextual evidence—leaning in the direction of autobiography. Even as he stresses that the *Recherche* as a whole cannot be unqualifiedly assigned to that genre (and in fact proposes applying to it the hybrid term "autofiction"), he maintains that the narrator-hero's namelessness must be understood as "an autobiographical turn"[34] and even that "this enunciatory mode . . . clearly draws the register of this narrative close to a pure and simple autobiography."[35]

But a few years later, in *Fiction and Diction* (his last publication to date dealing with narrative theory), Genette takes a radical turn in the opposite direction. In the brief passage devoted to the *Recherche* in the chapter entitled "Acts of Fiction," its narrator is decisively declared to be "fictional," and his discourse is considered entirely representative of "the discourse of first-person fictional narrative." He adds: "in fact here . . . *no* speech act belongs to Marcel Proust . . . no matter how the narrative content may happen to relate to the biography, the life and opinions of its author."[36]

This turnabout on Genette's part is by no means incidental or capricious; it is dictated by the new angle of his vision in *Fiction and Diction*— now forthrightly directed to literarity and fictionality itself rather than to

---

31. *Narrative Discourse*, 249.
32. In *Figures III*, 50; my translation.
33. *Narrative Discourse Revisited*, 15.
34. Gérard Genette, *Palimpsestes*, 293.
35. Genette, *Seuils*, 279; my translation.
36. Genette, *Fiction and Diction*, 34.

narrativity in general.[37] Nonetheless it illustrates—as do Genette's earlier oscillations in this matter, not to mention those of the Proust scholarship as a whole—the extreme difficulty of stabilizing, or normalizing, the generic position of the *Recherche*.

IDEATIONAL COMMENTARY

An important critical approach to the *Recherche* that I have not mentioned to this point is the one that examines it principally for its ideas. On the face of it, this type of philosophical study of Proust's work would seem to have little concern for the question of its genre, for whether it is to be understood as a novel or an autobiography. Yet as we will see, the fact that Proust's narrator is an essayist at least as much as a story teller—that he may, in fact, be telling his story *for the sake of* his interpretive reflections—has essential implications for our problem.

A glance at any of the many volumes and essays that deal with the philosophical (psychological, aesthetic, sociological) discourse in the *Recherche* quickly reveals that—although their authors as a rule pay lip-service to the notion that it is a novel—its ideas are almost invariably attributed to Proust.[38] Giles Deleuze's well-known book *Proust and Signs* is entirely typical in this respect, punctuated as it is with such phrases as "Proust says," "Proust speaks of," "Proust states," "Proust's reaction to," usually followed by direct textual quotations. A reference to the recurrences of sensations in the courtyard of the Guermantes reads, "Proust says: 'And I felt that this must be the sign of their authenticity. I had not sought out the uneven cobble stones where I stumbled.'" And here is an allusion to the narrator's sexual attitudes: "And we recall the power with which Proust characterizes male homosexuality as accursed, 'a race anathematized, and which must live in deception.'"[39] Philosophical studies of Proust, in effect, usually take it for granted that the author of the *Recherche* is in direct communication with his reader, no less direct than the writer of an essay or a treatise: it is *his* voice that sounds in all reflective statements, *his* beliefs that inspire the innumerable gnomic articulations of general "truths." This kind of unqualified narrator-author identification is not commonly found these days in sophisticated discussions of works

---

37. This is not the place to examine Genette's evolution in this respect, except to note the important role that Käte Hamburger's *Logic of Literature* (French translation, 1986) has played in it.

38. This holds true even for Muller, one of the strongest advocates of the novelistic reading of the *Recherche* (see note 23 above). He understands the essayistic passages as "interventions" of the author, speaking in his own voice (see esp. *Les Voix narratives*, 91, 105, and 167–69).

39. Giles Deleuze, *Proust and Signs*, 161 and 181.

that are clearly understood (and overtly signaled) as novels: Werther's ideas are not automatically attributed to Goethe, nor Clamence's to Camus—let alone Felix Krull's to Thomas Mann.

It would not be accurate to say, however, that critics who study the *Recherche* for its ideational content read it autobiographically. The narrator's *"je"* is taken to refer, not to a concrete person, whose life and opinions are shaped by his individual personality and specific circumstances, but to an abstract self, not unlike the one heard in Kant's *Critiques* or Hegel's *Phenomenology of the Mind*. In studies of this kind, one often finds such terms as *thinking subject, absolute being,* or *pure formula* applied to the narrator in seemingly willful disregard for the highly particularized person and experience conveyed by the self-narration that embeds the reflective language.[40]

These philosophical readings suggest, at any rate, that there is a major (and perhaps insuperable) obstacle that stands in the way of understanding the ideological statements of the *Recherche* as the discourse of an invented fictional character rather than the author's own and/or those of a generalized philosophical subject. Could this difficulty be related to the fact that no fictional character (self-narrating or not) has ever articulated his ideas quite so volubly?[41] Such massively reflective and yet personal outpourings are known from the essayistic oeuvres of writers like Montaigne, Emerson, Kierkegaard. They are not likely to appear on a novel reader's horizon of expectation, perhaps because it is not easy to imagine the genesis of a novel of this type:[42] an author who sets out to fashion an elaborate philosophical system of gigantic proportions that is to be articulated by a fictional narrator figure.

Despite the abundant attention that the ideational content of the *Recherche* has received, relatively little has been said about its singularity in this respect. A notable exception is the previously mentioned Proust essay by Roland Barthes, who may, however, be overstating the

40. For one of the most recent philosophical readings, specifically concerned with the question of the self in the *Recherche,* see Pierre Campion, "Le 'Je' proustien: Invention et exploitation de la formule."

41. A possible exception is *The Man without Qualities*—a work whose author is often called "the Austrian Proust." But in this novel the essayistic discourse is, as often as not, voiced by the heterodiegetic narrator rather than by the protagonist himself; and when the latter's own gnomic language comes to the fore in the second part, it is largely cast in spoken dialogue (with his sister) rather than silently directed at the reader.

42. This is true despite the attention that has been given to the genetic origin of this singularity in *Contre Sainte Beuve,* which many critics regard as an early version of the *Recherche.* For the juxtaposition of the fictional and the essayistic in the former, see the "Introduction générale" to the Pléiade edition (I:xl–xli).

case when he describes Proust's work as follows: "Once the chrono-logy is shaken, intellectual and narrative fragments will form a series shielded from the ancestral law of Narrative and Rationality, and this series will spontaneously produce the *third form*, neither Essay nor Novel."[43] Barthes, in fact, gives precedence to the essayistic over the narrative to the point where he regards the latter as a mere illustration—"starring" (*étoilement*)—of the former, forgetting that the commentary is at every point elicited by, and subordinated to, the telling of outer and inner events.[44]

Even less attention has been given to Proust's ways of imbricating ideas into the narrative itself.[45] These ways are closely related to the semantic pluri-significance of the first-person pronoun—ranging from the most intimate self-reference to the most generalizing gnomic enunciation. As a recent linguistic study of early versions of the *Recherche* points out, Proust passes with unusual ease—and without any manner of "grammatical scandal"—from the meaning of *I* as a literally personal pronoun to its meaning as an impersonal pronoun akin to *one* (*on*).[46] The linguist authors of this study also argue that this recurring shift from self-narrative to philosophical language, far from signifying the (recently fashionable) "death of the subject," forcefully stresses the single and unified subject origin of the entire discourse—its philosophizing no less than its mnemonic language.

Viewed in this light, the profuse philosophic discourse intermittently featured in the *Recherche* in no sense ejects it from the domain of autodiegetic narrative texts—texts of a kind that constitutionally incarnate the subjectivity of their speaker. It seems to me, however, that this discourse makes the question of its speaker's fictionality even more essential. For if we understand the *Recherche* as a novel, we can no longer assume—in the unreflective manner of philosophical readers—that the ideological views it expresses are necessarily and invariably Proust's own. We are prompted—on theoretical grounds, reader expectations notwithstanding—to consider the possibility that Proust may have created the vocal figure of an ideologically unreliable fictional narrator.

43. *The Rustle of Language,* 281.
44. A more balanced assessment of the relationship between the reflective and narrative aspects of the *Recherche* is provided in Volker Roloff, "Die Entwicklung von 'A la Recherche du temps perdu'" (see esp. 190–94).
45. Genette touches on this subject only fleetingly, noting that Proust may have opted in favor of autodiegetic narration in order to make the "omnipresent speculative discourse" appear less intrusive (*Narrative Discourse,* 251).
46. A. Grésillon, J. L. Lebrave, and C. Viollet, *Proust à la lettre.*

ALTERNATIVE RESOLUTIONS

Before I point up the interpretive implications (briefly alluded to earlier) of this possibility for the *Recherche*, a few general remarks concerning the notion of fictional unreliability are in order. The concept stems from Wayne Booth, who summarily defines it as applying to fictional narrators who do not speak for "the norms of the work (which is to say the implied author's norms)."[47] A narrator is unreliable in this Boothian sense when his non-mimetic language (his commentary, his judgments, his generalizations) does not relate to his mimetic language in convincing ways, creating the impression that he is unable or unwilling to provide a correct interpretation of the events he narrates.[48] Needless to say, an impression of this sort does not arise only in the reading of fictional narratives; untrustworthy explanations are often spotted in historical (including autobiographical) texts as well. But when a narratorial interpretation appears to be faulty in a fictional text, there is a difference: for here we are not obliged to attribute its incongruity to the author himself; we are free to attribute it to the narrator, now conceived, not as the author's mouthpiece, but as an artfully created vocal organ—whose author is meanwhile tacitly communicating the correct interpretation to us behind the narrator's back.

Fictional unreliability—as my wording above is meant to suggest—is most appropriately viewed in light of a reader-oriented approach.[49] A reader, faced with a seemingly invalid nonmimetic discourse in a homodiegetic fictional text, is given a choice between two different options: he may hold the author responsible, motivating the incongruity by way of the latter's historical or personal circumstances; or he may hold the narrator responsible, thereby not only exempting the author but also crediting him with creative mastery and control over the fallibility of his narrator-character. It is one of these two mutually exclusive hypotheses—the genetic resolution and the perspectival resolution, as they have been called[50]—that a reader more or less consciously adopts when he is confronted with this type of discrepancy.

47. *The Rhetoric of Fiction*, 158–59. As can be seen from the quotation, Booth's concept applies solely to the ideology—"the norms"—expressed by the narrator, not to the facts he narrates. Though it is possible, on theoretical grounds, to conceive of a fictional narrator as factually unreliable as well, this rarely occurs in practice; there is, at any rate, no reason to suspect Proust's narrator on these grounds—provided, of course, that we do not understand the *Recherche* as Proust's autobiography.

48. For the distinction between mimetic and nonmimetic language, see Félix Martínez-Bonati, *Fictive Discourse and the Structures of Literature*, 32–39.

49. I owe this approach to Tamar Yacobi, "Fictional Reliability as a Communicative Problem."

50. Ibid., 114–15 and 118–19.

The reason such an approach is relevant to Proust's work is that the concordance between the narrator's philosophical commentary and the events he recounts, long taken happily for granted, has in recent years been thrown into doubt. Critics increasingly question the fit, particularly where the aesthetic theories of the final volume are concerned.

Vincent Descombes's book *Proust: Philosophy of the Novel* clearly exemplifies the stance of a critic who opts for the genetic resolution to this problem. Motivating what he takes to be Proust's philosophical shortfall historically, he essentially blames him for clinging to outmoded ways of thinking that fail to account for the internal happenings he recounts—happenings that are strikingly "modern" in terms of analytic philosophy, whereas the explicit ideology contained in the *Recherche* is "scarcely intelligible," the novel itself is "an elucidation . . . of the obscure, paradoxical, and misleading propositions of Proust [!] the theorist" (6–7).

Other critics ground the genetic resolution more specifically in personal circumstances, particularly in facts that relate to Proust's dilatory composition of the *Recherche*. In his early essay "Proust palimpseste," Genette explains that Proust initially set out to exemplify a specific aesthetic theory by way of his work—"the *Recherche du Temps perdu* was to be the illustration of a doctrine, the demonstration, or at least the gradual unveiling of a Truth"—but was unable to remain entirely faithful to this intention. The tragic nature of the narrator's erotic life ultimately determined a deeply pessimistic worldview: "the negative experience that was to be no more than a stage in the overall progress of the work sweeps it up whole and entire into a movement that is the reverse of the one proposed." This is where (and why) the surface clarity—the "message in plain language"—of the *Recherche*'s final aesthetics becomes obscured and is left unresolved. Genette nonetheless ends this essay with a contradictorily positive formulation: Proust's greatest triumph, we are told, is precisely that "of having succeeded in the failure of his undertaking, and of having left us the perfect spectacle of that failing, namely his work."[51] This paradoxical conclusion is clearly aimed at salvaging the image of Proust's mastery in the face a major inconsistency. Genette does not seem, at this point, to conceive of the possibility of resolving this inconsistency differently: perspectivally rather than genetically, by attributing the "failure" to a fallible narrator-figure rather than to the failing (yet perfect) master himself.

The perspectival resolution has, in fact, never been explored insistently or consistently by *any* critic. Still, I have found a few incidental and

51. In *Figures of Literary Discourse*, 225–26.

fleeting hints of it. Here and there—most often in their final paragraphs—some critics briefly envision that Proust may have deliberately created a flawed ideological discourse for his narrator, a discourse designed to be read critically, ironically, against the stream.

There is, for example, a moment (quite possibly the first of its kind) toward the end of Germaine Brée's book, where, after remarking that Proust rather overdoes it when it comes to generalizations, she adds: "Yet here also the structure of the novel sets up its guard rails. The narrator alone is involved in the decrees of reason. . . . Proust, however close he may be to the narrator, remains distinct from him. . . . When the narrator . . . tries to extend to our lives the conclusions he has drawn from his, we can perfectly easily take exception to them without shaking the foundations of the Proustian world."[52] Brée here clearly reaches for the perspectival resolution—in preference to blaming Proust for what she regards as an aesthetic flaw in his work.

There is another, to my mind rather more significant instance of a critic moving in this direction. In the final paragraph of his Proust essay, Paul de Man insists that there is an "unbridgeable gap between the narrator and Proust" whenever the narrator refers to his having understood *"plus tard"* (later) something he misinterpreted at an earlier moment of experience. De Man now introduces the quote—from the narrator's reflections in *Le Temps retrouvé* (IV: 489; III: 948)—with which he ends his essay as follows: "Marcel is never as far from Proust as when the latter has him say: 'Happy are those who have encountered truth before death and for whom, however close it may be, the hour of truth has rung before the hour of death.'"[53] For de Man, in other words, the narrator of the *Recherche* is maximally distanced from his author at the moment when the former, having just conceived the vision of his future *oeuvre*, experiences his felicitous moment of truth.[54] And although the belief that Proust could not have shared in such a moment is no doubt inspired by de Man's deconstructive skepticism, his conclusion nonetheless suggests—*in extremis*—that the narrator of the *Recherche* is deluded in a way his author was not, could not have been. This reading is altogether sur-

---

52. *Marcel Proust and the Deliverance of Time*, 230–31.
53. "Reading (Proust)," in *Allegories of Reading*, 76.
54. At first reading, it may not seem as though the narrator actually counts *himself* among those for whom "the hour of truth has rung before the hour of death," but that he merely envies those who experience such an hour. When one reads this passage in context, however, it becomes clear that the time at which he conceives his work—no matter how intense his fear that death will cut short its execution—signifies the attainment of absolute truth (see esp. IV:612–15; III:1091–95).

prising, given the fact that it comes from a critic who (as we have seen) denies that there is any kind of generic difference between autobiography and fiction. But—even though de Man would no doubt refuse to acknowledge it—his interpretation does strongly imply that the *Recherche* is a work of fiction, a novel with a fictional narrator expressly created to appear unreliable. Had he taken it as an autobiography, he would have had to hold Proust himself responsible for every one of its narrator's ideas.

De Man's loaded remark, based as it is on a sentence from the narrator's cogitation about his future creation, opens to what is no doubt the weightiest interpretive question raised by Proust's generic ambiguity: Is the work before us—the work whose last narrated scene is the Guermantes' matinée—in fact the work the narrator plans to write in the course of this scene? I would suggest that this question, which lies at the heart of numerous Proust studies, is intimately tied to the narrator's problematic ontological (real versus fictional) status and to his problematic reliability.

The above question has traditionally been answered in the affirmative. The narrator, waiting in the Guermantes' library before entering the social gathering, is understood to verbalize in his mind the very ideas on which he bases the work we have just read—ideas that are often, and quite casually, called "Proust's art poétique." In this reading, the *Recherche* concludes with the account of its genesis; the work as a whole is structured as a circuitous *recorso,* with its ending representing the threshold of its beginning. Clearly, this is a "happy" ending: art saves life, literature transfigures the pain and suffering of existence, the creation of the beautiful *oeuvre* bestows meaning on meaningless experience.

This widely accepted and, in its way, powerfully satisfying interpretation, already questioned by Genette in "Proust palimpseste" (see above), has recently been insistently undercut by Rainer Warning. In several articles—all published in Germany and not yet widely known to Proust scholars—Warning argues that the "official poetics" (*offizielle Poetik*) of Proust's final volume stands in "essential contradiction" (*Grundwiderspruch*) to the implied poetics of the *Recherche* as a whole. The explicit poetics adheres to a positive, traditionally Romantic ideology: belief in essentialism, cognitive certainty, absolute values, and stable self-identity, with memory serving as the secure and supreme conduit to a state of cognitive and emotive euphoria. By contrast, the ideology that tacitly informs the narrator's entire prior discourse is devoid of all idealistic absolutes, bearing throughout the signature of post-Romantic modernity: akin to the insights of Bataille and Foucault, it manifests a perspectivism ruled by desire, a cognitive void, unstably contingent values, absolute hopelessness, and (most important of all) a dispersed and riddled notion of self that memory is powerless to capture and unify. In consequence of this profound self-contradiction between its theory and its practice, Warning maintains that the *Recherche* is far from corresponding to the unified *oeuvre* the narrator intends to write at its closure. The overall structure of Proust's work, far from forming a coherent whole, is cleaved by a deep "epistemological rupture" (*epistemologischer Riss*).[55]

It remains to be seen whether Warning's diagnosis of this essential flaw in the *Recherche*—which he attempts to demonstrate by means of extensive textual analyses—is sufficiently convincing to affect future Proust scholarship. What makes his thesis relevant for my present concerns is the urgency with which it confronts one with the decision of accounting for it on genetic or perspectival grounds. Warning himself, in unfortunate analogy to other Proust critics, never formulates or faces up to the choice, but tacitly passes from one alternative to the other. In the concluding pages of one of his essays, he seems to be leaning toward the perspectival resolution: Proust appears as an author intent on drawing attention to the incongruity of the narrator's ultimate idealistic stance, a stance meant to be understood as nothing more than a limited, self-servingly biased rationalization.[56] With the stage thus promisingly set for a reading that can apply solely to a *fictional* autobiography, however, Warning draws back from the actual performance of such a reading. In a later essay, he reverts to the genetic resolution, calling on Freud and Derrida to propose various reasons that Proust was unable or unwilling to part from the Romantic aesthetics of his early years.[57]

Highlighting as it does the critical reluctance to sever the *Recherche* decisively from the autobiographical matrix, Warning's work leads me to a cluster of concluding questions—without conclusive answers.

Granting that Proust enters into no binding pact concerning the generic status of the *Recherche,* that contractually his work remains ambiguous; granting as well that other criteria (of content and narrative mode) incontestably signal its novelistic status—how can we explain the inhibition on the part of critics to read Proust's masterwork "simply" as a novel? Such a reading would have to assume that the narrator of the *Recherche* produces—in Genette's words quoted earlier—"*no* speech act

55. Warning, "Supplementäre Individualität," 456.
56. Warning, "Romantische Tiefenperspektivik," 321–24.
57. Warning, "Vergessen, Verdrängen und Erinnern," 190–95.

[that] belongs to Marcel Proust." Following the interpretive options opened by other first-person fictions, it would have to open to the possibility of an unreliable narrative discourse, in the sense I have defined it.

In the course of this essay I have suggested two possible answers to this question. The first—explicitly proposed in "Ideational Commentary" above—is that the sheer mass of essayistic, philosophical discourse in the *Recherche* discourages the mental construction of a narrator who is not identified with the author. The second—implied in "The Textual Dilemma" above—is that criteria of narrative content and narrative mode are too weak, as compared to contractual criteria, to enforce a bona fide fictional reading. What speaks in favor of these factors—whether they are understood to act separately or in concert—is that both are based on distinct peculiarities of Proust's work. I nonetheless question whether they are (either or both) sufficiently weighty, wondering whether they might be supplemented (or replaced) by others. This doubt does not, however, reduce my certainty that such inhibiting factors must exist.

This is not to say, however, that these obstacles to a genuinely fictional reading of the *Recherche* are insuperable. Given the problems opened by such critics as Genette, de Man, and Warning, the terrain is prepared. But would such a reading be fully convincing, fully sustainable, or would it, in turn, be countered by a return to autobiographical readings? Most important of all: would it dispel once and for all the ambiguity between autobiography and novel created by the *Recherche,* or would it renew the critical attempts to sustain the—to this point unsustainable—suspension on the horns of the generic dilemma?

5

Breaking the Code of Fictional Biography

Wolfgang Hildesheimer's *Marbot*

In 1982 the *London Review of Books* featured a lengthy review by the British Germanist J. P. Stern of a new work by Wolfgang Hildesheimer that tells the life of one Andrew Marbot, an unduly forgotten aesthetician and art critic of the younger generation of English Romantics who is presumed to have committed suicide in 1830, at the tender age of twenty-nine. A later issue of the same journal published a letter to the editor that begins like this: "Sir: to my dismay, I find that the reviewer of my latest book, *Marbot,* has missed the point of the book: namely the fact that the hero of this biography has never existed. He is purely fictitious. . . . The quotations from his writings, his letters, the letters from Lady Catherine, his diaries etc. are *my own*." After further stressing his paternity of this impressive brainchild, Hildesheimer adds: "In my view, it speaks for the book that the reviewer has taken Marbot's existence for granted." The editor of the *London Review* appended the following reply: "It speaks for the reviewer that the author of the book should take for granted an assumption, on the reviewer's part, of Marbot's existence."

Clearly an uncommon reception-historical instance: a reviewer pretends to be caught in an author's game, only to find that he has caught the author in his own game. This singular imbroglio begins to suggest the uncommon nature of the work in question: the life story of an imaginary person presented in the guise of a historical biography, a guise that the author evidently intended to be recognized and admired for what it is: a masterful *dis*guise.

This disguise sports all the historiographic trappings of the biographer's craft: both the book cover and the title page of the first German edition (1981) are adorned with a portrait labeled "Sir Andrew Marbot (1827)," reproduced from a lithograph by Delacroix; the final pages consist of a carefully annotated *index nomini*; a center-folded gallery contains paintings of family members (including one of Marbot's mother, the lovely Lady Catherine, by Sir Henry Raeburn), photographs of the family's manor houses, portraits of friends, acquaintances and mistresses (the former include de Quincy, Byron, and Leopardi, the latter Goethe's daughter-in-law Ottilie and Byron's one-time mistress Teresa Guiccioli). This pseudoauthentic iconographic documentation matches and sustains the textual documentation, a veritably luxuriant paper trail manufactured to interweave Marbot's life with the lives of his contemporaries: eyewitness accounts of meetings with the young Englishman are cited from such real historical texts as Henry Crabbe Robinson's and Schopenhauer's correspondence, Berlioz's and Delacroix's diaries, not to mention Goethe's *Conversations with Eckermann*. Conversely, autobiographical sources describe encounters with these same and other illustrious figures, such as Blake, August von Platen, Corot, and Turner. But these sources also contain documentation of a rather more intimate nature: notably telltale evidence, blacked out in a manuscript notebook, but recently deciphered with the aid of quartz lamps, of Marbot's incestuous relationship with his mother. It is this discovery that has induced the biographer to write Marbot's life, since it alone can explain the originality of his works, notably his astonishingly proto-Freudian insights into the depth-psychological roots of artistic creativity.

A few gullible early reviewers aside, critics quickly saw through Hildesheimer's mock-historiographic travesty. But the elaborateness of his performance had the effect of orienting its reception far more to the matter than to the manner of his generic trompe l'oeil. It was, in other words, reviewed in the manner historical biographies are usually reviewed. For Stern this approach was obviously dictated by his reviewing spoof. But other critics too have been most preoccupied by such issues as the accuracy of the historical data, the validity and originality of Marbot's aesthetic theory and art-critical practice, and, of course, the anomaly of his erotic life: the psycho-scandalon of an incest perpetuated (unlike its classical prototype) by a mother and son *en toute connaissance de cause*.[1]

---

1. Hildesheimer's historical data were checked by (among others) Peter Wapnewski. For the most knowledgeable discussion of Marbot's aesthetics, see Ulrich Weisstein, "Wolfgang Hildesheimer's *Marbot:* Fictional Biography and Treatise on Comparative Literature." Marbot's psychopathology is central to Hans-Joachim Beck, *Der Selbstmord als eine schöne Kunst begangen: Prolegomena zu Wolfgang Hildesheimers psychoanalytischem Roman "Marbot. Eine Biographie,"* a monograph that attempts a tracing of all the intertextual lines that connect Marbot's psyche to the various myths and archetypes of Western culture (more often than not by way of overinterpretations and tenuous analogies).

For further secondary literature concerning *Marbot*, see Patricia H. Stanley, *Wolfgang Hildesheimer and His Critics*, 62–74.

Granting the interest of these historical and thematic questions, for me the true originality of *Marbot* lies less in its matter than in its manner, more precisely in the way its matter relates to its manner. In my formalistic perspective, its distinction lies in the fact that it creates the life of a wholly imaginary character by way of the standardized discourse of historical biography.[2] In this respect *Marbot*—despite its conventional appearance— represents a generic anomaly, a one-of-a-kind experiment in fictional form that deviates from the entire novelistic tradition as we know it, including the tradition of the historical novel. That Hildesheimer himself thought of *Marbot* in these terms is confirmed by his cryptic announcement—in an interview two years prior to publication—that his work in progress was intended to create a new literary species: "It belongs to a category that does not as yet exist."[3]

Before I try to substantiate these large claims (Hildesheimer's and my own), I will enlarge them even further, in terms of the double meaning of this chapter's title. For even as I understand *Marbot* as a work that breaks the code of fictional biography in the sense of departing from the norms that rule the genre, I also understand it as a work that can induce the reader to break this generic code in the sense now of deciphering the way it functions.

NARRATIVE NESCIENCE

To put it most directly, *Marbot* breaks the code—in both senses of the phrase—by excluding all the signal devices we have come to expect from fictional works. In this respect Hildesheimer's work can be said to define the third-person novel by what it isn't, by conspicuously excluding its distinctive features. This severe abstinence may be taken as both the necessary and the sufficient condition that enables Hildesheimer to create his "category that does not as yet exist." Any slippage on his part into specifically fictional narrative discourse would have derailed his experiment, making *Marbot* into just another historical novel, remarkable only for its fancy makeup.

Hildesheimer's vigilance concerns first and foremost his epistemological credibility. He allows himself to include only biographical data for which he can plausibly claim documented knowledge. Marbot's

2. On this matter, my focus in this chapter overlaps with Käte Hamburger, "Authenticity as a Mask: Wolfgang Hildesheimer's *Marbot*." In this study the author briefly applies to *Marbot* some of the basic generic criteria she developed in *The Logic of Literature*, a work that has influenced my own thinking in such fundamental ways (acknowledged elsewhere) that the coincidence of our views in this instance is far from coincidental.

3. "Gespräch mit Wolfgang Hildesheimer," 190; my translation.

physical appearance, his public bearing, even what he said to whom can be known quite readily from the fake entries quoted from real memoirs and letters. His intellectual portrait can be credibly drawn on the basis of quotations from his notebooks and correspondence. But Hildesheimer will allow his biographer no scenes of a kind that escape the gossip of witnesses or that would not or could not have been recorded by his subject himself. This applies above all to the two climactic moments of Marbot's life: his overstepping of the incest barrier and his—probable, never certified—suicide.

But the strictest prohibition enabling Hildesheimer's game is his pretended ignorance of Marbot's psyche. Lacking what he calls "die Schlüssel zum inneren Erleben" ("the keys to the inner life"),[4] his biographer refuses to force his way in by illegitimate—read fictional—means. This does not, however, prevent him from trying to penetrate Marbot's mind in the manner of modern psychobiographers: as a psychoanalytically trained observer who uses every shred of available evidence to build depth-psychological hypotheses. But these interpretations are insistently cautious, self-critically disabused, as befits a sophisticated psychobiographer in our age of suspicion. His psycholoquacious discourse is dotted with ignorance-asserting phrases: "wir wissen es nicht" ("we don't know"), "es bleibt ungewiss" ("it remains uncertain"), "wir werden nie wissen, ob . . ." ("we'll never know whether . . ."). He modalizes almost every psychological interpretation: "so scheint es" ("so it seems"), "vieles spricht dafür" ("there is much to support this"), "ich bin nicht sicher, ob . . ." ("I am uncertain if . . ."). Many passages consist of a flurry of unanswered questions. Here is a typical instance concerning Marbot's possible relations with women (after circumstances force him to leave his mother-mistress and his homeland):

> In seinen Aufzeichnungen findet sich . . . die verräterische Notiz, von der wir aber nicht wissen, was sie verrät: "He whose innocence is raped by an angel loses by every novel experience." . . . Hat er daher auf die "neue Erfahrung" lieber verzichtet, um das wunderbare Bild des Engels nicht auszulöschen? Oder hat er den Verlust in Kauf genommen, im Versuch dieses Bild endgültig aus seiner Seele zu bannen? Wahrscheinlich doch das letztere, denn er hätte kaum von der Erfahrung gesprochen, hätte er sie nicht gemacht. Oder handelt es sich um eine Selbstwarnung? Wir wissen es nicht. (100)

---

4. Wolfgang Hildesheimer, *Marbot. Eine Biographie,* 156; *Marbot: A Biography,* 114. Subsequent page references to these editions will appear parenthetically in the text.

In his notes . . . there is the tell-tale jotting—though we do not know what secret it reveals: "One whose innocence was raped by an angel loses by every further experience." Did he then prefer to do without the "further experience" in order not to blot out the exquisite image of the angel? Or did he accept the loss in an attempt to expunge that image from his soul for ever? Probably the latter, since he would scarcely have spoken of the experience had he not had it. Or is it a warning to himself? We do not know. (70)

The biographer's nescience is peculiarly in evidence as he approaches the *scène à faire,* the mutual seduction of mother and son. Distancing and modalizing phrases begin to multiply, leading eventually to a brief paragraph that opens with a promising "Ich stelle mir vor:" (74) ["I picture it thus":] (51)—a phrase that, ever since Max Frisch's *Gantenbein,* has come to function in Germanophone literature as a metanarrative topos for introducing an imaginary scene. But *what* he imagines remains singularly flat, almost clinically depersonalized. It concludes with the words "wer wen ins Schlafzimmer zieht, ist ungewiss, das Unerhörte nimmt seinen Lauf—" (75) ["who draws whom into the bedroom is uncertain, the unnameable deed takes place—"] (51). Inevitably the manner in which this scene is—or isn't—told has drawn the attention of critics otherwise quite unconcerned with matters of narrative form, but only to voice their puzzled disappointment. One of them comments: "The reticence Hildesheimer imposes on himself for the presentation of the erotic limit-situation is totally incomprehensible. . . . Can one narrate more fussily, less erotically?"[5] And another: "I have rarely seen such a weighty, libidinous, erotic event described so unerotically."[6] These comments betray the degree to which these critics have missed the crux of Hildesheimer's venture: the fact that it is wholly dependent on this self-imposed "reticence," on inhibiting the narrative voice from telling Marbot's erotic experience—erotically.

We might remember in this connection what Henry James once, in an uncharacteristically libidinal image, described as the novelist's true achievement: "the intensity of the creative effort to get into the skin of the creature; the act of personal possession of one being by another at its completest."[7] Marbot's narrator could not allow himself to penetrate "into the

---

5. Hanjo Kesting, *Dichter ohne Vaterland: Gespräche und Aufsätze zur Literatur,* 79; my translation.
6. Helmut Heissenbüttel, "Die Puppe in der Puppe oder der Hildesheimer im Marbot"; my translation.
7. Henry James, *The Art of the Novel,* 37.

skin of the creature," least of all at this supremely transgressive moment, without transgressing the biographer's norms. Such penetration would have been tantamount to admitting, precisely, that Marbot *is* his creature. In this sense, the fake biographer's failure to successfully "imagine" the bedroom scene spells the success of the real author's fictional experiment.

By now my insistence on the Marbot narrator's antiomniscient stance must have brought into view what I view as the deep chasm that separates the biographer's enterprise from the novelist's. To deepen this perspective further still, imagine for a moment the unimaginable: what the fictional lives of memorable characters would be like if their authors had treated them in the manner Hildesheimer treats Marbot—the lives, say, of Stephen Dedalus, Raskolnikov, Isabel Archer, Emma Bovary, Aschenbach. Without episodes packed with their gestures and words, without moments of lonely self-communion minutely tracing spiritual and emotional conflicts, these characters would no doubt never have come to life or become engraved in our reading memories.

Among the memorable characters just mentioned, Aschenbach is an especially illuminating counterexample to Marbot, since his narrator does at one point take on the pose of a historical biographer: in the extended flashback that follows the opening scene, summarizing the life of the protagonist up to the moment when we first encountered him. The narrator's discourse in this section is quite comparable to that of Marbot's biographer: he analyzes, evaluates, and speculates on Aschenbach's works and ways, limiting himself strictly to what he may have learned from witnesses and inferred from documents, including Aschenbach's own writings; in short, he tells us only what a biographer can plausibly know about his subject. But this distanced account—confined to a single expository chapter—contrasts sharply with what precedes and follows. Had this biographical discourse continued throughout *Death in Venice,* we would carry a very different image of its protagonist in our reading memory: no prophetic jungle vision with crouching tiger, no magic transfiguration of time and space, no erotic ecstasy and shame, no Platonic meditation on the Lido beach, no Dionysian dream, no famous last thoughts. In sum, had Mann renounced the novelist's privilege of making his protagonist's mind transparent to his reader's eyes, there would be no *Death in Venice.*

In all but its flashback section, then, Mann's novella follows the code of fiction cast in third-person form, more specifically the focalization on and by a single character that gives its distinctive stamp to fictional biographies (see Chapter 8 below). We can readily check the stability of this code by running through our mind all the works of this type we know—including those that center on the lives of actual historical persons. As I mentioned earlier (see Chapter 2 above), this biographical form of historical fiction on occasion features daring experiments in the presentation of the inner life, some famous examples being Georg Büchner's *Lenz,* Thomas Mann's Schiller novella *Weary Hour [Schwere Stunde]* and his Goethe monologue in *The Beloved Returns [Lotte in Weimar]*, Hermann Broch's *The Death of Virgil [Der Tod des Vergil]*, and most recently J. M. Coetzee's Dostoevsky novel, *The Master of Petersburg.*

It now becomes clear that, in respect to the relationship between its matter and its manner, *Marbot* is the exact inversion of the type of fictional biography exemplified by *Lenz* and *The Death of Virgil*. In these works, distinctively fictional discourse narrates the life of a historical figure. In *Marbot*, by contrast, distinctively nonfictional (historiographic) discourse narrates the life of a fictional figure. To reflect this inversion, we might call the *Lenz* type *fictionalized historical biography,* the *Marbot* type *historicized fictional biography* (at least until someone proposes more elegant generic tags).

The relationship of *Marbot* to its three typological counterparts can now be diagrammed as follows:

protagonist discourse	historical	fictional
historical	historical biography *Mozart*	historicized fictional biography *Marbot*
fictional	fictionalized historical biography *Lenz*	fictional biography *Death in Venice*

But valid as this schema may be on theoretical grounds, it is invalid on empirical grounds. Its symmetry obscures the fact that *Marbot* is—to date, to my knowledge—the lone inhabitant of its box, whereas the three other boxes are thickly populated. And it is this textual population that has inscribed in our reading minds the codes by which we read, activating different expectations according to whether we read (or think we read) fiction or history, fictional or historical lives.

I will not go so far as to claim that we had to wait for *Marbot* to decipher the generic code of fictional biography. The idea that free access to the minds of its characters is the distinctive feature of the novel has been around at least since the eighteenth century, when it was proposed by one of the earliest theorists of the genre, Friedrich von Blanckenburg. More recently (some thirty years ago) another German theorist, Käte Hamburger, placed this distinctiveness of fictional discourse at the vital center of a newly designed generic system in her *Logic of Literature* (see Chapter 2 above). If I nonetheless feel that *Marbot* has a heuristic role to play, it is because so many contemporary theorists of fiction have closed their eyes to the essential difference between factual and fictional narrative that *Marbot* brings into view.[8]

AUTHOR AND NARRATOR

I now pass on to another problem that opens to a somewhat less clearly encoded aspect of the generic code. It concerns the narrator—or better, the reader's image of the narrator. Do we (and are we meant to) understand this biographer's voice as the author's own, or do we (and are we meant to) attribute it to a fictional person or persona of sorts?[9]

We must note, first of all, that if *Marbot* were a real biography, this question would not arise. As in all nonfictional forms of discourse—not only historiographic narratives, but also philosophical treatises, cookbooks, travel guides, program notes, and so forth—the ideas and judgments expressed in a historical biography are unquestioningly attributed to the author whose name appears on the title page. The fact that he stands behind the work as its signatory instructs the reader to assume that he stands behind the views textually expressed.

There is at least one class of fiction where this is clearly not the case: novels and stories cast in first-person form. We recognize such a work—even when it does not announce its fictional status by way of a subtitle—by the fact that its narrator bears a different name from its author. This is also the only way we can distinguish, on purely textual grounds, fictional from historical autobiographies—recognize, say, that *Lolita,* whose narrator is named Humbert Humbert, is a novel, whereas *Speak, Memory* is Nabokov's self-narration of his life. And we are no more entitled to attribute Humbert's opinions to Nabokov than those of any of his charac-

8. I discuss the work of these theorists in Chapter 2 above. The ignorance of textual distinctions between historical and fictional biography is also strikingly illustrated by the analytic philosopher Arthur Danto when he imagines potentially identical texts resulting from a historian's research and a novelist's imagination concerning a "Polish noblewoman of the last century" named Maria Mazurka, whom Danto expressly invents for this purpose; see his "Philosophy as/and/of Literature" (1–23).
9. I take up this problem in a more general and theoretical context in Chapter 7 below.

ters in third-person novels. Had Hildesheimer chosen to cast Marbot as the teller of his own life—perhaps publishing the book under the title "Confessions of a Romantic Oedipus"—the problem of vocal attribution would not have arisen, nor would the generic ambiguity. Marbot's life story would instantly have been recognized as a fiction; unless of course Hildesheimer had reverted to the early-eighteenth-century practice of leaving his own name off the title page. A distance—or at least a clearly marked distinction—between author and narrator would likewise have been created if Marbot's life had been told by someone who had known him personally, as a witness biography in the manner of Thomas Mann's *Doctor Faustus: The Life of the German Composer Adrian Leverkühn as told by a Friend*. (See Chapter 2 above for a definition of this type of novel.)

Such clear fictionalizations of his biographer, and the disengagement from the authorial self it entails, are models Hildesheimer evidently chose *not* to follow in *Marbot*. That this was a deliberate choice is indicated in a prepublication interview. Referring to a conversation about his work in progress with his friend and fellow writer Walter Jens, he quotes the latter as saying, "Then you must of course work on two different levels, that of the represented figure and that of the first-person narrator, so that you can produce a contrastive effect." Whereupon Hildesheimer comments, "That would result in too much of a fiction for me."[10] What he did intend—as he further explains in a postpublication essay significantly entitled "Working protocols for the 'Marbot' proceeding" ["Arbeits protokolle des Verfahrens 'Marbot'"]—was to create the impression that he spoke throughout as himself, a process he calls at one point "my act of identification with the biographer," at another "my personal self-narrative role."[11] What he does *not* say (but surely also intended) is that this voice would be recognized as his own by extratextual evidence that lay close at hand: his best-selling *Mozart* biography, published only four years before *Marbot* and similarly punctuated by a rash of phrases of the "We-don't-know-this"-type applied to the psyche of the protagonist.[12] Hildesheimer could thus count on many of his readers perceiving the intertextual emulation of his own biographical stance in the earlier work, understanding that, as the biographer of Marbot, he was, so to speak, pos-

---

10. "Gespräch mit Wolfgang Hildesheimer," 189; my translation.
11. "Arbeitsprotokolle des Verfahrens 'Marbot,'" 27; my translations.
12. The biographer's inability to penetrate the consciousness of his subject is explicitly underlined throughout *Mozart*. See also Hildesheimer's remarks appended to *Mary Stuart: Eine historische Szene*: "What did things look like inside Mary Stuart? . . . The question remains without an answer, like all questions regarding the inner life of historical figures" (76); my translation.

ing as himself. In this respect, the choice of his hero's name—a near-scramble of Mozart's—was surely meant as an *avis au lecteur*. But more importantly, the self-pastiche is underlined by the Marbot biographer's almost verbatim repetition of the Mozart biographer's didactic comments on his craft, including such adages as the following:

> Ich habe niemals die Ansicht vertreten, dass der Biograph vor dem Schlafzimmer haltzumachen habe, da das erotische Leben seines Helden zu ihm gehört und wesentlich—wenn nicht gar den wesentlichsten—Aufschluss vermittelt. (152)
>
> Es ist der Welt immer schwer geworden, mit ihren Skandalen zu leben, daher ist es der Geschichte und Kulturgeschichte immer wieder gelungen, die Anomalien ihrer Helden und Opfer zu verdrängen . . . Auch die Biographie ist durchsetzt von diesen furchtbaren Vereinfachern, die schiefe und daher falsche Bilder entwerfen oder dafür sorgen, dass sie sich potenziert fortzeugen. (155f)

> I have never supported the view that the biographer should stop outside the bedroom door, for the erotic life of his hero belongs to him and provides essential—if not the most essential—information. (111)
>
> It has always been difficult for the world to live with its scandals, which is why historians and cultural historians have succeeded again and again in suppressing the anomalies of their heroes and victims. . . . Biography too is beset by these "terribles simplificateurs" who draw lopsided and therefore false pictures, or take care that they are perpetuated in intensified form. (113)

What Hildesheimer, as he himself admitted, failed to foresee is that the readers' reception of such normative language is willy-nilly affected when it is transplanted to newly fictional surroundings. "A number of my friends," he tells us in "Arbeitsprotokolle," "have taken this or that passage, which I myself had meant absolutely seriously, for the discourse of a rather pompous, conceited, and somewhat pedantic Other. In these passages I apparently failed. I was intent on always having full control over my own self as object, but it seems to have turned into someone different from the one I had planned." He furthermore notes with particular distress that the comparison of *Marbot* with Mann's *Doctor Faustus* novel—which he himself encourages on other grounds—was applied to the neuralgic matter of his narrator: "There were even some friends who were reminded of Serenus Zeitblom [the narrator of *Doctor Faustus*]. That's a thought that would never have occurred to me. The last thing I wanted was to write a novel in which there would be a fictional frame with a narrator figure."[13]

Hildesheimer's surprise at what he himself calls his "failure" in this regard is not itself surprising if we believe his repeated assertion that he is not nearly as versed in literary theory as in the aesthetics of music and art.[14] Those of us who are acquainted with theoretical perspectives on fictional narrators and their potential unreliability will readily understand that the readers to whom Hildesheimer refers quite legitimately took advantage of an option he gave them by the mere act of becoming the narrator of a fiction: the option to disengage this narrator from the author, opening a gap that casts an ironic (and in this case also self-parodic) light on his normative discourse.[15] There is no way Hildesheimer could have guarded against this critical move on his readers' part, save one: to limit himself to purely narrative language. Since this novel, however, includes a prominent "didactic I"[16] that articulates numerous passages of normative language, the reader may understand the voice that speaks here as originating in an expressly constructed figure of an unreliable narrator, rather than in the author himself. This move may, in fact, work in the author's favor: for then he will no longer be held responsible for any flaws or discrepancies the reader might discover in his ideological discourse.[17]

In this regard, it is surely significant that Hildesheimer attributes the (mis)understanding of his narrator as a somewhat ridiculous Zeitblom-like figure to *friendly* readers—"a number of my friends." For I would maintain that it opens to a far more positive evaluation of his work, by way of a reading that refers all the weaknesses in the Marbot-biographer's performance to a fallible narrator-figure of the author's own making. Resolved perspectively, the flaws in the narrator's discourse can now work in the author's favor.[18]

---

13. "Arbeitsprotokolle," 27–28; my translation.
14. See, for example, "The End of Fiction," where Hildesheimer states: "I would have preferred to talk about fine arts and music. I have reflected and speculated about these two fields, but not about literature. I am a writer and an occasional reader, but not a theoretician" (59); my translation.
15. This theoretical perspective is developed with particular clarity in Félix Martínez-Bonati, *Fictive Discourse and the Structures of Literature*, 32–39; see my discussion of this work in Chapter 7 below.
16. "As the author of a book about him [Marbot], I am as it were a didactic I that writes his biography" ("Arbeitsprotokolle," 30; my translation).
17. A reader-oriented perspective on the unreliability of fictional narrators is developed in Tamar Yacobi, "Fictional Reliability as a Communicative Problem."
18. For a perspectival reading that "salvages" a much greater work than *Marbot* in this manner, see Chapter 8 (on *Death in Venice*) below.

One of these flaws—which I will mention merely in passing—is this psychobiographer's rather shaky mastery of psychoanalytic language (notably his misuse of such Freudian concepts as repression and sublimation). But far more central to the thematic structure of *Marbot* is the incongruity that attends the narrator's stated reason for writing his psychobiography in the first place—bedroom secrets and all. His motivation, as he tells us more than once, is that Marbot's aesthetic writings—about to be published for the first time in an undoctored edition—cannot be fully understood without knowledge of their depth-psychological genesis:

> Gewiss stellt sich hier auch wieder die Frage, ob Marbots Bedeutung, sein Stellenwert in der Kulturgeschichte, Angabe und Kenntis der letzten intimen Einzelheiten seines Lebens rechtfertige. Es dürfte sich aber schon bisher ergeben haben, dass diese Frage zu bejahen ist, denn ohne Kenntnis dieser Einzelheiten wären—und waren!—Marbots Schriften einer Tiefendimension beraubt. (152–53)

> Here again, it may be asked, does Marbot's significance, his rank in cultural history, justify the knowledge and recital of the most intimate details of his life? It should be obvious by now, however, that the answer will be in the affirmative, for without the knowledge of these details Marbot's writings would be—or have been!—robbed of their dimension of depth. (111)

The reader who repeatedly encounters statements of this sort naturally expects that they will be sustained by the wide sampling of Marbot's own writings directly quoted by his biographer. This is, however, far from being the case: Marbot's pronouncements on the process of artistic creativity, no less than his innovative interpretations of specific art works, are penetrating and illuminating in themselves, and in no sense dependent on—or even enlightened by—knowledge of his pathological love life. Accordingly, the biographer, who doth protest too much, stands exposed as something of a self-promoting fop, who—in a manner known from some of his colleagues—overinflates the explanatory value of biographical data for understanding the products of a creative mind.

Two further sources cast ironic light on the Marbot-biographer's self-inflating discourse. The first stems from Hildesheimer himself, who defended a diametrically opposite thesis concerning the power of biographical explanations in his *Mozart* book. Here he demonstrates precisely the unbridgeable abyss that separates the life from the work, arguing that there is radical discontinuity between the Mozart we know from biographical and autobiographical sources and the Mozart we know from his music. In this respect the intertextual relationship between *Mozart* and *Marbot* is clearly antithetical, and the reader who attributes the didactic discourse of these two works to the same mind—as he is encouraged to do on other grounds—cannot help but conclude that this mind has reversed itself in the four-year interval.

But this would be to forget that this same mind also created the mind of Marbot, a mind (clearly fictional this time) that in turn is made to create an aesthetic theory. And Marbot's own theory matches the Mozart-biographer's far more closely than the one held by his biographer. For even though Marbot insists (like Freud a century later) that every work of art originates in its creator's unconscious conflicts—"das Kunstwerk als Diktat der unbewussten Regungen seines Schöpfers" (15) ["the work of art as the dictate of the unconscious impulses of its creator"] (7)—he emphasizes the insoluble mystery of this psychic origin with at least equal force: "Bilder erscheinen mir immer wie gerahmte Rätsel, . . . ich glaube der Art des Rätsels auf der Spur zu sein, nämlich der Seele des Künstlers" (119) ["Paintings strike me more and more as framed enigmas, . . . I believe that I am on the scent of the nature of the enigma, namely the soul of the artist"] (85). Beyond this general intuition, the enigma will allow for no answer. It has a way of thickening whenever Marbot tries to decipher it in a specific work. A Giorgione self-portrait that he probes with particular intensity returns his gaze with the words: "In Wirklichkeit wirst du nichts über mich erfahren, du kannst es nicht" (185) ["In reality you will learn nothing about me, you cannot"] (135). Finally, prominently displayed on the final page of the biography, the following quotation from Marbot's notebook:

> die Frage nach dem grössten Geheimnis beantwortet es [das Kunst-werk] niemandem, nämlich die nach jener seelischen Notwendigkeit, dem es seine Entstehung verdankt. Daher werden wir mit Gewissheit nichts von dem erfahren, was im Künstler vorgegangen ist, ausser seinem Gebot, was in uns vorzugehen habe. Der Künstler spielt auf unserer Seele, aber wer spielt auf der Seele des Künstlers? (320)

> To no one does it [the work of art] answer the question as to the greatest mystery, namely the spiritual necessity to which it owes its being. Therefore we shall not learn with certainty of anything that has taken place within the artist, other than his injunction as to what should take place in us. The artist plays on our soul, but who plays on the soul of the artist? (237)

"Mystery," "enigma": these are, of course, the very terms Freud himself—unlike some of his followers—invariably employs when he speaks of the origin of a work of art. In this regard the proto-Freudian Marbot is much more in tune with the master's voice than his post-Freudian biographer.

What I am suggesting is that Hildesheimer has endowed his imaginary protagonist with far greater wisdom and subtlety than his biographer. If we took the author at his word and understood his narrator as a self-impersonation, we would be forced to conclude that he has created for Marbot a mind superior to his own.[19] This unlikely possibility points up in a backhanded way that the narrator of a fictional biography is on principle distinct from its author—a deep-seated, tenacious feature of the generic code that even the code-breaking author of *Marbot* was not able to break.

PARATEXTUAL PRESENTATION

Finally, surfacing from the deep, a few words about the most obvious, but perhaps also the most vexatious, of Hildesheimer's code-breaking practices: the duplicitous nature of his text's paratextual presentation that simultaneously asserts and denies its fictional status (and its historical status). This problem leads me, in conclusion, to consider the class of modernist literary experiments with which *Marbot* could rightfully be classed.

Did Hildesheimer want his readers to be caught in his game? Not if we judge from his protest against Stern's (as he mistakenly believed gullible) review, quoted at the beginning of this discussion. Nor if we believe another even clearer postpublication pronouncement: "If some of my readers and critics were duped, I can only assure them that the fault isn't mine. Granted that my intention was to bestow life on Marbot; but it wasn't to commit a fraud." He immediately concedes, however, "that my demonstration of the fictional nature [of the work] was perhaps too hidden and too weak."[20] This "demonstration," he now explains, consisted of two paratextual items: a single phrase in the first sentence of the (German) book-jacket text, which reads: "Sir Andrew Marbot, the hero of this biography, is as it were woven into the cultural history of the early nineteenth century" (my translation); and the omission from his *index nomi-*

---

19. Martin Swales reaches precisely this paradoxical conclusion in his review of *Marbot*. After demonstrating the cogency of Marbot's aesthetic theories as compared to his biographer's simplistic psychologisms, he suggests (tongue in cheek?) that we need to defend Marbot against his creator. Swales also remarks on the fact that Marbot's writings, as quoted by his biographer, can easily dispense with the depth-psychological explications proposed by his biographer.

20. Hildesheimer, "Arbeitsprotokolle," 28; my translation.

ni of all the Marbot family members' names. What Hildesheimer does *not* mention here (or in any other place) is another paratextual item that easily outweighs the discreet and less than decisive signals he mentions: the subtitle *Eine Biographie* (*A Biography*) featured on the title page. This is surely the factor most immediately responsible for the fact that some readers and even some early reviewers were misled.

Generic subtitles, as Gérard Genette explains in a study that deals with the various verbal thresholds surrounding and supporting the body of a text, tend to play a decisive role in the reception of literary works. Their status is official, in the sense that the reader is meant to understand them as a kind of contractual agreement on the author's part. They signal the author's intention or decision concerning the generic nature of his work, with a view to determining a definite horizon of expectation.[21] In light of this convention, the tag *Eine Biographie* (*A Biography*) on the title page of *Marbot* would have to be understood as a deception on the author's part. But there is, of course, an alternate way of understanding it, the only way one *can* understand it once one has become apprised—by whatever means—of the real state of affairs, namely that *Marbot* is a fictional and not a historical work. *Eine Biographie* (*A Biography*) must then be understood, not as a generic subtitle that stands underneath the main title, but as part and parcel of the main title itself, which reads correctly: *Marbot. Eine Biographie* (*Marbot: A Biography*). Its appropriate generic subtitle— *Roman* (*Novel*)—has simply been omitted, subtitles not being obligatory (for novels or any other types of publications). Another way of conceptualizing the ambiguity attending Hildesheimer's title page would be to say that it overtly frames *Marbot* as a biography—with the term *framing* here used in Erving Goffman's sense of contextualizing—but that this overt frame is surrounded by another *covert* frame that, once it is discovered, transforms this biography (including its title page) into a novel.[22]

I doubt that Hildesheimer set up this titular prestructure inadvertently. Clearly the effect of the work depended on a complex, if not a perverse, manipulation of his reader: explicitly inviting him to believe in the historicity of *Marbot* at the outset and sustaining that belief by all the means at his disposal; but inviting him as well, by fainter signals, to suspect its *counterfeit* historicity. He seems, in effect, to have aimed for an ideal read-

21. See Gérard Genette, *Seuils,* 89ff.

22. The relevance of Erving Goffman's *Frame Analysis* for ambiguous title pages is proposed by Lennard J. Davis in *Factual Fictions: The Origins of the English Novel,* 20ff. Davis applies it to eighteenth century fictional autobiographies whose title pages more or less "duped" the reader into understanding the work as the life history of a real person.

er who, Janus-eyed, could alternately conceive Marbot as a real *and* as an imaginary figure, on the analogy with the viewer of the rabbit-and-duck in Gombrich's iconic illustration of absolute ambiguity. Such a reader, needless to say, could not survive the move of checking on Marbot in the *Dictionary of National Biography*. Still, a hypothetically innocent reading would create a condition of hesitation between two dissimilar visions of the world: one that did and one that did not include Andrew Marbot. Such an "ontological flicker" is the reader reaction that Brian McHale attributes to the postmodernist genre of "apocryphal history," a form of historical fiction that "contradicts the official version [of history] . . . [by] claiming to restore what has been lost or suppressed."[23] *Marbot* could be regarded as a biographical variant of this genre, by dint of the new look the existence of its protagonist gives to the history of aesthetics as well as to the history of the Romantic movement.

But at the same time its mock-biographical presentation also affiliates *Marbot* with another postmodern experimental trend: the writing of lives that play on (and with) the border between history and fiction. The most prominent breakdown of generic distinction since the nineteen-sixties has been occurring between historical and fictional *auto*biography. Here a number of crossbreeds have appeared — under such tags as "Autofiction" (Serge Doubrovsky, *Fils*), "A Fictional Memoir" (Frederick Exley, *A Fan's Notes*), or simply "A Novel" (Ronald Sukenik, *Up*) — that adopt the contradictory practice of naming their fictional self-narrators after their authors, thereby effectively ambiguating the distinction between fiction and nonfiction for self-narrated lives.[24]

But to subvert the codes that separate fiction from history in telling lives of *others,* more subtle rules must be broken. Here experimental transgression has proceeded unilaterally, by appropriating fictional devices (including even stream-of-consciousness techniques) to tell about the inner life of real persons — movie actresses, convicted murderers, astronauts, sports heroes — in works that bear appropriately oxymoronic subtitles: "True Life Novel," "Novel Biography," "Nonfiction Novel," and the like.[25] To my knowledge, *Marbot* is the only work to date that clearly reverses this direction. Whether others will follow remains to be seen. But there is reason to doubt that it will be (or was meant to be) a pacesetter:

23. Brian McHale, *Postmodernist Fiction,* 90.
24. See Jonathan Wilson, "Counterlives: On Autobiographical Fiction in the 1980s."
25. For a discussion of this contemporary practice, see Ina Schabert, "Fictional Biography, Factual Biography, and their Contaminations" and Tom Wolfe, "The New Journalism" in *The New Journalism,* 1–52. See also Chapter 2 above.

unlike the experimental biographies just mentioned, it depends, as we have seen, not on permissive freedom but on forbidding constraint: renunciation of the imaginative omniscience traditionally granted to the creator of imaginary beings. On this account, *Marbot* may well remain the sole specimen of its species.

6

"I Doze and Wake"

The Deviance of Simultaneous Narration

Life tells us that we cannot tell it while we live it or live it while we tell it. Live now, tell later. On existential grounds this *différance* may be a source of despair. Sartre's Roquentin says: "You have to choose: live or tell. . . . I wanted the moments of my life to follow and order themselves like those of a life remembered. You might as well try and catch time by the tail."[1]

On aesthetic grounds this same dilatory constraint may become a source of value. Thomas Mann writes in his "Foreword" to *The Magic Mountain:* "Stories must be past, and the more past, one could say, the better for them in their quality as stories, and the better for their narrator, that droning wizard of the past tense."[2] Narrative theorists denote this state of affairs more dispassionately. Shlomith Rimmon-Kenan writes: "Common sense tells us that events may be narrated only after they happen";[3] Paul Ricoeur: "Every story is told in the past for the voice that tells it";[4] and Robert Scholes: "It is a formal feature of narrative texts—a part of their grammar—that the events are always presented in the past tense, as having already happened. . . . narrative is past, always past."[5]

Such apodictic statements notwithstanding, a number of theorists acknowledge that the axiomatic pastness of narrative needs to be variously qualified. Some question its validity in fictional as compared to historiographic (and generally nonfictional) narrative. Others probe its local suspension in traditional narratives of all types when they shift from the past to the so-called historical present. Still others allow for the global displacement of the past by the present in such modern genres as interior monologue novels and eyewitness news reports.

1. *Nausea,* 39–40.
2. My translation.
3. *Narrative Fiction,* 89.
4. *Time and Narrative,* II:98.
5. "Language, Narrative and Anti-Narrative," 209–10.

Narrative poetics, however, has as yet failed to account for the most serious challenge to the accepted truth that "narrative is past, always past":
the mounting trend in modernist first-person fiction to cast a distinctively narrative (not monologic) discourse in the present tense from first to
last.[6] This deviant narrative manner has been applied to narrative matter
of the widest diversity by such well-known contemporary writers as Margaret Atwood (*Surfacing*, 1972; *The Handmaid's Tale*, 1985), J. M. Coetzee
(*In the Heart of the Country*, 1977; *Waiting for the Barbarians*, 1980),
Nathalie Sarraute (*Portrait of an Unknown Man*, 1948; *Martereau*, 1953),
Robert Pirsig (*Zen and the Art of Motorcycle Maintenance*, 1974), and Percy Walker (*The Moviegoer*, 1960).[7] Granting that each of these instances
calls for separate examination and may ultimately be found to involve
quite different thematic and ideological motivations, this chapter will address the more general questions introduced above: How does this new
fictional form relate to narratological norms? Can it be made to fit into
established systems, or does it call for systematic revision? What are its
principal effects, and how do they depart from, and compare to, accepted discursive practices?[8]

AN UNACKNOWLEDGED CATEGORY

I begin by assessing whether the above-mentioned amendments flex the
rule of narrative pastness sufficiently to allow for a first-person narrator
who tells his or her entire story in the present tense.

The theorist who advocates the separate status of *fictional* narration in
respect to the pastness-axiom most forcefully is Käte Hamburger. As
readers of *The Logic of Literature* will recall, however, her thesis concerning the "timelessness of fiction" (and the consequent indifference of its
narrative tense) applies exclusively to the *third*-person novel.[9] In the *first*-
person novel, which Hamburger conceives on principle as adhering to
the logic of real-world discourse (reality statement), the obligatory temporal distance between the past of experience and the present of narration

6. The profusion of the present as narrative tense in anglophone fiction may be gauged from
   two front-page articles published in the *New York Times Book Review* some years ago (11 October 1987 and 10 August 1986), as well as from a remark in the *New York Review of Books* (16
   January 1992) that singles out a new novel under review for "avoiding the use of the first person and present tense common among young novelists."
7. Like all formal innovations, this one is not lacking in predecessors. One finds it heralded in
   certain stories by Chekhov and Kafka, for example, and in Erich Remarque's novel *Nothing
   New on the Western Front* (1928).
8. Some of these questions are touched on in Monika Fludernik, *Toward a "Natural" Narratology*, 249–56.
9. See Hamburger, *The Logic in Literature*, 105–9.

remains fully in effect; events can only be narrated retrospectively.[10] It turns out, then, that the theorist who most decisively rules against the pastness of fictional reference is also the one who most decisively rules *out* first-person/present-tense narration—in fiction and nonfiction alike.

Though other theorists have proposed more flexible and inclusive models of fictionality, those who have given due attention to differences between third- and first-person narrative situations have generally agreed that there is an essential distinction between the functioning of tenses in the two principal fictional domains. The departure from the tensual norm (whether local or global) in *third*-person novels does not affect their temporal structure in essential ways; for, to the degree that the past tense creates the experiential present of fictional minds, it becomes semantically (i.e., temporally) moot, hence indifferently replaceable by the present tense. In *first*-person novels, by contrast, the past tense of narration ineluctably refers to the speaker's own past—to a time that is necessarily understood as anterior to the present moment in which the discourse is uttered. This tensual logic binds the language of fictional narrators (Werther's letters, Humbert Humbert's confession) no less than that of autobiographers like Goethe or Nabokov. Michál Glowínski, like Hamburger, attributes this linguistic homology between fictional and real self-historians to the fact that first-person novels traditionally imitate discursive genres of real life (memoirs, oral confessions, letters, journals), a process he calls "formal mimetics."[11] On this basis, the narratological dicta I quoted at the outset—"events may be narrated only after they happen"; "every story is told in the past for the voice that tells it"—would apply to first-person fiction with equal force, and on the same grounds, as to all manners of historiographic narration.

Nor is this force in any sense weakened if and when the past tense momentarily yields to the present in a first-person novel. When, after his mother's death, David Copperfield returns home in the past, buries her in the present, then reverts to the past as the discourse takes up his now orphaned life, the temporal distance of the burial scene is not in question. The reason is obvious: embedded as it is in past-tense narration, out of which and into which it shifts at start and finish without interrupting the narrative continuity, the past-time reference of this present tense is contextually marked with unambiguous clarity. The suspension of normal tensual semantics in historical present—reflected in the oxymoronic term itself—has been acknowledged by most linguists concerned with this

10. Ibid., 311–18.
11. "On the First-Person Novel," 106.

phenomenon. Characterizing it by such phrases as "temps comme si," "jeu littéraire," "Tempusmetapher," and "stylistic device,"[12] they recognize that its intermittent effacement of temporal distance is not to be taken (and is not in danger of being taken) literally. The highlighting impact generally attributed to the use of the historical present—variously expressed in terms of enhanced vividness, dramatic effect, or presentification—is accordingly understood as being wholly dependent on its intermittence: if it were not embedded in normal tensual surroundings, its tensual deviance would not stand out.[13]

Understood in this fashion as a structurally harmless stylistic device, the historical present within first-person fiction is readily assimilated without in the least perturbing the basic narrative situation that determines this formal type. This is no doubt the reason why leading narratologists have generally set up their basic categories without giving much attention to this tensual variant; curiously, it does not even figure among the more or less striking narrative "figures" in Gérard Genette's system. By the same token, however, the standard interpretation of the historical present may have discouraged theorists from envisioning the virtuality of a first-person novel *globally* narrated in the present tense. In the absence of any framing past-tense context, can such a text still be understood as structurally innocuous? Can its tense be regarded simply as a historical present extended over the entire length of the work, differing merely in degree, not in kind, from the local use of the present in certain scenes of traditional self-narrated fictions? I leave these questions suspended for the moment, noting merely that the possibility of normalizing this deviant practice would seem to depend on the way they are answered.

In contrast to the lack of attention narratologists have given to the *narrative* functioning of the present tense in first-person novels, they have given considerable attention to a first-person fictional form where the present functions as a *nonnarrative* tense: the autonomous interior monologue, as exemplified by Schnitzler's *Fräulein Else* or the "Penelope" section of *Ulysses*. Genette, who labels this form "immediate speech" (where the potentially misleading term *speech,* however, clearly signifies silent

---

12. The first two of these phrases are from Paul Imbs, *L'Emploi des temps verbaux en français moderne,* 201; the third is from Harald Weinrich, *Tempus: Besprochene und erzählte Welt,* 125; the fourth is from Emile Benveniste, *Problems in General Linguistics,* 309.

13. Nessa Wolfson, in "Tense-Switching in Narrative," even suggests that the "vividness" effect associated with the historical present should be attributed to "tense switching" rather than to the grammatical tense itself. This idea is based on her observation of oral narrative practice, in which speakers punctuate their stories by alternating their tenses "in either direction," present to past as well as past to present.

mental self-address) understands its language to be "emancipated . . . from all narrative patronage."[14] Stanzel, who inscribes this form within the segment of his circle that extends between two typical narrative situations—first-person and figural—likewise describes it in a manner that clearly foregrounds its nonnarrative discourse: "In interior monologue the reader encounters a self that already exhibits the characteristic features of a reflector-character: *it does not narrate* or address a listener or reader, but reflects in its consciousness its own momentary situation."[15]

Both of these theorists, then, quite correctly in my perspective, deny the status of "narrator" to Else, Molly Bloom, and the other fictional characters whose monologizing voices we hear in this type of text, and accordingly deny the narrative structure of these texts themselves. It is nonetheless by way of the autonomous monologue form that both Genette and Stanzel (though in rather different ways) come closest to conceiving a virtual systematic space for a narratively structured first-person type that would be cast in the present tense throughout. Genette approaches it by misstepping, as it were, when he assigns monologic texts to a category he labels "simultaneous narrating,"[16] contradicting the nonnarrating character he attributed to them earlier (see the passage referred to above). We thus owe to him a concept that, at least in respect to self-narration, remains an empirically void abstraction in his system, and whose problematical structural implications he fails to explore. Stanzel, for his part, though he never uses the term "simultaneous narration," does at one point seem to glimpse its potential location. Visualizing "several degrees of disengagement from the first-person model of narrative transmission" as his circle moves toward the unmediated "interior monologue," he describes one of these transitional stages as "the transition of tense from the past to the present."[17] But here too, this virtuality remains unexplored in theory and practice.[18]

14. *Narrative Discourse*, 174.
15. Franz K. Stanzel, *A Theory of Narrative*, 212; my emphasis. For my own perspective on this nonnarrative form of fiction, see *Transparent Minds*, 174 and 217–47.
16. Genette, *Narrative Discourse*, 218–19.
17. Stanzel, *A Theory of Narrative*, 227.
18. In contrast to their disregard of self-centered present-tense narration, both Genette and Stanzel clearly identify a type of present-tense narration focused on a visual field from which the speaker remains effaced. Genette labels it "behaviourist" (*Narrative Discourse*, 219); Stanzel labels it "camera eye" (*A Theory of Narrative*, 294–99); others have called it "current report" (Christian Casparis, *Tense without Time*, 43–45) and "tabular present" (Hamburger, *The Logic of Literature*, 123). This narrative type is not limited to fiction; it includes, for example, sportscasting. On account of its exclusion of self-reference—which clearly makes it a form of third-person narration—it does not present the peculiarly perturbing features that mark first-person/present-tense novels.

It turns out, then, that despite the qualifications that have been applied to the axiom of narrative pastness, the global first-person/present-tense form remains narratologically in limbo: neglected (if not denied) in theory, mis- or un- identified in practice, its anomaly falls between the cracks of established discursive norms.[19]

INADEQUATE READING OPTIONS

We may now ask how, in the face of these norms, a theoretically informed reader is apt to react to the "abnormal" novelty of first-person novels cast, from first to last, in the present tense. My textual paradigm will be a representative passage from J. M. Coetzee's *Waiting for the Barbarians*. It occurs at the moment when the nameless narrator of this novel—a minor official in a nameless, autocratically ruled country—has just escaped from prison and is about to hide in the room of a girl he has formerly known:

> As boldly as I can, but wincing despite myself, I mount the stairs. How must I look to the world with my dingy shirt and trousers, my bare feet, my unkempt beard? Like a domestic, I pray, an ostler come home after a night's carousing.
>
> The passageway is empty, the door to the girl's room open. . . .
>
> The bed is made up. When I slip my hand between the sheets I imagine I can feel the faint afterglow of her warmth. Nothing would please me more than to curl up in her bed, lay my head on her pillow, forget my aches and pains, ignore the hunt that must by now have been launched for me, and like the little girl in the story tumble into oblivion. How voluptuously I feel the attraction of the soft, the warm, the odorous this morning! With a sigh I kneel and coax my body in under the bed. Face down, pressed so tightly between the floor and the slats of the bed that when I move my shoulders the bed lifts, I try to compose myself for a day of hiding.
>
> I doze and wake, drifting from one formless dream to another. By mid-morning it has become too hot to sleep. . . .

19. Significantly, this neglect also pervades Suzanne Fleischman's linguistically based study *Tense and Narrative: From Medieval Performance to Modern Fiction*, the most systematic and sophisticated approach to narrative tense we have to date. Reiterating from the outset the established precept concerning narrative pastness—"Narration is a verbal icon of experience viewed from a *retrospective* vantage; the experience is by definition 'past' . . . for this, I submit, is the only way one can *narrate*" (23–24, her emphases)—she denies that the present tense in its narrative function can ever become "cotemporal with now" and concludes that works globally cast in the present tense must be understood as "something other than narration" (306). While her textual corpus—mainly drawn from the medieval epic and the *nouveau roman*—tends to sustain this thesis, I don't see how it could account, without major modifications, for the deviant fictional type examined in the present chapter.

A torpor is already beginning to settle over the town. The morning's work is over: anticipating the heat of midday, people are retiring to their shaded courtyards or to the cool green of their inner rooms. . . .

Sighing I lay myself down on the bed in the sweet remembered scent of flowers. How inviting to join the rest of the town in its siesta! These days, these hot spring days already becoming summer—how easily I slip into their languorous mood! How can I accept that disaster has overtaken my life when the world continues to move so tranquilly through its cycles? . . . "*Why?*" I groan into the pillow: "*Why me?*" Never has there been anyone so confused and innocent of the world as I. A veritable baby! (ll. 92–94)

If one tries to make a work of this kind conform to the law that says "narration is past, always past," one has two principal ways to go: either to deny that its tense is a genuine present, or to deny that its discourse is genuine narration. I will call the first way out the *historical present resolution,* the second way out the *interior monologue resolution.* Both these ways offer escapes from the apparent illogicality of present tense narrative language in a first-person novel. But as we will see, they both lead away from the way actually followed by this passage, the way followed by Coetzee's and many other entire novels for hundreds of pages—lead away from it precisely by choosing between two mutually exclusive ways of reading one and the same language.

The historical present resolution understands the tense of the quoted passage not as a real present that refers to the time in which the discourse ostensibly takes place, but as a metaphorical "as if" present that stands in for the past tense and refers to past time. This resolution no doubt draws its force from habit: though, in the absence of a past context, Coetzee's novel provides no intrinsic reason for attributing past meaning to events referred to in present tense, the massive experience of most readers with *local* use of the present as narrative tense seems to carry over onto its *global* use, inclining the reader to an unreflectively normalized understanding of the present tense as referring to past history. This, at any rate, appears to me as the most plausible explanation for the pervasive disregard of its tensual deviance in the reception of *Waiting for the Barbarians.*[20]

---

20. A notable exception to this disregard is Anne Waldron Neumann's "Escaping the 'Time of History'? Present Tense and the Occasion of Narration in J. M. Coetzee's *Waiting for the Barbarians.*" Neumann proposes a highly perceptive ideological interpretation of the tensual peculiarity of its narrative language.

A closer look at the textual reality of our sample passage brings certain shortfalls of this reading into view. Several moments encourage us to take its tense literally, in the precise sense signified by Benveniste when he defines the present as "the time when one speaks," explaining: "this 'present' . . . has only a linguistic fact as temporal reference: the coincidence of the event described with the instance of the discourse that describes it."[21] The synchrony of language and event in the quoted passage obtrudes itself most strongly when the text seems to render the speaker's unspoken thoughts and perceptions: "How must I look to the world with my dingy shirt and trousers?"; "Nothing would please me more than to curl up in her bed"; "These days, these hot spring days already becoming summer." The effect here is of overhearing an immediate verbalization of what is felt and thought, an effect known to the modern reader from "Penelope" and its analogously structured progeny—texts that present themselves as mental quotations from start to finish, as unmediated mimesis of consciousness. This analogy prompts the alternate interior monologue resolution, the attempt to understand the present tense of this passage (and of the entire novel that contains it) as the normal tense of silently expressive self-communion, a language that emerges in a fictional mind without aiming at communicative narration or narrative communication.

But although the interior monologue resolution is encouraged by certain textual moments, it in turn becomes implausible for the text as a whole. For one thing, the speaker's thoughts are at times not directly rendered but explicitly quoted: "'*Why?*' I groan into the pillow: '*Why me?*'" At other times the inner happenings are mediated by a knowingly analytic voice: "I imagine I can feel"; "I try to compose myself." But the introspective instance that most strongly resists the interior monologue reading is no doubt the one that reads: "I doze and wake, drifting from one formless dream to another." Here semantic incongruence combines with the formal feature that most forcefully counteracts the impression of an unrolling mental quotation in this passage as a whole: the pace of its discourse is not consistently synchronized with the pace of the events it conveys, but time and again compresses extended stretches of time in summary sentences, on occasion even leapfrogging the passing hours: "By mid-morning it has become too hot to sleep."[22] Perhaps more than anything else, the temporal structure of this passage, evoking as it does a

21. Emile Benveniste, *Problems in General Linguistics*, 227.
22. Elsewhere in Coetzee's novel, summaries apply to even larger units of time: days, even weeks; for example, see 57–63 and 122–25.

teller who stands away from—looks back on—his experience, induces us to de-literalize its tense and to revert to the historical present resolution—but only until the textual moments that resist this reading again obtrude themselves and insist that the present language must after all coincide with the speaker's presently lived experience.

The mutual exclusiveness of the two reading options I have just outlined for the passage from *Waiting for the Barbarians* points up the difficulty of subsuming texts of this type under established narrative categories. I will now propose a way to escape from the horns of this reading dilemma: a way that takes first-person/present-tense narration literally, even as it calls for certain modifications in our theoretical conception of fictional norms that allow us to normalize the paradoxical term "simultaneous narration."

AN ATTEMPT AT NORMALIZATION

We must note, first of all, that though both of the reading strategies described above try to normalize simultaneous narration in terms of conventions of fictional realism, these conventions are not the same in each case. The historical present resolution calls on the norms of formal mimeticism that the realist tradition ties to *first*-person fictional narration: the imitation of an autobiographical discourse where the narrating self refers to the past life of an experiencing self. The interior monologue resolution calls on the norms of verisimilar psychological presentation that mark the tradition of *third*-person realist fiction: the transparency of fictional characters that grants inside views into their consciousness. As I have suggested elsewhere,[23] in this respect the realist novel assumes a highly artificial privilege that categorically differentiates it from all manners of natural or real-world discourse. Heightening, even radicalizing its fiction-specific artificiality, this device was lifted out of its third-person context by the autonomous monologue and—in the wake of Dujardin (*Les Lauriers sont coupés*), Schnitzler (*Leutnant Gustl, Fräulein Else*), and Joyce ("Penelope")—became a generally accepted vehicle for the fictional mimesis of mental life.

I would suggest that simultaneous narration breaks with *both* of these two conventions of fictional realism. Its innovation, to state it bluntly, is to emancipate first-person fictional narration from the dictates of formal mimetics, granting it the same degree (though not the same kind) of discursive freedom that we take for granted in third-person fiction: the li-

---

23. *Transparent Minds*, 3–9; see also Chapter 2 above.

cense to tell a story in an idiom that corresponds to no manner of real-world, natural discourse. It seems clear that its detachment from the autobiographical matrix allows first-person narration to create certain effects denied to its classical form: effects that follow directly from the adoption of its fiction-specific artifice (its "artifictionality," as we might call it) and that are no less singular than those that differentiate fictional lives in third-person form from their counterparts in historical biography (as explained in Chapter 2). To bring to light the fiction-specific effects inherent in simultaneous narration, I will now briefly focus on three principal and closely interrelated features of simultaneous narration: the incongruity of its narrative situation, the semantic implications of its narrative tense, and the absolute focalization of its narrated experience.

Unlike the autonomous monologue—where the nonnarrative quality of the silent, self-addressed discourse annuls a priori all semblance of mediated presentation—simultaneous narration does imply a narrative situation, but one that defies all manners of picturing it on verisimilar lines. Every conceit the reader may try out with a view to finding a pragmatically acceptable origin for this discourse—contemporaneously written script, continuous tape-recording, nonstop oral diary—breaks down when it is matched with the textual realities. The relationship of the narrative language to its source remains vexingly elusive, irretrievable on realistic grounds.[24]

We must note, however, that fiction cast as simultaneous narration almost always allows its unimaginable narrative situation to remain in the shadows. Unlike standard fictional autobiographies, with their often obtrusively foregrounded narrational and mnemonic stance, these deviant texts themselves tend to discourage questions concerning their ostensible origin. Their stories are generally presented without calling attention to any manner of temporal relation between narrated experiences and narrating instance, reference and utterance, what is said and where, when, and how it is said. This discretion concerning the narrator's "impossible" verbal stance seems to facilitate the unreflective acceptance of simultane-

---

24. A kind of proof by the absurd of this "impossible" relationship is inadvertently provided by Gerhart Hauptmann in his travel journal *Griechischer Frühling* [*Greek Spring*]. Its closely paced present-tense entries—regularly clocked: "Es ist jetzt fünf Uhr" ["It is five o'clock now"]; "Jetzt 7 1/2 Uhr" ["7.30 now"]—at times give way to an ambulatory writing pose: "Ich schreibe, meiner Gewohnheit nach, im Gehen, mit Bleistift diese Notizen. Mein Auge weidet" ["I write, as is my habit, while walking, using a pencil. My eyes are feasting"]. If a venerable author's affected synchronicity of writing and sight-seeing rather stretches the imagination, such synchronicity goes far beyond imaginable limits for the narrators presented in *Waiting for the Barbarians* and other fictional texts of this type.

ous narration as a fictional device. In this respect, as suggested above, its artifice is comparable to the one the narrators of third-person novels invariably pass in silence: their unnatural power to see into their characters' inner lives.[25]

The imponderability of its narrative situation in turn affects the effect (or effects the affect) of the tense that hallmarks simultaneous narration. As previously suggested, when the present is used narratively over the entire length of a first-person novel, there are no compelling reasons to understand it as a substitutionary tense referring to past time, let alone one that bears a highlighting function. With its global consistency dissolving the semantic specificity that attends the historical present, one is free—and, I think, rather compellingly encouraged—to understand the present as a temporally indeterminate or "absolute" narrative tense,[26] for which the most appropriate term—highlighting its fiction-specificity—would seem to be "fictional present." This understanding has the advantage of dislocating the narrated text from a temporally fixed point of origin, much as Hamburger's interpretation of the past tense in third-person fiction detaches it from the obligatory retrospection it signifies in nonfictional discourse.

Beyond their commonly distinctive fictionality, however, one discovers that the tense of simultaneous narration opens onto far more heterogeneous linguistic vistas than the past tense of standard third-person fiction. As most grammars tell us, the present is the most pluri-significant of all tenses. Aside from the equivoque mentioned earlier—does it refer authentically to the speaker's "now" or vicariously to his past?—its aspectual fluidity—does it signify the singular moment of the speech-act or its durative-iterative context?—can create vexing interpretive problems.[27] So can the so-called *irrealis* present that cloaks fantasies and imag-

---

25. Inevitably, however, the unnaturalness of its narrative situation obtrudes itself in the rare instances when it is referred to in a simultaneously narrated novel. This happens, for example, in Margaret Atwood's *The Handmaid's Tale,* when its narrating voice comments: "I would rather like to believe this is a story I'm telling. . . . It isn't a story I'm telling. It's also a story I'm telling, in my head, as I go along. Tell, rather than write . . . " (52). See also the appended "Historical Notes," where a future fictional scholar comments about the text we have just read: "There is a certain reflective quality about the narrative that would to my mind rule out synchronicity" (384).

26. I take this term (and this idea) from Daniel M. Bellos, "The Narrative Absolute Tense." He proposes it, however, as a more accurate tag for (and understanding of) the historical present itself, i.e., for local shifts from the past to the present, rather than the *global* use of the present in the texts that concern me here.

27. Notably in certain Kafka stories (see J. M. Coetzee, "Time, Tense and Aspect in Kafka's 'The Burrow'") and Sarraute novels (see André Allemand, *L'Oeuvre romanesque de Nathalie Sarraute,* 54–90).

ined scenarios in the same tensual grammar as perceptions and descriptions of the real world.[28] Used as a global fictional tense, the present can potentially bring into play all these meanings and more, fusing and confusing, consuming and subsuming them to create a grammatically homologous field of unparalleled semantic tension, instability, flexibility, and ambiguity.

These interpretive vagaries created by the present tense in first-person fiction may well be one of the principal attractions simultaneous narration holds for modern writers. But another is surely its surpassing aptitude for presenting consistently focalized self-narration, a mode rarely (if ever) sustained throughout a standard (past-tense) fictional autobiography.[29] For here the temporal hiatus between the narrating and the experiencing self—which diary and epistolary novels may shrink to days, hours, even minutes—is literally reduced to zero: the moment of narration *is* the moment of experience, the narrating self *is* the experiencing self. One effect of this fusion is the seamless continuity that simultaneous narration achieves between outer and inner reality, report and reflection. It is precisely this continuity that retrospective first-person narration can never fully achieve, since—even when the narrator's past thoughts and perceptions are rendered in free indirect style—the past tense itself inevitably reminds the reader that they are mediated by memory, presented when they are no longer literally present. In this respect simultaneous narration may be said to attain, within the first-person domain, analogous aims to those notoriously attained by figural narration in the third-person domain. On this score, one may well be led to wonder whether Henry James himself—had he known this deviant way with self-narration—might not have relented on his critique of the form as "foredoomed to looseness." Perhaps he would even have conceded that this newly conceived self-historian is "encaged and provided for as 'The Ambassadors' encages and provides" for Strether, its central consciousness.[30]

28. This ambiguity is especially prominent in J. M. Coetzee's *In the Heart of the Country*. See Susan Wright, "Tense Meaning as Style in Fictional Narrative: Present Tense Use in J. M. Coetzee's *In the Heart of the Country*" for an interesting, if not in every respect convincing, analysis.

29. Though a focalized type of first-person narration in fiction is generally included in narratological systems, it has proved empirically elusive in the extreme. Granted that most fictional autobiographies alternate freely between the perspectives of the narrating and experiencing self, very few novels maintain the vantage point of the experiencing self from beginning to end. Knut Hamsun's *Hunger* is a rarity in this respect, for which reason it served me as paradigm for focalized (or, as I prefer to call it, consonant) first-person narration in *Transparent Minds* (155–58). But it is surely significant that this novel (in the Norwegian original) includes extensive passages in which the present tense substitutes for the past.

30. *The Art of the Novel*, 320–21.

This frivolous speculation aside, my intention in this chapter has been to highlight a break in traditional norms. It yet needs to be integrated into narratological systems, especially those that aim for a "combinatory potential . . . of narrative possibilities" (Gérard Genette)[31] or those that want to encompass "various possibilities of narrative which are gradually being realized in the historical development of the novel and the short story" (Franz Stanzel).[32]

---

31. *Narrative Discourse Revisited,* 127.
32. *A Theory of Narrative,* 237.

7

Signposts of Fictionality

A Narratological Perspective

Narratology has been largely disregarded by modern theorists in the ongoing discussion of fictionality. Far more often than not, borderlines between the fictional and the nonfictional realms of narration have been drawn, withdrawn, retraced, and re-effaced on various grounds—logical, ontological, phenomenological, pragmatic, speech-actional, deconstructive, semantic—without looking to the discipline that has dug most deeply into the ground of narrative itself.

There is a certain poetologic justice to this snub: narratologists themselves have, to a quite astonishing degree, ignored the question of demarcation between fiction and nonfiction. One can hardly deplore this omission in works that openly (by way of title, subtitle, or prefatory remarks) limit their area of investigation to fictional narratives.[1] But most narratological studies, including such classics of the discipline as Roland Barthes's "Introduction to the Structural Analysis of Narrative" and Gérard Genette's *Narrative Discourse,* don't explicitly restrict their field, and some even quite expressly announce that they intend to encompass nonfiction as well.[2] In the absence of counterindications of any sort, a narrative poetics of this overarching kind leads one to believe that the entire panoply of conventions, "figures," structural types, and discursive modes that it identifies applies equally within and without fiction, even though its textual exemplifications are drawn exclusively from the novelistic canon.[3] In view of this tendency to homogenize the entire narrative domain, it must appear unlikely that narratology can contribute substantially to a debate concerning the differential nature of fictional narrative.

1. For example, Seymour Chatman, *Story and Discourse*; Shlomith Rimmon-Kenan, *Narrative Fiction*.
2. For example, Gerald Prince, *Narratology: The Form and Functioning of Narrative*; Mieke Bal, *Narratology: Introduction to the Theory of Narrative*. It should be noted that Genette himself has lately acknowledged his "guilt" in this respect in *Fiction and Diction,* 55–56.
3. On account of this restriction of its textual repertoire, one might want to question whether *narratology,* the name Todorov created for the discipline, is not in fact misleading. I am not about, at this late date, to propose a more accurate neologism (fictiology? fictionology?) but

My attempt in this chapter to counteract this impression, particularly in regard to the branch of the discipline that has been labeled "discourse-narratology,"[4] will accordingly involve a pointed critique of the most important narratological systems: a critique that questions whether existing categories are or are not fiction-specific, that points up ways in which existing tools need to be qualified or modified before they can be applied to nonfictional narrative, and that spotlights discursively inscribed fault lines between the two narrative domains. But although my aim is to develop criteria of fictionality from within the confines of narratology itself, I do not consider these confines as rigid and impenetrable. The development of such criteria seems to me perfectly compatible with theories that base fictionality on "literary communication as a system of norms,"[5] provided only that their spokesmen do not deny a priori (as many unfortunately tend to do) that fiction-specific signals may be found within texts themselves.

Of the three criteria I explore below, only the second is squarely embedded in discourse-narratological terrain: it concerns narrative situations (voice and mode). The first involves the most basic working assumption that underlies narratological studies: the distinction between levels of analysis (story and discourse). The third criterion, even as it centers on the concept of the narrator—a clearly narratological instance—relates that concept to its extratextual origin and effect.

In all three of my explorations, I profile fictional narrative against the foil of historical narrative (with only occasional glances at other types of nonfictional narrative). I choose this perspective because it corresponds to the front where the borderline of fictionality has been most hotly disputed and most nearly stamped out. In the process, though I pretend to no expertise in the field, I will at times move the contrastive backdrop to the forefront of attention, proposing some rudiments for a historiographic narratology.

LEVELS OF ANALYSIS

No conceptual tool has been more fundamental for the formalist-structuralist approach to narrative than the distinction between the two levels (or aspects) of analysis that anglophone critics commonly label *story* and *discourse*—signifying respectively the events referred to by the text

---

a qualified "*fictional* narratology" might help to counteract the current tendency to identify all narrative as fiction (see Chapter 1 above).

4. This name was proposed by Thomas Pavel in *The Poetics of Plot,* 14–15.

5. Siegfried J. Schmidt, "Toward a Pragmatic Interpretation of 'Fictionality,'" 171.

and the way these events are presented. To question the validity of this distinction is to question the validity of this approach itself.[6] Ever since its first appearance in the guise of the *fabula-sjuzhet* dichotomy, this partition has functioned as the initiating and enabling move of all major narratological studies, including, of course, Barthes's "Introduction" to the publication that launched this entire movement in France. Moreover, it has dictated the organization of all studies that overarch both levels, notwithstanding certain terminological and subdivisional variations.[7]

In contrast to its centrality for fictional narratology, the story-discourse separation has remained marginal at best for the analysis of historical (or generally nonfictional) narrative. Significantly, Paul Ricoeur, whose *Time and Narrative* has been called "the most important synthesis of literary and historical theory produced in our century,"[8] never touches on the bi-level model at all in the part of his work devoted to narrative history (vol. 1), whereas in the part devoted to narrative fiction (vol. 2), he gives it its full due in a long chapter entitled "Games with Time."[9] Here he introduces it by explaining that the redoubling of narrative into utterance and statement (*énonciation* and *énoncé*) is the "privilege" of fictional over historical narrative. To my mind, this rather overstates the case. While one must grant that the two levels relate in more stable and accordingly less absorbing and arresting ways in historiography than in fiction, the distinction is relative, not absolute. As I will argue below, the features that set the two domains off from each other cannot be clearly perceived unless full comparative attention is given to both levels in both domains.

As I see it, the essential reason that theorists of history neglect the bi-level model of narratology is not that it is inapplicable or irrelevant to their discipline but rather that it is insufficient and incomplete. The fact is that

6. For an antinarratological polemic based on a critique of the "two-level model," see Barbara Herrnstein Smith, "Narrative Versions, Narrative Theories."
7. The divisional correspondence between different narratologists can be summed up as follows:

Russian Formalism	*fabula* vs. *sjuzhet*
Barthes	functions + actions vs. narration
Genette (English)	story vs. narrative + narrating
(French)	*histoire* vs. *récit* + *narration*
Chatman	story vs. discourse
Prince	narrated vs. narrating
Rimmon-Kenan:	story vs. text + narration
Bal	fabula vs. story + text

8. Hayden White, *The Content of the Form*, 170.
9. Paul Ricoeur, *Time and Narrative*, II:61–99.

a text-oriented poetics of fiction excludes on principle a realm that is at the very center of the historiographer's concern: the more or less reliably documented evidence of past events out of which the historian fashions his story. It is this other relationship, between the story level and what we might call the referential level (or data base), that has riveted the attention of historiographers ever since it has become problematized by modern poetics.

The possibility of viewing this relationship along narratological lines, in terms of two levels of analysis, is graphically confirmed in an article by Robert Berkhofer.[10] This historian systematizes what he titularly calls "The Challenge of Poetics to (Normal) Historical Practice" with the help of a series of increasingly complex layered diagrams, displaying the historian's two-way trajectory between a level initially labeled "Past→Evidence" and another initially labeled "History←Synthesis." Berkhofer, moreover, confirms my sense that the relationship between these two levels complements, rather than replaces, the fiction-oriented narratologist's focus on the story/discourse relationship. Even as he acknowledges, in a footnote, the importance of the story/discourse distinction to historical productions, he explains that "it would only complicate my argument without greatly affecting its main points."[11]

It becomes clear at this point that historical narrative, if it is to be viewed in terms of a stratified model at all, needs to add an extra level to the story/discourse model that has dominated fictional narratology.[12] Whether such a tri-level model—reference/story/discourse—would serve to clarify historiography per se will have to be assessed by specialists in the field. I propose it here merely on account of what seems to me its heuristic value for a comparative perspective on historical versus fictional narrative. For the tri-level model points up the basic dissymmetry between the semiotic concerns that must enter the study of the two narrative domains, a dissymmetry that the standard narratological focus on the story/discourse relationship too readily disregards.

In postulating a referential level of analysis for historical narrative and denying such a level to fictional narrative, I do not mean to oversimplify the vexing problem of reference in either narrative domain. But the idea that history is committed to verifiable documentation and that

10. Robert Berkhofer, "The Challenge of Poetics to (Normal) Historical Practice."
11. Ibid., 443.
12. Significantly, it was a theorist of literature, not of history, who first proposed a model of this kind in a brief intervention at a symposium on historical narrative; see Karlheinz Stierle, "Geschehen, Geschichte, Text der Geschichte," 530–34. To my knowledge, this proposal has not been further developed by its author, nor has it been taken up by other theorists.

this commitment is suspended in fiction has survived even the most radical dismantling of the history/fiction distinction. In historiography the notion of referentiality, as Mink, Ricoeur, and Berkhofer have shown, can, and indeed must, continue to inform the work of practitioners who have become aware of the problematics of narrative construction.[13] And in fictional poetics, though the concept of reference has recently been reinstated, its qualification by such terms as *fictive, nonostensive,* or *pseudo-* sufficiently indicates its nonfactual connotations, even when it denotes components of the fictional world taken directly from the world of reality.[14]

A good starting point for clarifying the divergent relational concerns of historical and fictional narrative poetics is the conceptual-analytic level that historiography and narratology most clearly hold in common: the story level. Prior to the advent of "metahistory," this was the level at which theorists preferred to locate the line of demarcation between the two narrative domains, in accordance with the Aristotelian criterion of unity of plot. But in the wake of the discovery and emphasis (by such theorists as W. B. Gallie and Hayden White) of *plot* as the moving force of historical narration, we have become increasingly aware of the extent to which history and fiction overlap in this respect and that indeed some historical works (including many autobiographies) are no less artfully plotted than their novelistic counterparts. For this reason narrative theories restricted to the story level — and this applies to plot grammars of the type fashioned by Brémond, Prince, and Pavel no less than to the plot typologies proposed (on entirely different grounds) by Northrop Frye and Todorov — can in no way serve to delineate a divide between fiction and nonfiction.

But can the closing of the divide on this single level be taken to signify the undividedness of the narrative domain? Clearly, only if we take the overlap of history and fiction on the level of story as the whole story. This limited perspective can easily lead to the "characterization of historiography as a form of fiction making" and inspire Hayden White to write: "Readers of histories and novels can hardly fail to be struck by the similarities. There are many histories that could pass for novels, and many novels that could pass for histories, considered in purely formal (or I

13. See Louis Mink, "Narrative Form as Cognitive Instrument," esp. 148–49; Paul Ricoeur, *Time and Narrative*, III:142–56; Robert Berkhofer, "The Challenge of Poetics," 450.

14. I take this to be the consensus among the most differentiated approaches to the problem of fictional referentiality; see especially Benjamin Harshaw, "Fictionality and Fields of Reference"; Thomas Pavel, *Fictional Worlds*; Linda Hutcheon, "Metafictional Implications for Novelistic Reference." For more on fictional referentiality, see Chapter 1 above.

should say formalist) terms. Viewed simply as verbal artifacts histories and novels are indistinguishable from one another."[15] Here White expressly blocks out the referential level of historical narrative, signaling its disregard with the phrases "considered in purely formal[ist] terms" and "viewed simply as verbal artifacts." But what he signifies with these phrases is solely structuration on the story level: the level of analysis at which White discovers that narrative histories and novels can take on analogous archetypal forms. He never looks to the level of discourse, where (as I will soon show) narratology can come into play to define highly differentiated formal features that do, in our daily reading practice, prevent histories from passing for novels and vice versa. But before we look at that level, a few remarks are in order on distinctions that the differently stratified models themselves can bring into view.

Modern theorists concerned with the construction of historical narrative from the traces of past events (the referential level) have coined a number of conceptual terms for this process: "configurational act" (Mink), "emplotment" (White), *mise en intrigue* (Ricoeur). All these terms essentially signify an activity that transforms preexisting material, endows it with meaning, makes it into "the intelligible whole that governs the succession of events in any story."[16] These same theorists also stress the decisive role played by selection in a historical text, what it includes and what it excludes, with its all-important temporal corollary: where it begins and where it ends. Even this summary account of the relationship between the level of story and the level of reference in historical narrative makes it clear that its terms do not apply to the structure, or even to the construction, of fictional narrative. A novel can be said to be plotted, but not *em*plotted: its serial moments do not refer to, and can therefore not be selected from, an ontologically independent and temporally prior data base of disordered, meaningless happenings that it restructures into order and meaning. In this respect the process that transforms archival sources into narrative history is qualitatively different from (and indeed hardly comparable to) the process that transforms a novelist's sources—whether they be autobiographical, anecdotal, or even historical—into his fictional creation. The former process is highly constrained and controlled, subject to the author's justification and the reader's scrutiny, with its obligatory correspondence to the happenings it narrates overtly displayed in the text itself. The novelist's relation to his sources is free, remains tacit, or, when mentioned, is assumed to be spu-

15. Hayden White, *Tropics of Discourse,* 121–22.
16. Paul Ricoeur, "Narrative Time," 171.

rious; its true origination may (and often does) remain forever unknown—sometimes to the writer himself.

The level of reference introduces a diachronic dimension into the trilevel model of historical narrative that is absent from the bi-level model of fictional narrative. Story and discourse are conceived as synchronous structural aspects of fictional texts with no presumption of priority of story over discourse. When the story/discourse model is applied to nonfictional narrative without the postulation of an additional narrative level, the transfer can easily result in a misleading perception of parity between the two domains.[17] For outside the realm of fiction, the synchronous interplay of story and discourse is undergirded—no matter how shakily—by the logical and chronological priority of documented or observed events.

The varied and potent impact of referential constraints on the discursive level of historical narratives—which ranges from the most overt and direct to the most covert and indirect—can only be fully assessed when one looks at history in the comparative light of fiction. What most immediately jumps into view is, of course, the presence of an entire "perigraphic" apparatus (foot- or end-noted, prefatory or appended) that constitutes a textual zone intermediating between the narrative text itself and its extratextual documentary base.[18] But this base also penetrates into the textual terrain itself, which, as Michel de Certeau puts it, "combines the plural of quoted documents into the singular of *quoting* cognition."[19] This citational process can be more or less smoothly integrated, less so when archival sources are quoted directly, more so when they are paraphrased or summarized. But the stratum of testimonial evidence obligatorily lines even the most homogeneously surfaced historical narrative.

There is, as a rule, nothing that corresponds to this testimonial stratum in fictional narrative. Needless to say, this rule, like all rules, can be broken: authors of historical novels have on occasion felt moved to include a referential apparatus, usually in the form of an afterword explaining the extent to which they have followed (or, more often, the reason they have decided *not* to follow) archival source materials. This pattern—found in

---

17. This is what happens, in my view, when Jonathan Culler discovers an overriding "double logic" in *all* narrative texts: a paradoxical structuration that dictates an understanding of every story as both the cause and the effect of the discourse that renders it ("Fabula and Sjuzhet in the Analysis of Narrative"). Enlightening as this mutuality can be for the interpretation of fictional narrative, its application to historical narrative seems to me to occlude the perception of difference between the two domains.

18. The term *périgraphie* is used in Philippe Carrard, "Récit historique et fonction testimoniale."

19. Michel de Certeau, *L'Ecriture de l'histoire*, 111; my translation.

works as diverse in other (including formal) regards as Yourcenar's *Hadrian's Memoirs,* Broch's *Death of Virgil,* and Gore Vidal's *Lincoln*—seems to be on the rise and to deserve serious investigation. As is generally true for generic borderline cases, such works, far from effacing the border they straddle, offer an opportunity to study the historical and theoretical grounds for its existence. And I would suggest that such a study might profit from the differentiation proposed above between a bi-level and a tri-level model for fictional and historical narrative respectively.

Up to this point I have mentioned only features that historical narrative *adds* to the discursive virtualities of fiction, not the ways its referential constraints may alter or restrict these virtualities themselves. This impact of referentiality on the relation between discourse and story does not directly affect the structures of temporality. Here the narratological system (as standardized by Genette) seems to me to apply outside no less than inside the fictional domain. No narrative genre makes the order of its discourse consistently adhere to the chronological sequence of an abstracted story, nor does it make its discursive pace advance with isochronic regularity. Barthes, glancing at varying relationships between the two temporal levels in the works of classical historians, finds all manners of accelerations, inversions, and zigzags not only performed, but self-consciously alluded to in their discursive language.[20] But although his suggestive remarks could be further elaborated, filled in, systematized, and expanded to other narrative genres (journalistic reports, autobiography), I doubt that such a survey would yield any temporal "figures" not already identified by Genette in fictional texts.

This is not to say that historians "play" with time in the same sense as novelists: their departures from chronology and isochrony tend to be functional, dictated by the nature of their source materials, their subject matter, and their interpretive arguments rather than by aesthetic concerns or formal experimentation. No history of early twentieth-century Dublin swells discourse time over story time in the manner of *Ulysses*; no family monograph twists it in the manner of *The Sound and the Fury*; no account of the years preceding World War I programs its acceleration in the manner of Hans Castorp's seven *Magic Mountain* years. But such artful perturbations of the temporal structure are, as a rule, conditioned by the narrative situation through which the story is transmitted to the reader: the combined modal and vocal structures that convey the fictional world and

20. Roland Barthes, "Historical Discourse," 146–48.

the characters that experience it. This is where the discourses of history and fiction take on a qualitative difference, where the former's ties to the level of reference and the latter's detachment from this level determine distinct discursive parameters that narratology has thus far failed to chart.[21]

NARRATIVE SITUATIONS

Among the many theorists of various persuasions who have reiterated the thesis that fictional and nonfictional narratives are look-alikes, it will serve my purpose to single out one who provides an example to prove his point. In his well-known essay "The Logical Status of Fictional Discourse," John Searle writes: "There is no textual property, syntactic or semantic, that will identify a text as a work of fiction" (325). And again: "The utterance acts in fiction are indistinguishable from the utterance acts of serious discourse, and it is for that reason that there is no textual property that will identify a stretch of discourse as a work of fiction" (327). These statements appear in a speech-act-theoretical discussion of the following "stretch of discourse":

> Ten more glorious days without horses! So thought Second Lieutenant Andrew Chase-Smith recently commissioned in the regiment of King Edwards Horse, as he pottered contentedly in a garden on the outskirts of Dublin on a sunny Sunday after-noon in April nineteen-sixteen.

Searle, who tells us that he picked this passage (the inception of Iris Murdoch's *The Red and the Green*) "at random," seems quite unaware of how effectively it disproves his case. To mention only the most obvious: what "serious" discourse ever quoted the thoughts of a person other than the speaker's own? Even if the genre-tagged cover page of this novel were removed, we would know from its first sentence that this scene tells of a *fictional* second lieutenant—a character who is known to his narrator in a manner no real person can be known to a real speaker.[22]

21. In this respect, *Time and Narrative*—despite the scrupulous and prolonged attention Ricoeur devotes to the findings of narratology in the course of his investigation of the history/fiction relationship—is not entirely satisfying. I attribute this shortfall to Ricoeur's intense focus on the phenomenology of time and his relative neglect of vocal and modal structures. Although in volume 2 he points to the omniscient presentation of fictional characters' minds as the "magic" that most clearly separates fiction from history, he retracts this distinctive marker when he scumbles the borderline between the two narrative domains in volume 3.

22. Needless to say, not all novelistic beginnings are fiction-specific in the manner of *The Red and the Green*. Most novels written before 1900 initially adopt the manner of a historical narrative before focalizing on (and with) one or several characters. In this connection, see my argument against Barbara Herrnstein Smith in Chapter 2 above.

This is not, at any rate, the manner in which historical figures are known to historians. Here is how a master practitioner—even as she announces her intention to forego it—labels and samples the historian's standard manner of presenting the inner life of his human subjects:

> I have tried to avoid . . . the "he must have" style of historical writing: "As he watched the coastline of France disappear, Napoleon must have thought back over the long . . . " All conditions of weather, thoughts or feelings, and states of mind public or private, in the following pages have documentary support.

Thus writes Barbara Tuchmann in her "Author's Note" to *The Guns of August:* a history of the beginning of World War I, where every phrase of the type "Krafft was 'stunned,'" "Bülow was furious," "a horrid doubt entered the mind of General von Kuhl" is referentially annotated for verification. And it is indeed only when such privately revealing sources as memoirs, diaries, and letters *are* available that a scrupulous historian will feel free to cast statements touching psychological motives and reactions into the past indicative tense. In the absence of reference, the historian will have to make do with inference (and its conjectural "must have" grammar)— or else opt for history devoid of any allusions to individual psychology.

In their different ways, the examples just cited—of a theorist's blind spot and a practitioner's insight—point up a distinction that, obvious as it may appear, has somehow gotten lost in the narratological shuffle: that the minds of imaginary figures can be known in ways that those of real persons can not. As will become clear, this distinction itself, as well as its far-reaching implications for the modal structure of historical as compared to fictional discourse, has never been clearly formulated or analyzed in narratological terms, despite the ever more refined typologies of narrative situations that have been devised for the fictional domain itself.

This holds true even for the one incursion into the historical domain that sets out by asking the right question, Barthes's previously mentioned essay "Historical Discourse": "Is there in fact any specific difference between factual and imaginary narrative, any linguistic feature by which we may distinguish on the one hand the mode appropriate for the relation of historical events . . . and on the other hand the mode appropriate to the epic, novel or drama?" (145). As may be surmised from the rhetorical form of the question, Barthes is heading for a negative answer. He reaches it in part by equating the historian's standard pose as "objective subject" with that of the Realist novelist: both make it appear as though the story "writers itself," as though (in Benveniste's phrase) "nobody speaks" (148–49).

What Barthes passes in silence here is that this stance is characteristic and stable only for the historical narrator, not for the fictional narrator. As none other than Barthes himself had shown on an earlier occasion—in a passage that has become a *locus classicus* for discourse narratology[23]— fiction is able to alternate between this "a-personal" mode and another "personal" mode, where it adopts the vantage point of a character. This omission of *the* distinctive modal feature of fictional discourse from his answer to the question regarding "any linguistic feature by which we may distinguish . . . " places Barthes's "Historical Discourse" at the precise blind spot that has obfuscated the vision of modern theorists ever since.[24]

Still, if we combine (as Barthes does not) the passing insights of the two passages mentioned above, we can catch a glimpse of the parting of the modal ways of history and fiction. And if we remember that Barthes's "personal mode" became Genette's "focalized" mode (or "internal focalization"), then a correlation between a mainstream category of discourse narratology and the principal history/fiction distinction begins to emerge.[25] This category, however, designates only what history *cannot* be or do: it cannot present past events through the eyes of a historical figure present on the scene, but only through the eyes of the (forever backward-looking) historian-narrator. In this sense we may say that the modal system of historical (and other nonfictional) narration is "defective" when compared to the virtual modalizations of fiction.

When it comes to characterizing the narrative mode of historiography in positive terms, however, neither one of the remaining Genettean types of focalization—zero or nonfocalization, and external focalization—seems entirely adequate. Zero focalization is a notoriously vague category, which Genette comes closest to defining clearly when he concedes (if I understand him correctly) that it is no more than a kind of floating relay station between narrative segments variously focalized by different characters (his formula for this being "zero focalization = variable, and sometimes zero, focalization") and that accordingly no fictional work can

---

23. The famous *Goldfinger* analysis in "Introduction to the Structural Analysis of Narrative"—originally published in 1966, a year prior to the original publication of "Historical Discourse" in 1967.

24. One can only speculate as to why Barthes's vision failed him here. My hunch is that it was because the problematic story/reference relationship of historical narrative—with which his essay (despite its title) is largely concerned—drew his attention away from the story/discourse relationship.

25. In what follows, I use Genette's widely known typology of focalizations as a paradigm. My critique would apply equally to the modal categories of other narratologists (Stanzel, Bal, Rimmon-Kenan, Chatman, etc.).

remain nonfocalized in its entirety.[26] This clearly discourages its application to works of history, where the mode remains stably unfocalized from start to finish. In this regard, external focalization would seem to offer a more promising fit: this type, which Genette identifies with what some theorists call "neutral" and others call "camera eye,"[27] by definition excludes the presentation of the characters' inner lives. But the unsuitability of this fictional type for describing historical narration becomes clear from the texts most often cited to exemplify it: works that consist of a single scene (Hemingway's "The Killers") or a series of scenes without intervening summaries (Duras's *Moderato Cantabile*), and that feature nothing but dialogue linked by behavioral descriptions of the characters' gestures. At most, one might see a narrow zone of overlap between this liminal fictional mode and the narrative situation that pertains on those rare occasions when historians narrate a scene in great detail (with due documentary reference to their observer-source).[28]

It appears, then, that Genette's typology of focalizations would have to be considerably modified to make it applicable to historical narration: that is, enlarged to include a type conjoining nonfocalization and external focalization in a manner that I have not found described in any discourse-narratological work to date—which goes to show how slim the chances are of its being identified (and given its due) in any study based on a textual repertoire limited to fictional works. Avoiding an unprovable negative, I will resist declaring that no fictional narrative has ever been (or ever could be) written that adhered to the historical mode from beginning to end. The fictional history of an other-worldly or future-worldly society, for example, or, for that matter, an "apocryphal history" of our own world might be effectively told by a narrator posing as a historian.[29] But if an author imposed this role on the narrator of a historically realistic novel, the result would be a generic anomaly; for unless it announced its fictional status para- or peritextually, nothing would prevent such a work from passing for a historical text.[30]

This is clearly *not* the case with the genre we normally refer to as "historical novel," least of all when such a novel includes "real" historical

26. Genette, *Narrative Discourse Revisited*, 74.
27. Ibid., 120–21.
28. For Genette's own retrospective awareness of the fiction-specific nature of his modal categories, see *Fiction and Diction*, 65–67. Note that this work postdates the original proposal of his modal system by some twenty years.
29. See Brian McHale, *Postmodernist Fiction*, chapters 3, 4, and 6 for discussion of numerous postmodern novels of this type, none of which, however, seem to conform to mock-historiographic presentation.
30. This was very nearly the fate of Wolfgang Hildesheimer's *Marbot*; see Chapter 5 above.

figures in its cast of characters. In such "documentary historical novels,"[31] as the *matter* comes closest to narrative history, the *manner* becomes unmistakably and distinctively fictional. Typically, this occurs in one of two ways: either the historical figure is itself the focalizing subject, the central consciousness through which the events are experienced (the case of fictionalized historical biographies, like Büchner's *Lenz* or Burgess's Shakespeare novel *Nothing like the Sun*);[32] or else the historical figure is the focalized object, observed by another character, who may be himself either historical or invented (the case of novels in the Scott tradition favored by Lukács). In neither case are historical novels presented as (or as though they were) history, as one is so often told in discussions of this genre. Nor is this relationship accurately described by saying that the reader grants the documentary historical novelist "greater freedom than the historian to speculate."[33] Marked by their distinctive discursive modes, historical fiction and history are different in kind, not merely in degree.[34]

Beyond the bare recognition of its peculiarity (when seen from the vantage point of fictional narratology) lies the larger task of describing the modal system of historical discourse (not to mention nonfictional discourse generally).[35] Though the categories identified in various discourse narratologies would no doubt be useful for this task, I doubt that they would be sufficient. Two of the parameters with which a historiographic narratologist would have to deal are, first, the fact that history is more often concerned with collective "mentalities" than with individual minds, a focus that creates altogether distinctive discursive conventions requiring detailed examination; and second, and related, the massive prevalence of summary over scene in historical narration, where external focalization is maintained over rather vaster (and less closely paced) temporal stretches in the lives of individuals or nations than the tense hour in Henry's lunchroom covered by "The Killers." But even where historical narration concerns individual figures and singulative moments—Napoleon watching the coastline of France disappear, Queen Elizabeth giving orders to

---

31. A term proposed in Joseph W. Turner, "The Kinds of Historical Fiction: An Essay in Definition and Methodology," 337.

32. See Chapters 2 and 5 above.

33. See Turner, "The Kinds of Historical Fiction," 349.

34. Further discussion of the differential between historical fiction and history will be found in Chapter 9 below.

35. Some important steps in this direction have recently been taken by scholars who examine specific historical topics and schools (see esp. Ann Rigney, *The Rhetoric of Historical Representation,* and Philippe Carrard, *Poetics of the New History*).

execute Mary Stuart, the young Dostoevsky facing the firing squad on Se-
menovsky Square—it draws on a language of nescience, of speculation,
conjecture, and induction (based on referential documentation) that is
virtually unknown in fictional scenes of novels (including historical novels) cast in third-person form.

This is the point where the category of person (or voice) must enter
our comparative discussion of narrative situations in fiction and history.
In all I have said until now, I have taken it for granted that the historian-
narrator can be contrastively compared to the narrator of third-person
fiction or—to use Genette's more precise term—to the heterodiegetic
narrator. It is in this perspective that the modal system of history may be
said to be "defective" when compared with fiction. At this juncture we
would do well to recall that the constrictions and constraints under which
the historian writes are not entirely unknown from (or to) fictional narrators. The pages of certain novels abound in laments concerning the limits of knowledge, particularly where the psychic opacity of protagonists
is concerned. The narrator of Günter Grass's *Cat and Mouse* says of his
mysterious friend Mahlke: "And as for his soul, it was never introduced
to me. I never heard what he thought" (40). The voices that emit such
complaints, however, belong, not to narrators who are alien (*hetero-*) to
the world of the stories they tell, but to those who inhabit these same
worlds, those Genette calls *homo*diegetic narrators. They are themselves
presented as human beings with human limitations, including the inability to perceive what goes on in the minds of their fellow beings, to perceive what others perceive. In this respect they are comparable to historians, who can likewise only tell their protagonists' stories—to the extent
that they are not their own (autobiographical) protagonists—in external
focalization, and for the same reasons.

This analogy with homodiegetic narrators becomes more plausible
when we call to mind the plain fact that historians do, after all, live in the
same (*homo-*) world as their narrative subjects—a fact that we tend to forget when their stories deal with faraway times and places, but that we cannot forget when their stories verge on those we read in the morning paper. A particularly instructive work in this regard is Hannah Arendt's
Eichmann in Jerusalem, which intertwines a report on the contemporary
events of a trial at which the author was physically present a year before
the book's publication in 1963 and a history of the Holocaust (1938–45).
In its first sentence—"'*Beth Hamishpath*'—the House of Justice: these
words shouted by the court usher at the top of his voice make us jump to
our feet . . . "—the homodiegesis of the narrative situation is expressly

marked by the first-person forms. And although Arendt was not herself present at the scenes of the earlier historical events she recounts, her relation to them is nonetheless homodiegetic if—following Genette—we take *diegesis* to mean "the universe in which the story takes place."

Returning from this vantage point to the comparison between the modal behavior of the historical narrator and the narrator of a third-person (heterodiegetic) novel, their difference now appears in a new light. It is grounded quite simply in the fact that the former (the historian) is a real person who inhabits the real world, and that he is separated from all other beings in that world, living or dead, by what Proust called "those opaque sections impenetrable to the human spirit." The historian's modal restrictions, in other words, result from (and in) his adherence to what the speech-act theorists call "natural" or "serious" discourse. These restrictions apply equally to the homodiegetic fictional narrator—who is, by definition, a figure whose fictional "reality" determines (and is determined by) his imitation of real-world discourse and whose status in the world he inhabits is analogous to the historian's status in our real world. But the same restrictions become null and void for the heterodiegetic narrator, whose voice (if we take the term *diegesis* in its exact meaning) is by definition otherworldly, by nature unnatural or artificial, or, as we might say, "artifictional."

NARRATORS AND AUTHORS

In what follows, I will disregard the deconstructive critique (by Barthes, Foucault, Derrida, and others) of the author concept, but not without noting in passing that this critique, addressing as it does the personified source of *all* written texts—narrative and nonnarrative, fictional and nonfictional alike—has tended to erase the very borderline that I am attempting to retrace. For by questioning the unitary origin and authority of textual discourse in general, regardless of genre, one is inevitably led to ignore, if not to deny outright, the *added* equivoque that attends the origin of fictional texts in particular.[36] I will assume, then, that the reader of a nonfictional narrative understands it to have a stable univocal origin,

36. In this regard it is interesting to note that Roland Barthes, in his seminal article "The Death of the Author," launches his thesis that "the voice [of the text] loses its origin" with a quotation from a *fictional* work (a Balzac story), and one cast in free indirect style at that. Yet his death sentence explicitly extends to authors of nonfictional works as well (*Image—Music—Text,* 144–45). Only two years earlier—in "Introduction to the Structural Analysis of Narrative" (*Image—Music—Text,* 79–124)—Barthes had seemingly limited the absence of the author to fiction, merely explaining that "the (material) author . . . is in no way to be confused with the narrator" since "narrator and characters . . . are essentially 'paper beings'" (111).

that its narrator is identical to a real person: the author named on its title page.

The notion of a cleavage of this vocal unity in fiction is actually of fairly recent vintage, having entered the mainstream of narrative poetics (at least in Germany) when Wolfgang Kayser declared, in answer to the titular question of his essay "Who Narrates the Novel?" (1958), "not the author . . . the narrator is a created character [*eine gedichtete Person*] into which the author has transformed himself."[37] Though Kayser's trope of metamorphosis has given way to less surreal and also less kinetic images, the general idea of a functional distinction between the two narrative instances has become widely accepted. It informs, in particular, a variety of graphic models that distance narrators from their authors spatially, place them on different levels, segregate them in concentric frames, align them at separate points on transmission diagrams—more often than not with an "implied author" standing guard between them (quite unnecessarily, as Genette has, I think, convincingly demonstrated).[38] But although the author/narrator differential by now appears to be a widespread poetological axiom, one often finds it invoked quite incidentally, as though postulated anew and ad hoc for clarifying certain specific theoretical and critical problems, including such diverse matters as narrative motivation, unreliable narration, fictional tense, heteroglossia, the specific characteristics of a particular period, an individual novelist, or an individual novel.

There are, however, at least two theorists who have explicitly applied the author/narrator distinction to the question that concerns me in this essay. The first of these is Paul Hernadi, who suggests that the distinction might serve as a basic criterion for segregating fictional from historical narrative: "I submit that a workable theoretical distinction between historical and fictional narratives can be based on the different relationships they prompt us to postulate between the author implied by a given text and the *persona* of the narrator emerging from it. . . . Fictional narratives demand, historical narratives preclude, a distinction between the narrator and the implied author."[39] Though this idea is clearly and aptly stated—with the phrase "prompt us to postulate" meaningfully pointing up the mutual interdependence between text- and reader-oriented approaches to this problem—it is proposed only in passing, in an article that deals mainly with historiography per se. A far more detailed elaboration

37. Wolfgang Kayser, "Wer erzählt den Roman?" 91; my translation.
38. Gérard Genette, *Narrative Discourse Revisited*, 137–54.
39. Paul Hernadi, "Clio's Cousins," 252.

of this separatist thesis may be found (without reference to Hernadi's work) in Genette's *Fiction and Diction* (72–79), where it is both narratologically qualified and theoretically fortified.[40] The final part of this chapter will take the idea of the fiction-specific separation of authors and narrators in directions that may help to consolidate a unified model of fictionality.

First of all, it must be emphasized that there is a world of difference between the two vocal domains of fiction in respect to the explicitness of the author/narrator distinction. For in homodiegetic fiction the unified vocal existence of the historical author-narrator is clearly and literally equivocated, most clearly of all in fictional as compared to real autobiography. David Copperfield, Humbert Humbert, and Felix Krull are the narrators of their own lives; they are also the principal characters of novels authored by Dickens, Nabokov, and Thomas Mann. The nominal differentiation between narrators and authors of fictional autobiographies is, as Philippe Lejeune has extensively demonstrated, a decisive signal for the reader's recognition of their novelistic status: a status that is determined by the presence of an imaginary speaker incarnated as a character within the fictional world.[41] This embodied self is brought to life by a discourse that mimes the language of a real speaker telling his past experiences. It is therefore easy to visualize the structure of a fictional autobiography like *The Confessions of Felix Krull* as an imaginary discourse directly quoted by the author, implicitly introduced by a phrase like "Here is the story Felix Krull told." In this sense, all homodiegetic novels can be imaged as being inset within a surrounding frame of discourse, even though they are, in fact, surrounded by nothing but silence—the silence that allows, as Wayne Booth puts it, for the "secret communion of the author and reader behind the narrator's back."[42]

The duplicate vocal origin of fiction—and the corollary conception of fiction as embedded discourse—becomes far more controversial when we pass from homo- to heterodiegesis. Here most theorists who insist *on principle* that fictional narrators are never to be identified with their au-

---

40. The chapter of this work entitled "Fictional Narrative, Factual Narrative" was first published in the same issue of *Poetics Today* in which an earlier version of this chapter appeared. Genette's chapter and my own article were thus conceived simultaneously and independently, with their overlap indicating the degree of analogy between our approaches to narrative matters. As readers of these two pieces will note, however, Genette tends to draw the line between fictional and nonfictional narrative rather less firmly than I do, as indicated (among other things) by his critique (in n. 43, pp. 83–84) of an earlier version of Chapter 2 above.

41. See Philippe Lejeune, *On Autobiography*, 3–30.

42. *The Rhetoric of Fiction*, 300.

thors tend to collapse the distance that separates them.[43] In critical *practice,* at any rate, the separateness of authors and narrators has been demonstrated almost exclusively where it is most readily visible to the naked eye, namely where the narrator-figure is a physical and nominal presence, central or peripheral, in the fictional world.

Yet the disjunction of the narrator from the author can hardly constitute a valid touchstone of fictionality unless it is theoretically validated (and shown to be more than a mere virtuality) for heterodiegetic fiction as well. For it is only here that the disjunctive model (as I will call it) runs up against rival conceptions of "who narrates the novel," most obviously against the common assumption—seemingly never questioned by eighteenth- and nineteenth-century novelists (let alone their readers)—that a novel is quite simply narrated by its author. This assumption, though swathed in linguistic and philosophical qualifications, is still very much alive in the works of speech-act theorists. A clear case in point is the essay by Searle cited earlier, where he argues that "in the standard third-person narrative . . . *the author pretends* to perform illocutionary acts. . . . *Murdoch* . . . tells us a story; in order to do that, *she pretends* to make a series of assertions about people in Dublin in 1916."[44]

The shortfall of this way of visualizing the novelistic text as the pretended discourse of its author has been forcefully demonstrated by Félix Martínez-Bonati.[45] This same theorist also constructs a rigorous philosophical foundation for the disjunctive model.[46] Its decisive shape may be gauged from the following statements: "Between the author and the language of the work [of fiction] there is no immediate relationship, as there is between a speaker and what he says." "The author, a real being, is not and cannot be part of an imaginary situation. Author and work are separated by the abyss that separates the real from the imaginary. Consequently, the author of works of narrative is not the narrator of these works."[47] Fortunately for those of us interested in theory primarily for the light it can shed on the characteristic features of fictional language, Martínez-Bonati devotes the major portion of his book to exploring the

43. Meir Sternberg, for example, believes that in third-person novels the distance between authors and narrators is reduced to "a zero sign of unrealized potential"; see "Mimesis and Motivation," 145–88.

44. "The Logical Status of Fictional Discourse," 327–28; my emphases.

45. "The Act of Writing Fiction."

46. *Fictive Discourse and the Structures of Literature.* For a carefully calibrated presentation and critical assessment of this work as a whole, see Marie-Laure Ryan, "Fiction as a Logical, Ontological, and Illocutionary Issue."

47. Martínez-Bonati, *Fictive Discourse,* 81 and 85.

discursive implications of his systematic conclusions. In this respect, the yield of his book is comparable to that of Käte Hamburger's equally phenomenologically grounded *Logic of Literature,* from which, however, its theoretical proposals diverge on a number of crucial points. The most important among these is that Hamburger argues against the disjunctive model no less vigorously than Martínez-Bonati argues in its favor, presenting in its stead a *narratorless* model for third-person fiction that seems to me a far more challenging alternative than the author-pretense model of the speech-act theorists.[48]

I don't think this model can be dismissed merely on account of its surreal overtones—in the manner of Genette, who declares that, if he ever encountered a tale told by "nobody," he would run for the nearest exit.[49] This attitude forgets that the attribution of a tale to a narrator—a vocal source one cannot help but conceive in more or less anthropomorphic terms—assumes an at least equally fantastic conceit: a "somebody" who is capable of looking through the skulls (or with the eyes) of other human beings. It is precisely because this "somebody" assumes optical and cognitive powers unavailable to a real person that we feel the need to dissociate the statements of a fictional text from its real authorial source. Ultimately we are compelled to accept that the language transmitted to us in heterodiegetic fiction cannot be imaged in analogy to *any* plausible real-world discourse situation, no matter whether we personalize or depersonalize its origin. This being the case, the best we can do is to conceptualize its origin in the manner that accounts in the most functional and flexible way for the variable reality of our reading experience. It is on these pragmatic grounds that I find good reason to resist the ejection of the narrator from the poetics of fiction and to agree with Brian McHale when he says: "The thesis that narrative sentences have speakers explains more phenomena more adequately, with less violence to the reader's intuitions."[50] Two of these phenomena (intimately interrelated) deserve particular attention in the context of the present chapter: first, the presence of normative language as a potentially integral component of heterodiegetic fiction; and second, the possibility of understanding this language as "unreliable." Particularly the latter phenomenon can, as we will see, bring the fiction/history borderline more clearly into view.

48. See Käte Hamburger, *The Logic of Literature,* 134–75. Regrettably, Martínez-Bonati does not take up the challenge. A comparative examination of these two important theories of fictionality would seem to me an essential and potentially highly enlightening task.
49. *Narrative Discourse Revisited,* 101.
50. "Unspeakable Sentences, Unnatural Acts," 22.

It may be granted, I think, that the narratorless conception of heterodiegetic fiction can account quite cogently for the reader's experience
of those textual moments where the narrative discourse, whether internally focalized or not, is purely "reportive" and uninterrupted by any
manner of commentary: those moments—sometimes extended over the
entire length of a novel—when one gets the sense that the story "tells itself." The cogency of the narratorless model ends only if and when such
moments are interrupted, as they frequently are in certain third-person
novels. To illustrate this point, here is a passage from *Death in Venice*
(where the enamored Aschenbach reacts to news reports that confirm his
suspicion that the plague has broken out in the city):

> "They want it kept quiet!" thought Aschenbach in some agitation,
> throwing the newspapers back on the table. "They're hushing this
> up!" But at the same time his heart filled with elation at the thought of
> the adventure in which the outside world was about to be involved.
> *For to passion, as to crime, the assured everyday stability of things is not op-*
> *portune, and any weakening of the civil structure, any chaos and disaster af-*
> *flicting the world, must be welcome to it, as offering a vague hope of turning*
> *such circumstances to its advantage. Thus* Aschenbach felt an obscure
> sense of satisfaction at what was going on in the dirty alleyways of
> Venice, cloaked in official secrecy.[51]

Despite its segmented structure, the vocal continuity of this passage
is strongly in evidence: the generalizing present-tense statement is explicitly linked to the past-tense narrative language that it interrupts by
the "For" that introduces it and the "Thus" that immediately follows it.
If we personalize the source of the weighty intervention into a "narrator," as I think the text prompts us to do, then it would be illogical not to
attribute the purely narrative sentences to this same personalized source
as well. Granted that its vocal presence fluctuates: fades away when it
simply narrates, becomes obtrusive when it comments—at which moment it takes shape as a rather narrow-minded and opinionated moralist
who compares lovers to criminals. Still, the positing of a narrator—in
turn both covert and overt—seems to me the most cogent way of accounting for the narrative situation of Mann's novella as a whole and for
works similarly structured. By extension and analogy, third-person
fictions that consist of purely narrative sentences and that consistently
omit all semblance of normative commentary—say *The Castle* or *A Por-*

---

51. Thomas Mann, *Death in Venice and Other Stories,* 246; my emphasis.

trait of the Artist—can then be described as having covert narrators throughout.[52]

But the postulation of a narrator, over and above its functional advantage for conceptualizing the vocal origin of heterodiegetic narration, also enables a theoretical move that seems to me of the utmost importance for the interpretation of works like *Death in Venice:* the possibility of considering that a narrator's explicitly stated norms may not coincide with the implicit norms of the author. The theory that provides a methodology for considering a narrator unreliable in this sense of the word is developed by Martínez-Bonati, who differentiates between two different strata of fictional language: mimetic sentences, which create the image of the fictive world—its events, characters, and objects—and nonmimetic sentences, which create nothing more nor less than the image of the narrator's mind. Whereas mimetic statements are objective, "as though transparent," and unreservedly accepted by the reader as fictional truth, nonmimetic sentences are subjective, opaque, and received by the reader with the qualified credence one grants to the opinions of an individual speaker. On this basis, to produce an unreliable narrative all an author has to do is "to create a perceptible difference between the impression of the events derived by the reader solely from the mimetic moments of the basic narrator's discourse, and the view of the same events present in the non-mimetic components of the same discourse."[53]

This analysis opens the way for discovering unreliable narration in heterodiegetic (as well as homodiegetic) fictional texts, in works, that is, where a narrator, though not a character physically present in the fictional world, nonetheless takes on a conspicuous mental presence by uttering nonmimetic, "opaque" sentences. As can be seen from the passage quoted above, Thomas Mann's narrator in *Death in Venice,* with his obtrusively sententious and judgmental discourse, is a prime candidate for the charge of unreliability. And indeed, when one examines the novella as a whole with this virtuality in mind, one finds that the mimetic language that tells

52. The opposition between overt and covert narration is developed in Chatman, *Story and Discourse,* 196ff.

53. Martínez-Bonati, *Fictive Discourse,* 44–46. This purely *normative* unreliability of a fictional narrator—which corresponds to the unreliability concept as originally proposed by Wayne Booth in *The Rhetoric of Fiction,* 158ff—must be differentiated from the *factual* unreliability (or lack of "circumstantial credibility") that Martínez-Bonati discusses later in the same work (103–11). Unlike normative unreliability, factual unreliability (which does not concern me here) can normally be ascribed solely to first-person narrators, and only under quite special circumstances. For a systematic investigation of the specific narrative situations that reduce a narrator's "authentication authority," see Lubomír Doležel, "Truth and Authenticity in Narrative."

the story of Aschenbach's love and death in Venice creates responses that disagree (and ultimately even clash) with the narrator's evaluative commentary.[54] We must grant, I think, that a critic faced with this kind of incongruity is always free to attribute it to the author rather than to the narrator. I would maintain, however, that the aesthetic and ideological integrity of the work in question can only be upheld if we opt for the separation of its narrator from its author. This may well be the reason why the discovery of unreliable narrators in heterodiegetic novels has of late been on the rise, fulfilling Booth's prediction that the "pervasive irony hunt" would ultimately reach "even the most obviously omniscient and reliable narrators."[55]

This is not the place to argue against Booth's deploring of this critical tendency or even to ponder (as I began to do just now) the interpretive implications of the alternatives outlined above. It is more germane to the argument advanced in this final section of this chapter to stress that the severance of normatively vocal narrators from their authors is an option that can be fully validated, both on theoretical and on discourse-narratological grounds, in hetero- no less than in homodiegetic fictions and to propose that this option is one of the factors that makes the reading of fictional narratives a qualitatively different experience from the reading of univocally authored narratives: that it burdens its performance with a uniquely stressful interpretive freedom.

Thus my case for the relevance of narratology to the fictionality debate is conditional. It depends on the discipline's awakening to what I consider its principal shortfall: its lack of awareness of the places where its findings apply solely to the fictional domain and need to be modified before they can apply to neighboring narrative precincts. I have (without aiming for completeness) identified three such places: the synchronic bilevel (story/discourse) model, which cannot claim equally encompassing validity for texts that refer to events that have occurred prior to their narrative embodiment; the dependence of certain prominent narrative modes (notably for the presentation of consciousness) on the constitutional freedom of fiction from referential constraints; and the doubling of the narrative instance into author and narrator—a meaningful con-

54. For a detailed interpretation of Mann's novella on this basis, see Chapter 8 below. *Death in Venice* is clearly a more appropriate work for exemplifying the virtual unreliability of a narrator in a heterodiegetic fictional text than Martínez-Bonati's own illustration, *Doctor Faustus*, with its highly embodied narrator, Serenus Zeitblom (see *Fictive Discourse*, 112).
55. *The Rhetoric of Fiction*, 369.

ception of the vocal origin (and an important option for the interpretation) of fictional narratives. As I have tried to suggest, these three signposts, even as they point to the differential nature of fiction, also point to
each other. Their mutual consistency will have come into view without
my articulating it in a single sentence of causally connected clauses that
could be permuted at will. Were I to formulate such a conclusive sentence,
it would take on an air of bold (and bald) finality quite out of keeping with
the exploratory spirit of this chapter, and of the poetics on which it is
based.

8

The "Second Author" of *Death in Venice*

In his review of a now-forgotten work published in 1923, Thomas Mann emphatically separates the voice that narrates a novel from the author who writes it: "Narrating is something completely different from writing; the distinction of the former is its indirectness." This indirectness, he now explains, is most slyly effective when it veils itself in directness: when the author interposes between himself and his reader "the voice of the second, interpolated author." What happens then is that "a *monsieur* is heard perorating, not the author of the work, but a feigned and spectral observer."[1] By this "spectral observer" Mann cannot mean a narrator who—like his own Felix Krull—bears a name, a body, a civic identity. He clearly means one who remains disincarnated, nameless and faceless—the kind that we hear perorating loudly and volubly in Mann's own third-person novels and to whom we are inclined to attribute the mind, if not the body, of the author whose name appears on the title page. Like so many of his comments concerning the works of other writers, the distinction Mann draws in his review looks suspiciously as though it were meant *pro domo*.

Though modern literary theory has taught us to resist identifying such narrating "monsieurs" with their authors, in critical practice the distinction has been slow to sink in. The voice that tells the story of *Death in Venice*—including the stand it takes on weighty problems of morality—has, at any rate, almost invariably been attributed to Thomas Mann himself. Encouraged by the author's comment quoted above, this chapter proposes a "second author" reading of his novella. It engages the question of its narrator's identity as far as possible *en vase clos*, with little attention to Mann's (notoriously ambivalent) contemporaneous views on art and the artist, or to the (largely contradictory) self-interpretations he provided for his story.[2]

My principal focus will be the relationship of the narrator to his protagonist as it emerges from the language he employs in telling the story

1. *Gesammelte Werke in zwölf Bänden*, X:631–32; my translation.
2. For Mann's self-interpretive comments, see T. J. Reed, *Thomas Mann*. Reed's genetically oriented chapter on *Death in Venice* (144–78) will be discussed in my conclusion to this chapter.

of Aschenbach's Venetian love and death. His personality stands out most clearly at those textual moments when he departs furthest from straightforward narration, when he moves from the mimetic, storytelling level to the nonmimetic level of ideology and evaluation.[3] In this respect, as we will see, the narrator of *Death in Venice* provides a profusion of data for drawing his mental portrait: generalizations, exclamations, homilies, aphorisms, and other expressions of normative attitudes. These will ultimately allow us to assess his objectivity, to decide whether he is, ideologically speaking, a reliable narrator and thus a spokesman for the norms of the author who has invented both him and his story.[4]

NARRATOR AND PROTAGONIST

In briefest summary, the relationship of the narrator to his protagonist in *Death in Venice* may be described as one of increasing distance. In the early phases of the story it is essentially sympathetic, respectful, even reverent; in the later phases a deepening rift develops, building an increasingly ironic stance.[5] In this regard, Mann's novella evolves in a manner diametrically opposed to the typical Bildungsroman, where we usually witness a gradual rapprochement of the mind of the protagonist to the mind of the narrator. Here the protagonist, far from rising to his narrator's ethical and cultural standards, falls away from them. The events of Aschenbach's final dream, we are told, "liessen die Kultur seines Lebens verheert, vernichtet zurück" ["left his whole being, the culture of a lifetime, devastated and destroyed"]; and subsequently, as he shamelessly pursues Tadzio through the streets of Venice, "schien das Ungeheuerliche ihm aussichtsreich und hinfällig das Sittengesetz" ["monstrous things seemed full of promise to him, and the moral law no longer valid"].[6] The narrator, meanwhile — as the words he uses here to describe Aschenbach's moral debacle indicate — remains poised on the cultural pinnacle that had formerly brought forth his protagonist's own artistic achievement.

3. For the distinction between mimetic and nonmimetic language in fiction, see Félix Martínez-Bonati, *Fictive Discourse and the Structures of Literature,* 32–39. Mimetic language is "as though transparent; it does not interpose itself between us and the things of which it speaks"; the nonmimetic parts of a narrator's discourse, by contrast, "refer back to his presence, since they . . . are *his* language, his acts *qua* narrator, his perceptible subjectivity" (36f). See Chapter 7 above for a closer look at Martínez-Bonati's theory.

4. I here use the term *reliable narrator* in the sense defined in Wayne Booth, *The Rhetoric of Fiction:* "I have called a narrator *reliable* when he speaks for . . . the norms of the work (which is to say, the implied author's norms), *unreliable* when he does not" (158f).

5. The growing separation of the narrator from Aschenbach has been previously noted by Burton Pike in "Thomas Mann and the Problematic Self," 136.

6. *Gesammelte Werke in zwölf Bänden,* VIII:516 and 518; *Death in Venice and Other Stories,* 259 and 261. Henceforth page numbers in parentheses in my text will refer to these editions.

It should be noted from the outset, however, that this bifurcating narrative schema unfolds solely on the ideological or evaluative level of the story without in the least affecting the point of view (in the technical sense of the word) from which the story is presented.[7] On the perceptual level, the narrator steadfastly adheres to Aschenbach's perspective. From the initial moment when he observes the strange wanderer standing on the steps of the funeral chapel to the final moments when he watches Tadzio standing on a sandbar, we see the events and figures of the outside world through Aschenbach's eyes. The narrator also upholds from start to finish his free access to his protagonist's inner life (whereas he never so much as mentions what goes on in Tadzio's mind). In sum, he maintains his intimacy with Aschenbach's sensations, thoughts, and feelings even as he distances himself from him more and more on the ideological level.

I will now follow this relationship through the text in greater detail. The most obtrusive indicator of the narrator's personality—and the fact that he *has* a clearly defined personality—is the series of statements of "eternal truths" he formulates. There are in all some twenty glosses scattered throughout the text, and they express a consistent system of values. This narrator is for discipline, dignity, decorum, achievement, and sobriety, and against disorder, intoxication, passion, and passivity. In short, he volubly upholds within the story a heavily rationalistic and moralistic code, most strikingly in the maxims that culminate many of his statements *ex cathedra:*

> Denn der Mensch liebt und ehrt den Menschen, solange er ihn nicht zu beurteilen vermag, und die Sehsucht ist ein Erzeugnis mangelhafter Erkenntnis. (464)

> For man loves and respects his fellow man for as long as he is not yet in a position to evaluate him, and desire is born of defective knowledge. (242)

> Denn die Leidenschaft lähmt den wählerischen Sinn und lässt sich allen Ernstes mit Reizen ein, welche die Nüchternheit humoristisch aufnehmen oder unwillig ablehnen würde. (506)

> For passion paralyzes discrimination and responds in all seriousness to stimuli that the sober senses would either treat with humorous tolerance or impatiently reject. (251)

7. In this respect, *Death in Venice* is a remarkable illustration of the "non-concurrence of points of view articulated at different levels" that Boris Uspensky discusses in *A Poetics of Composition,* 101–8.

Wer ausser sich ist, verabscheut nichts mehr als wieder in sich zu gehen. (515)

To one who is beside himself, no prospect is so distasteful as that of self-recovery. (259)

With their causal inceptions—*denn* [for]—these sententiae profess full accountability for the case under discussion. They embed Aschenbach's story in a predictable world, a system of stable psychological concepts and moral precepts.

That the narrator's code of values closely matches the protagonist's own before his fall can be seen from the flashback on Aschenbach's authorial career provided in chapter 2. As other critics have noted, this summary biography sounds rather like a eulogy penned in advance by the deceased himself. The narrator clearly takes the role of apologist, and his gnomic generalizations—more extensive here than elsewhere in the text, and all concerned, as the subject demands, with the psychology and sociology of artistic achievement—serve only to heighten the representative import of Aschenbach's existence and to enhance the *laudatio*.

The ideological concord between the narrator and Aschenbach continues into the narrated time of the story proper: in the starting episodes—the voyage south, the early phases of the Venetian adventure—authorial generalizations are barely differentiated from figural thoughts. Notice Aschenbach's introspection while he awaits his Munich tramway:

Er [hatte] das Gefühl gezügelt und erkältet, *weil er wusste, dass es geneigt ist,* sich mit einem fröhlichen Ungefähr zu begnügen. Rächte sich nun also die geknechtete Empfindung, indem sie ihn verliess, indem sie seine Kunst fürder zu tragen und zu beflügeln sich weigerte . . . ? (449, my emphasis)

He had curbed and cooled his feelings; *for he knew that feeling is apt* to be content with high-spirited approximations and with work that falls short of supreme excellence. Could it be that the enslaved emotion was now revenging itself by deserting him, by refusing from now on to bear up his art on its wings . . . ? (201, my emphasis)

Note the tensual sequence in the first sentence: Aschenbach *knew* what the narrator knows to be (forever) true. Note also that the second sentence may be understood either as a question Aschenbach puts to himself or as a question posed by the analytic narrator. Again, during Aschenbach's first contemplation of the ocean, narratorial comment dovetails with figural emotions:

> Er liebte das Meer aus tiefen Gründen; aus Ruhebedürfnis des schwer arbeitenden Künstlers, der vor der anspruchsvollen Vielgestalt der Erscheinungen an der Brust des Einfachen, Ungeheuren sich zu bergen begehrt; aus einem verbotenen, seiner Aufgabe geradezu entgegengesetzten und darum verführerischen Hange zum Ungegliederten, Masslosen, Ewigen, zum Nichts. *Am Vollkommenen zu ruhen, ist die Sehsucht dessen, der sich um das Vortreffliche müht; und ist nicht das Nichts eine Form des Vollkommenen?* Wie er nun aber so ins Leere träumte . . . (475, my emphasis)

> There were profound reasons for his attachment to the sea: he loved it because as a hardworking artist he needed rest, needed to escape from the demanding complexity of phenomena and lie hidden on the bosom of the simple and tremendous; because of a forbidden longing deep within him that ran quite contrary to his life's task and was for that very reason seductive, a longing for the unarticulated and immeasurable, for eternity and for nothingness. *To rest in the arms of perfection is the desire of any man intent upon creating excellence; and is not nothingness a form of perfection?* But now, as he mused idly . . . (224, my emphasis)

Fused almost seamlessly at both ends with Aschenbach's oceanic feelings, the narrator's intervention creates not a trace of distancing irony. This is true despite the ominous notes he sounds with such phrases as "forbidden longing." Aschenbach is still the intensely working artist "intent upon creating excellence" and who may thus be allowed—by way of a vacation—a temporary indulgence in "nothingness."

The *entente cordiale* between authorial and figural minds is disrupted at just about the midpoint of the Venetian adventure, in a scene that I will consider in detail below. From this point on, the authorial commentary becomes emphatically distanced and judgmental. A clear example is the scene where Aschenbach, having followed Tadzio with the "wholesome" intention of striking up a casual conversation with the boy, finds himself too strongly moved to speak:

> Zu spät! dachte er in diesem Augenblick. Zu spät! Jedoch war es zu spät? Dieser Schritt, den zu tun er versäumte, er hätte sehr möglicherweise zum Guten, Leichten und Frohen, zu heilsamer Ernüchterung geführt. Allein es war wohl an dem, dass der Alternde die

Ernüchterung nicht wollte, dass der Rausch ihm zu teuer war. *Wer ent-*
rätselt Wesen und Gepräge des Künstlertums! Wer begreift die tiefe In-
stinktverschmelzung von Zucht und Zügellosigkeit, worin es beruht! Denn
heilsame Ernüchterung nicht wollen zu können, ist Zügellosikeit. Aschenbach war zur Selbstkritik nicht mehr aufgelegt. (493-94, my emphasis)

Too late! he thought at that moment. Too late! But was it too late?
This step he failed to take would very possibly have been all to the
good, it might have had a lightening, gladdening effect, led perhaps to
a wholesome disenchantment. But the fact now seemed to be that the
aging lover no longer wished to be disenchanted, that the intoxication
was too precious to him. *Who shall unravel the mystery of an artist's na-*
ture and character! Who shall explain the profound instinctual fusion of
discipline and license on which it rests! For not to be able to desire wholesome
disenchantment is to be licentious. Aschenbach was no longer disposed
to self-criticism. (240–41, my emphasis)

The narrator distances himself from Aschenbach explicitly and immediately when he questions the directly quoted "too late." He now provides
his interpretation for the failed action, reinforces his analysis by exclam-
atory rhetoric, grounds it in generalizations, and caps it with a sententious
judgment. Finally, returning to the individual case at hand, he explicitly
excludes Aschenbach from his wisdom, since the latter "was no longer
disposed to self-criticism." There are numerous instances in the later part
of the story that follow this general pattern: an inside view of Aschenbach's mind, followed by a judgmental intervention cast in gnomic present tense, followed by a return to Aschenbach's now properly adjudged
reactions.

A further device that underscores the narrator's progressive disengagement is his increasingly estranging and negative way of referring to
Aschenbach. In the early sections, distancing appellations appear spar-
ingly and remain neutrally descriptive: "der Reisende" ["the voyager"],
"der Wartende" ["the waiting man"], "der Ruhende" ["the man resting"].
After the narrator parts company with his character, ideologically speaking, we find time and again the more condescending epithets "der Al-
ternde" ["the aging man"], "der Einsame" ["the lonely man"]. And at crucial moments of his descent, Aschenbach becomes "der Heimgesuchte"
["the afflicted one"], "der Starrsinnige" ["the stubborn man"], "der
Betörte" ["the madman"], "der Verirrte" ["the lost one"], down to the
final "der Hinabgesunkene" ["the man who had collapsed"].

So far, the schismatic trend I have been tracing has, to all appearances, its objective motivation in the story's mimetic stratum. Faced with a character who manifests such progressively deviant behavior, this severely judgmental narrator can hardly be expected to react differently. Even so, the smugness and narrowness of his evaluative code in the passages already cited may cause some irritation in the reader, akin to the nauseated intolerance Roland Barthes attributes to the readers of Balzac at moments when this author laces his novels with cultural adages.[8] Perennial reactions of this type aside, however, there are at least two of the narrator's interventions in *Death in Venice* that give one pause on more substantial grounds. In these two instances the narrator indulges in a kind of ideological overkill that produces an effect contrary to the one he is ostensibly trying to achieve. It is to these two moments in their episodic context that I now turn for close inspection.

THE TURNING POINT

As previously mentioned, the turning point in the relationship between narrator and character on the ideological plane roughly coincides with the midpoint of Aschenbach's Venetian stay: the pivotal scene when the enamored writer, for the first and last time, practices his art. Before this point is reached, however, a long section intervenes where narratorial generalizations have disappeared from the text altogether. This section comprises mainly Aschenbach's abortive attempt to leave Venice (end of chapter 3) and the first quiescently serene phase of his love (beginning of chapter 4). In these pages the narrator goes beyond merely adopting Aschenbach's visual perspective; he also emulates the hymnic diction (complete with Homeric hexameters), the Hellenic allusions, and the mythical imagery that properly belong to Aschenbach's inner discourse. This stylistic contagion—technically a form of free indirect style—has often been mistaken for stylistic parody, an interpretation for which I find no textual evidence.[9] The employment of free indirect style, in the absence of marked distancing devices, points rather to a momentary "sharing" of Aschenbach's inner experience by the narrator—as though he were himself temporarily on vacation from his post as moral preceptor.

This consonance reaches its apogee in the moment of high intensity that immediately precedes the writing scene, when the Platonic theory of beauty surfaces in Aschenbach's mind as he watches Tadzio cavorting on the beach: "Standbild und Spiegel! Seine Augen umfassten die edle

8. Roland Barthes, *S/Z: An Essay,* 98.
9. The principal advocate of the "parodistic idiom" in *Death in Venice* is Erich Heller in *The Ironic German: A Study of Thomas Mann*; see esp. 99.

Gestalt dort am Rande des Blauen, und in aufschwärmendem Entzück-
en glaubte er mit diesem Blick das Schöne selbst zu begreifen, die Form
als Gottesgedanken, die eine und reine Vollkommenheit, die im Geiste
lebt" (490). ["A mirror and a sculptured image! His eyes embraced the
noble figure at the blue water's edge, and in rising ecstasy he felt he was
gazing on Beauty itself, on Form as a thought of God, the one and pure
perfection that dwells in the spirit"] (237). Both the initial exclamation in
this passage and the final present tense ("dwells") indicate the extent of
narratorial identification with figural thoughts. The Platonic montage
that now follows (combining passages from the *Phaedrus* and the *Symposium*) is largely cast in narrated monologue form, fusing the narrator *verbatim* with Aschenbach's mental language. An intensely emotive tone
thus pervades the text as the narrator, in concert with Aschenbach, approaches the climactic writing scene. His sudden *change* of tone in the
course of narrating this episode is therefore all the more discordant.

The scene opens with a strikingly balanced gnomic statement: "Glück
des Schriftstellers ist der Gedanke, der ganz Gefühl, ist das Gefühl, das
ganz Gedanke zu werden vermag" (492). ["The writer's joy is the thought
that becomes emotion, the emotion that can wholly become a thought"]
(239). No other narratorial generalization in the entire work is as harmo-
niously attuned to the mood of the protagonist. Its syntactical symmetry
reflects with utmost precision the creative equipoise between intellect and
emotion that Aschenbach himself is seeking. But already in the next sentences, with Aschenbach standing on the verge of this "joy," the
narrator begins to withdraw from the miraculous moment: "Solch ein
pulsender Gedanke, solch genaues Gefühl gehörte und gehorchte *dem
Einsamen damals*. . . . Er wünschte plötzlich zu schreiben" (492, my emphasis). ["*At that time the solitary Aschenbach* took possession and control
of just such a pulsating thought. . . . He suddenly desired to write"] (239,
my emphasis). Other, even more alienating phrases follow presently: the
writer is called "der Heimgesuchte" ["the afflicted one"], the moment of
writing is referred to as "an diesem Punkte der Krise" ["at this point of the
crisis"], the object of his emotion becomes "das Idol" ["the idol"], and so
forth.

When we consider the radical nature of Aschenbach's creative performance in this scene, it is hardly surprising that the narrator refuses to follow him in silent consonance: "Und zwar ging sein Verlangen dahin, in
Tadzio's Gegenwart zu arbeiten, beim Schreiben den Wuchs des Knaben
zum Muster zu nehmen, seinen Stil den Linien dieses Körpers folgen zu
lassen . . . und seine Schönheit ins Geistige zu tragen" (492). ["And what

he craved, indeed, was to work in Tadzio's presence, to take the boy's physique for a model as he wrote, to let his style follow the lineaments of this body . . . and to carry its beauty on high into the spiritual world"] (239).

As T. J. Reed has pointed out, Aschenbach here tries to enact (literally and literarily) the truth Diotima imparted to Socrates, that Eros alone can serve as guide to absolute beauty.[10] In this light, his act of "writing Tadzio" can be understood as his attempt at gaining direct access to the realm of Platonic ideas. But in following this mystic urge, Aschenbach breaks the aesthetic credo to which he had dedicated his working life and that the narrator had explicitly endorsed: that the artist is unable to create in the heat of emotion. At the same time, this move countermands the entire process of the mimetic art he had practiced throughout his life: the patient art of the novelist, weaver of Aschenbach's most important work, "Maja." In chapter 2, the narrator had admiringly described this work as "den figurenreichen, so vielerlei Menschenschicksal im Schatten einer Idee versammelnden Romanteppich" (450) ["the great tapestry of the novel, so rich in characters, gathering so many human destinies together under the shadow of one idea"] (202). The horizontal images here point up the radical contrast between the reflected phenomenal world Aschenbach had formerly created and the direct vertical ascension he presently performs by way of his scriptural intercourse with beauty.

But if all this helps to explain why the writing scene brings about the sudden change in the levelheaded narrator's attitude toward Aschenbach, it also draws attention to his limitations. These come to the fore when, in its immediate aftermath, he indulges in his drastic distancing move: when he momentarily, but quite literally, steps out of and away from his story. Not the least shocking aspect of this breakaway is that it breaks all the unities — of time, place, and action — to which the novella so classically adheres. Having flashed forward to the admiring reception the writer's performance was to receive after its publication, the narrator deflates this performance in almost brutally sobering terms: "Es ist sicher gut, dass die Welt nur das schöne Werk, nicht auch seine Ursprünge, nicht seine Entstehungsbedingungen kennt; denn die Kenntnis der Quellen, aus denen dem Künstler Eingebung floss, würde sie oftmals verwirren, abschrecken und so die Wirkungen des Vortrefflichen aufheben" (493). ["It is well that the world knows only a fine piece of work and not also its ori-

10. *Thomas Mann: The Uses of Tradition,* 160. The Platonic import of Aschenbach's creative moment is disregarded by Pike, who takes its diminutive yield of a page and a half as an ironic comment on Aschenbach's artistic potential ("Thomas Mann and the Problematic Self," 135).

gins, the conditions under which it came into being, for the knowledge of the sources of an artist's inspiration would often confuse readers and shock them, and the excellence of the writing would be of no avail"] (239). This is by far the least motivated, the most disconcerting of the narrator's interventions. It seems as though he were taking headlong flight onto familiar ground—the psychology of the reading public—from the mysteries of a creative endeavor that is beyond his comprehension.

The substance of his comment itself raises a number of questions. For one thing, is it not plainly contradictory within its context? Having just revealed to his own reading public the inspirational sources of Aschenbach's newly created piece, what is the sense of now declaring that these sources had better remain hidden? Furthermore, is not the attribution of confusing and repulsive effects to Aschenbach's Platonically sublimated procreation excessively, unnecessarily aggressive?

These questions are apt to arise in the mind of a *Death in Venice* reader who dissociates its narrator from its author. And since it is this, his most questionable intervention, that initiates the ideological schism, it tends to reduce the trustworthiness of the narrator's distancing comments from this point forward. At the very least, it encourages readers henceforth to divide their allegiance between the narrator and the protagonist. I would even suggest that Mann may have designedly made his narrator jump the gun: his overreaction within the episode that climaxes the Apollonian phase of Aschenbach's erotic adventure seems to encourage the reader to weld his sympathy more firmly to the protagonist than if the narrator had waited to make his distancing move until after Aschenbach had begun his Dionysian descent.

THE MOMENT OF TRUTH

A second, even clearer, instance of evaluative overstatement occurs when Aschenbach reaches his nadir: the paragraph-long sentence that introduces his second Socratic monologue (in the scene that immediately precedes the death scene). To demonstrate its rhetorical impact, it needs to be quoted in full:

> Er sass dort, der Meister, der würdig gewordene Künstler, der Autor des "Elenden," der in so vorbildlich reiner Form dem Zigeunertum und der trüben Tiefe abgesagt, dem Abgrunde die Sympathie gekündigt und das Verworfene verworfen hatte, der Hochgestiegene, der, Überwinder seines Wissens und aller Ironie entwachsen, an die Verbindlichkeiten des Massenzutrauens sich gewöhnt hatte, er, dessen

Ruhm amtlich, dessen Name geadelt war und an dessen Stil die Knaben sich zu bilden angehalten wurden,—er sass dort, seine Lider waren geschlossen, nur zuweilen glitt, rasch sich wieder verbergend, ein spöttischer und betretener Blick seitlich darunter hervor, und seine schlaffen Lippen, kosmetisch aufgehöht, bildeten einzelne Worte aus von dem, was sein halb schlummerndes Hirn an seltsamer Traumlogik hervorbrachte. (521)

There he sat, the master, the artist who had achieved dignity, the author of *A Study in Abjection,* he who in so paradigmatically pure form had repudiated intellectual vagrancy and the murky depth, who had proclaimed his renunciation of all sympathy with the abyss, who had weighed vileness into the balance and found it wanting; he who had risen so high, who had set his face against his own sophistication, grown out of all his irony, and taken on the commitments of one whom the public trusted; he, whose fame was official, whose name had been ennobled, and on whose style young boys were taught to model their own—there he sat, with his eyelids closed, with only an occasional mocking and rueful sideways glance from under them that he hid again at once; and his drooping, cosmetically brightened lips shaped an occasional word of the discourse his brain was delivering, his half-asleep brain with its tissue of strange dream-logic. (264)

The most obviously "destructive" feature of this passage is, of course, the grotesque height of the fall it builds between the before and the after, the former self-image and the present reality. The elevation itself is constructed by sardonically piling up phrases we have heard before in a different context: they are the very phrases the narrator employed in the laudatory curriculum vitae of the summary chapter 2.[11]

The entire weighty sentence finally leads up to the phrase signaling the inception of Aschenbach's inner language. The fact that the narrator quotes this language directly on this occasion is itself significant: no other mode of presentation could have disengaged him as effectively from the ensuing discourse. But the terms he uses to introduce it—"half-asleep brain," "dream-logic"—are, of course, meant to be more immediately alienating; they disqualify its meaning in advance, as much as to warn us that the words we are about to hear are arrant nonsense.[12] When one ex-

---

11. What is perhaps less obvious is that this sentence parodistically echoes the structure of that earlier chapter's opening sentence.

12. The dream concept bears emphatically negative attributes throughout the narrator's discourse. He had earlier used such phrases as "mit verwirrten Traumworten" ["with confused

amines the actual content of Aschenbach's mind, however, one is forced to conclude that his "dream-logic" produces nothing less than the moment of truth toward which the entire story has been moving: a lucidly hopeless diagnosis of the artist's fate.

Aschenbach's Socratic address takes us back again to the Platonic doctrine of beauty as found in the *Phaedrus* and the *Symposium*. But he now turns this doctrine to profoundly pessimistic account—at least so far as the poet is concerned. He tells Phaedrus: "Wir Dichter [können] den Weg der Schönheit nicht gehen, . . . ohne dass Eros sich zugesellt und sich zum Führer aufwirft, . . . denn Leidenschaft ist unsere Erhebung, und unsere Sehnsucht muss Liebe bleiben,—das ist unsere Lust und unsere Schande" (521–22). ["We artists cannot tread the path of Beauty without Eros keeping company with us and appointing himself as our guide . . . for it is passion that exalts us and the longing must be the longing of a lover—that is our joy and our shame"] (264–65).

Having acknowledged the poet's defeat on the Platonic path to the higher realm, Aschenbach now denounces with particular bitterness his own erstwhile pedagogic pretensions with words that clearly echo Plato-Socrates' ultimate decision (in Book 10 of the *Republic*) to exile the poet from the ideal state[13]: "Die Meisterhaltung unseres Stils ist Lüge und Narrentum, unser Ruhm und Ehrenstand eine Posse, das Vertrauen zu uns höchst lächerlich, Volks- und Jugenderziehung durch die Kunst ein gewagtes, zu verbietendes Unternehmen" (522). ["The magisterial poise of our style is a lie and a farce, our fame and societal position are an absurdity, the public faith in us is altogether ridiculous, the use of art to educate the nation and its youth is a reprehensible undertaking that should be forbidden by law"] (265). If we note that Aschenbach's self-criticism here is every bit as biting as the narrator's foregoing sarcasm—and in fact cast in almost identical terms—the introduction to his discourse must appear as gratuitous aggression, merely adding insult to injury.

When we look at Aschenbach's despairing statement at the conclusion of his monologue, the narrator's prefatory venom takes on an even more dubious air: "Form und Unbefangenheit, Phaidros, führen zum Rausch und zur Begierde, . . . zu grauenhaftem Gefühlsfrevel, . . . führen zum Abgrund, zum Abgrund auch sie. Uns Dichter, sage ich, führen sie dahin,

---

dream-words"], "komisch-traumartiges Abenteuer" ["comically dreamlike adventure"], "Traumbann" ["dream-spell"], not to mention the "furchtbaren Traum" ["frightful dream"] that leaves Aschenbach "kraftlos dem Dämon verfallen" (515) ["powerlessly enslaved to the daemon-god"] (261).

13. Cf. Heller, *The Ironic German*, 114.

denn wir vermögen nicht, uns aufzuschwingen, wir vermögen nur auszuschweifen" (522). ["But form and naiveté, Phaedros, lead to intoxication and lust, they may lead a noble mind to terrible criminal emotions, . . . they lead, they too lead, to the abyss. I tell you, that is where they lead us writers, for we are not capable of self-exaltation, we are merely capable of self-debauchery"] (265). For all its dream-logic, this conclusion is tragically clear—as well as clearly tragic.

Inevitably, if one equates the narrator with Thomas Mann, one is forced to denigrate Aschenbach's famous last words. Critics have generally done so, understanding his monologue as an inauthentic self-justification. Instead of facing up to his individual guilt, Aschenbach attributes his abysmal end to the fate of poets generally, the generic "us writers." In my opinion, this interpretation cannot be substantiated on the basis of the text itself. To open an alternate "moral" path for Aschenbach, one has to look *outside* the text: to Mann's other, more optimistic works (*Tonio Kröger* or the Joseph novels), or to certain autobiographical pronouncements.[14]

On the other hand, if one dissociates the narrator from Thomas Mann, one is free to denigrate the introduction to the monologue and to understand Aschenbach's last words for what they are: his (and the story's) moment of truth, which the narrator is unwilling and unable to share to the bitter end. It is surely significant that only Aschenbach can sound this truth, that he can sound it only with lips drooping under his makeup, and only after these lips have taken in the fatal germs of the plague. In this light his monologue takes on the meaning of an anagnorisis, the expression of that lethal knowledge the hero of Greek tragedy reaches when he stands on the verge of death. The irony that the narrator directs at Aschenbach at this moment can then be turned back on its speaker—by a reader who, for his part, is willing and able to share the tragic truth the *author* imparts to him with this story.[15]

14. See, *inter alia,* Pike, "Thomas Mann and the Problematic Self": "Considering Mann's attitude toward art as it emerges in his other writings—fiction, essays, and letters—is not an art which so peremptorily dismisses 'sympathy with the abyss' incomplete?" (133).
15. I cannot resist breaking my self-imposed interdiction to refer to extratextual evidence at this juncture. The one point that remains constant through the years in Mann's self-contradictory comments on *Death in Venice* is that Aschenbach's final monologue articulates the truth of the story. He pronounced on this in at least four different places: in a letter of 1915 to Elisabeth Zimmer: "I wanted to produce something like *the tragedy of masterfulness*. This seems to have become clear to you, since you take the address to Phaedros as *the kernel of the whole*"; in *Betrachtungen eines Unpolitischen,* speaking of a past work "where *I made* a 'dignified' artist *understand* that someone like him would necessarily remain frivolous and an adventurer of feeling"; in the Princeton address "On Myself" (1940): "The artist, tied to sensuality, cannot

FANTASTIC UNDERCURRENT

To this point my argument for the "second author" of *Death in Venice* has rested solely on what the narrator says and how he says it. But what he leaves *unsaid* is equally important for my case; it complements and completes the telltale evidence.

It is telltale in the literal sense, for with this story Mann (though not his narrator) gives us—among other things—a *fantastic* tale. His vehicle is the often-remarked-upon cast of mysterious figures Aschenbach encounters on his lethal journey, figures who acquire their ominous meaning less by way of their individual appearance—their death-like and/or devil-like features notwithstanding—than by their serial *re*appearance. The unlikeliness (on realistic grounds) of their uncanny likeness suggests cumulatively that they all represent the same sinister power, a power relentlessly bent on driving the protagonist to his ruinous end. Now these hints of supernatural doings, which even a first reader finds too strong to miss or dismiss, are never picked up by the narrator himself. Though he meticulously describes each stranger, he passes silently over their obtrusive likeness, to all appearances studiously closing his eyes to it. This willed blindness may readily be understood as the counterpart to the moralistic, realistic, and rationalistic views he voices throughout.

Yet for all the narrator's closely woven cover-up on the nonmimetic level of the text, the underlying mystery on the mimetic level keeps shining through the causal fabric. And these abysmal glimpses into a covert realm make the reader feel increasingly uneasy with the overt explanations he provides. The narrator's silence, in short, speaks louder than his words, undercutting his trustworthiness even more effectively than his normative excesses. For nowhere does it become quite as evident that the author *behind* the work is communicating a message that escapes the narrator *within* the work. The exact meaning of this message—whether it signifies an otherworldly, cosmic power or the power of Aschenbach's unconscious, myth or (depth-) psychology, or both at once[16]—is less important in the present context than the fact that it refers to a realm that escapes the narrator. It escapes him precisely because he is inclined to ignore

---

really become dignified: this basic tendency of bitter and melancholy skepticism *is expressed in the confession* (modeled on Plato's dialogues) *that I placed in the mouth of the already doomed hero*"; and finally, in a letter of 1954 to Jürgen Ernestus, where he again quotes and paraphrases the monologue, adding (this time with a shade of reserve): "There is much truth, perhaps exaggerated and thus only partial truth, in this skeptical and long-suffering pessimism." The above quotations (all in my translation and with my emphases) may be found in *Dichter über ihre Dichtungen,* 406, 411, 439f., and 448.

16. See André von Gronicka, "Myth Plus Psychology," 51–54.

all questions that point above or below his flat conception of the world and of the psyche. In this respect his disregard of the demonic figures corresponds exactly to his rhetorical standoff from Aschenbach's mental experience, at both its zenith (the writing scene) and its nadir (the final monologue).[17] By the same token, the demonic figures themselves reinforce the truth-value of Aschenbach's anagnorisis in the latter instance: for what can their dark presence intimate, if not that a fateful force is at work in the universe, a force that irresistibly draws those who strive for beauty into the abyss.

But the fantastic undercurrent in the fabula of *Death in Venice* also has an essential aesthetic function. As Christine Brooke-Rose suggests, every good story needs to keep back something: "Whatever overdetermination may occur in any one work . . . some underdetermination is necessary for it to retain its hold over us, its particular mixture of recognition-pleasure and mystery."[18] In Mann's novella it is clearly the series of mysterious strangers that creates underdetermination, counterbalancing the narrator's overdetermination on the ideological level. In terms of Roland Barthes's codes, to which Brooke-Rose refers in this same essay, the strangers would have to be assigned to the story's hermeneutic code, the enigma-creating code that the narrator disregards and that the text leaves unresolved. I would maintain that the *fact* that it remains unresolved tacitly ironizes—behind the narrator's back—the univocal interpretation he tries to impose on Aschenbach's story.

A THEORETICAL QUESTION

My reading of *Death in Venice* opens to a theoretical question that I want to face in conclusion: granted that the positing of a "second author" may explain in a plausible manner the discrepancies between the narrator's commentary on Aschenbach's story and the story itself, is this the *only* way to account for them? The answer is clearly no. An alternate way is to attribute the narrator's shortcomings to the *first* author, Thomas Mann himself; more precisely, to the circumstances—personal and/or historical—that attended the composition of *Death in Venice* and that made him fall short of crafting a flawless work.

Now this is precisely the way taken by T. J. Reed in *Thomas Mann: The Uses of Tradition*.[19] To my knowledge, Reed is the only scholar to have

17. Aschenbach himself, while he never relates the stranger-figures to his fate or to each other, does on several occasions reflect on them with puzzlement.
18. "The Readerhood of Man," 131.
19. In addition to this genetic interpretation, Reed has provided a more intratextually oriented

squarely faced the problems raised by the narrator's ideological excesses in the later parts of *Death in Venice*. Referring specifically to the sentence that introduces Aschenbach's final monologue (discussed in "The Moment of Truth" above), Reed points up the narrator's "emphatic judgment" and adds: "It is a shade too emphatic for the reader accustomed to Mann's ironic temper. Where are the reservations usually felt in every inflection of his phrasing? The finality with which Aschenbach's case is settled is positively suspicious. . . . Is it not crudely direct beside the informed survey of Aschenbach's development in Chapter Two . . . ? There are depths to be sounded under the polished surface of the story."[20] This passage serves as the opening gambit for a probing investigation into the genesis of Mann's novella. It clearly indicates that Reed's admirable study is an attempt specifically to account for the "positively suspicious" nature of the narrator's judgmental rhetoric. Significantly, Reed pursues his genetic interpretation without ever questioning the reliability of the narrator, whom he seems automatically to identify with the author.[21] What he questions instead is the coherence and aesthetic integrity of the work itself. By following through the stages of Mann's creative process, he reveals what he finds concealed beneath the "polished surface" of the final product—i.e., that Mann has superimposed "a moral tale" on a text he originally conceived "hymnically."[22] This "diametric change" explains for Reed what he describes as the novella's "ambiguity in the word's more dubious sense . . . uncertainty of meaning, disunity." Mann has "sought to work out a changed conception of the materials and language ideally suited to an earlier one."[23] And although Reed has by this point shifted the ground of his critique from the narrator's narrow moralism to what he calls "disharmony between style and substance,"[24] the fact remains that it was the vexing narrator who sent him on his way in the first place—sent him, that is, outside the text to investigate the vagaries of its composition.

---

interpretation in *Death in Venice: Making and Unmaking a Master*. In this more recent work he does not touch on the problems that concern me in this essay.

20. Reed, *Thomas Mann: The Uses of Tradition*, 149.
21. Except perhaps toward the end of Reed's discussion, when he states rather cryptically: "It has proved possible to detach Mann from the emphatic condemnations of the later pages. These formulations . . . are Mann's concession to more confident moralists than himself" (ibid., 173). Is Reed suggesting here that the moralistic narrator is a kind of hypocritical role that Mann adopted for public consumption? This seems to me a highly unlikely possibility.
22. Ibid., 151–54. The terms *moral tale* ["moralische Fabel"] and *hymnically* ["hymnisch"] are used by Mann himself to contrast the final product with the original creative impulse. See his letter of 4 July 1920, to Carl Maria Weber—the crown witness for Reed's argument.
23. Ibid., 173–74.
24. Ibid., 176.

On the face of it, Reed's extratextual approach to the textual ambiguities in *Death in Venice* would appear to differ radically from the intratextual approach I have followed in this essay. Yet from a certain theoretical perspective these two approaches can be related, if not reconciled, with each other. We owe this perspective to an article by Tamar Yacobi, where the problem of fictional reliability is discussed on the basis of a reader-oriented theory of literary texts.[25] According to Yacobi, a reader who attributes unreliability to a narrator is merely choosing one of several "principles of resolution" potentially available when faced with the "tensions, contradictions and other infelicities" of a literary work. A rival principle, equally available, is what Yacobi calls the "genetic principle," which places the blame on the biographical-historical background of the work. These two principles of resolution have in common that they "both resolve referential problems by attributing their occurrence to some source of report." The difference between them "lies in the answer to the question: who is responsible?" The reader who calls on the genetic principle will answer: the author; the one who calls on the "perspectival" principle will answer: the narrator.[26] This signifies, in the case of a third-person text like *Death in Venice,* that one refuses to regard the narrator as the mouthpiece of the author.

From this theoretical vantage point, then, Reed's genetic explanation appears—even to myself—no less (and no more) valid and plausible than my "second author" explanation. But my equanimity gives way when I return from the plane of abstract generality to the concrete singularity of Mann's novella. For within the interpretive arena of a specific text, these two explanations are mutually exclusive; the reader is forced to choose between them. This brings me—at the risk of stating the obvious—to mention some of my reasons for preferring my resolution over Reed's.

My principal reason is confidence in Thomas Mann's aesthetic control and integrity as manifested in the complexity of vision I generally find incarnated in his major works of fiction (though not always in his extraliterary pronouncements). The severance of the narrator from the author seems to me a necessary interpretive move for a reader bent on affirming that *Death in Venice* is a fully achieved, and in this sense "flawless" work. It is a move that allows one to ascribe the ideological simplicities voiced in this novella to an artfully crafted vocal source. The distancing of these simplistic views from the mind of Mann seems to me especially persua-

25. "Fictional Reliability as a Communicative Problem."
26. Ibid., 119–21.

sive in view of the fact that they address matters of his deepest concerns and of his most differentiated views—art and the artist. In his other novels and novellas, he always approaches this subject obliquely, most obliquely of all in his only other full-fledged tragedy of a creative artist, *Doctor Faustus*. I take it to be no coincidence that Mann reverted—three decades later—to the same basic narrative indirection I attribute to him in *Death in Venice*. Admittedly the ironic interval that separates Mann from Zeitblom (the narrator of *Doctor Faustus*) is more blatant than the one that separates him from the teller of the earlier tale. Yet the proximity of the narrative situations in these two works offers a kind of proof by the absurd of my "second author" hypothesis. For is it not equally difficult to imagine the narrator of *Death in Venice* to be the creator of Aschenbach as it is to imagine Zeitblom to be the creator of Adrian Leverkühn? Only a mind capable of Mann's "Ironie nach beiden Seiten" ["two-directional irony"] could have conceived both members of these pairs in dialectical unison.

9

Pierre and Napoleon at Borodinó

Reflections on the Historical Novel

"Can one see from there?" "Are those our men there? . . . Where, where?" "What? Has it begun?" "What's happening here?"[1] This is the voice of Pierre Bezúkhov, come from Moscow to "see" the Battle of Borodinó. His perceptions are all cast in negative terms: "Nowhere could he see the battlefield he had expected to find . . . nor could he even distinguish our troops from the enemy's" (849); "Despite the incessant firing going on there, he had no idea that this was the field of battle" (883); "For a long time he did not notice the killed and wounded" (883); "When ascending that knoll, Pierre had no notion that this spot . . . was the most important point of the battle" (884–85). Eventually Pierre is thrown to the ground by a grenade, faints, comes to himself, has an encounter with a French officer—"Am I taken prisoner or have I taken him prisoner?" (890)—and walks away from the battlefield.

Pierre is not the only participant in this battle who doesn't understand what is going on: "Napoleon, standing on the knoll, looked through a field glass, and in its small circlet saw smoke and men, sometimes his own and sometimes Russians. . . . But . . . it [was] impossible to make out what was happening . . . it was impossible to make out what was taking place" (892). Seeing his own dejection reflected on the faces of his men, Napoleon finally realizes that he is observing "a lost battle." At this point, "a terrible feeling like a nightmare took possession of him. . . . Yes, it was like a dream in which a man fancies that a ruffian is coming to attack him, and raises his arm to strike that ruffian a terrible blow . . . but then feels that his arm drops powerless and limp like a rag" (897).

The techniques employed by Tolstoy in this episode from *War and Peace* reflect his conviction that the fictional narration of historical events from the perspective of persons *involved* in these events comes closer to

1. Leo Tolstoy, *War and Peace,* 847, 849, 880, 883. Future references to this edition (the Norton Critical Edition) will be given parenthetically in my text.

the truth than any historical narrative. After reading *La Chartreuse de Parme,* where another battle (the Battle of Waterloo) is rendered through the eyes of the fictional Fabrice del Dongo, Tolstoy reportedly said: "Who before him [Stendhal] had described war like that, as it really is?"[2] This is not the only indication of Tolstoy's belief (at least at the time he was writing *War and Peace*) that the novelist can succeed in doing what the historian inevitably fails to achieve: to narrate the past truthfully. Both the narrator's discourse within *War and Peace* itself and the essay "Some Words about *War and Peace*"[3] contain passages suggesting why and how fiction can, in this respect, surpass history.[4]

Fiction enables a writer, first and foremost, to render historical happenings by way of the personalized and momentary experience of individual human beings. I find this idea underlying the mathematical imagery of the chapter that introduces Book XI of the novel. The narrator here envisions a different model of writing about history—a model that he sets in opposition to the historian's construction of "an arbitrarily selected series of continuous events": "Only by taking infinitesimally small units for observation (the differential of history, that is, the individual tendencies of men) and attaining the art of integrating them (that is, finding the sum of these infinitesimals) can we hope to arrive at the laws of history" (918).

The Borodinó section in *War and Peace* may be understood to illustrate this model. Pierre's perceptions and reactions here constitute the "infinitesimally small units for observation," the "individual tendencies" that would be negligible in conventional historical terms. The same holds with even greater force for the intimate glimpse we get into the psyche of Napoleon in the passage quoted above. In the sentence that begins "Yes, it was like a dream . . . " the narrator, in fact, uses a notoriously fiction-specific technique to render Napoleon's nightmarish thoughts, the technique known as free indirect style that transposes into the past tense of narration what a character says to himself: "Yes, it is like a dream . . . " Here the style itself reflects the distinction of the historical novel as compared to historiography.

2. Quoted in Gary Saul Morson, *Hidden in Plain View,* 288, n. 4.
3. This essay is reprinted in the Norton Critical Edition, 1366–74.
4. On this score, I understand Tolstoy's views on historiography and their relationship to *War and Peace* rather differently from Gary Saul Morson. The latter believes that for Tolstoy *all* narrative—fictional, no less than historical, only more openly—"necessarily falsifies" the past (*Hidden in Plain View,* 131). For this reason he applies the term "negative narrative" to the novel as a whole (130 ff.). Accordingly, he understands *War and Peace* as a work that is "deeply parodic": as a novel that "satirizes all historical writing, and all novels" (83).

But the "infinitesimally small unit" that escapes the historian's schematization involves more than the plunge into the singularized depth of fictional and/or historical psyches. It involves as well (and simultaneously) the temporally minute moment. As we know from the emergence of the stream-of-consciousness novel in the early twentieth century, the two go hand in hand: the inner lives of Bloom and Stephen, Clarissa and Septimus, depend on the slow motion of the novels that configure them.[5] And even though the narrated time of Tolstoy's immense novel covers a far larger temporal compass than the single day of *Ulysses* or *Mrs. Dalloway,* the Battle of Borodinó—like numerous other episodes in *War and Peace*—is presented scenically, lingering with intense attention on the instantaneous perceptions and reactions of the baffled participants.[6]

There is yet another feature of narration focalized on and by a fictional character that correlates with the ones already mentioned: the sense of presentness it creates and the ensuing impression that it opens on an unknown future. Tolstoy's awareness of this fiction-specific effect may be gauged from his objections to retrospective reports of historical events (battles in particular). Such reports are inevitably untrustworthy, and their distortions are greatly magnified in (and by) official *post factum* accounts: "After any battle the two sides nearly always describe it in quite contradictory ways, in every description of a battle there is a necessary lie. . . . Question a month or two later a man who was in the battle, and you will no longer feel in his account the raw, vital material that was there before, but he will answer according to the reports" (1369–70). Only fiction is able to create the impression of presenting historical events at the moment they happen, thereby bringing to life the "raw, vital material" of experience without the distortions of hindsight.[7]

In this respect, then, as in the others referred to above, the scenes in the Borodinó episode of *War and Peace* that are focalized by Pierre and

---

5. Even though he is unaware of the formal correlates of the analogy, I agree with Isaiah Berlin when he proposes that Tolstoy's attitude toward historians is comparable to Virginia Woolf's attitude toward contemporary social novelists; see *The Hedgehog and the Fox,* 19–20.

6. That in this respect *War and Peace* anticipates the stream-of-consciousness novel is noted by Gleb Struve, "Monologue intérieur," 1108. Morson refers to an early story by Tolstoy, "A History of Yesterday," where "the narrator comes to recognize the impossibility of thoroughly describing even one day in the life of one man" (*Hidden in Plain View,* 87).

7. Cf. Morson's perception that "Tolstoy portrays the ignorance of future significance as the most accurate perception of events" (ibid., 166).

Napoleon exemplify how Tolstoy constructed his historical novel in ways that match his philosophy of history.[8]

Though no other historical novelist has articulated the distinction of fiction for rendering historical events in the manner of Tolstoy, his novelistic practice in the Borodinó section of *War and Peace* is basically in line with the norms of the classical (realist) historical novel.[9] At the same time, the scenes from which I have quoted strongly refute the widespread notion that the historical novel is a kind of crossbreed between history and fiction or (as one critic typically expresses it) a "hybrid . . . strategically situated between the novel and historiography."[10] Instead, these scenes support the idea that Alfred Döblin (himself a practitioner of the genre) expressed in the following adage: "The historical novel is, in the first place, a novel; in the second place, it isn't history."[11]

This genre, for one thing, allows for the conjunction—in the same time and place, when and where they experience the same event—of figures that stem from different ontological realms: Pierre Bezúkhov, a character known only from his featured role in Tolstoy's novel, and Napoleon, a person whose past existence in the real world is attested by historiographic sources. Theorists have applied a variety of tags to these two different types of figures: Terence Parsons would call Pierre a "native" of the fictional world, Napoleon an "immigrant";[12] Ruth Ronen would call the former an "imaginary" character, the latter a "real-world counterpart";[13] for Ann Rigney the world of a historical novel is inhabited by "fictional supplements" in addition to real historical figures;[14] Marie-Laure Ryan's typology of narrative genres contrasts historiography and historical

8. The genesis of *War and Peace* suggests that Tolstoy's antihistorical views may in fact have grown with (and out of) his novelistic practice. As Eickhenbaum has shown, this work was initially conceived as an "English novel" (bearing the title "All's Well That Ends Well") that followed a "family plot" in the manner of Trollope and Thackeray. While working on this early version Tolstoy noted in his diary his intention to write "a psychological history-novel about Alexander and Napoleon." Eickhenbaum believes that these projects flowed together to produce the final version of *War and Peace*, which would explain why the narrator's antihistorical essays appear only in the second half of the novel (after book 9). See Boris Eickhenbaum, *Tolstoy in the Sixties*, 149 f., 175, 195, 233.
9. See Ansgar Nünning, *Von historischer Fiktion zu historiographischer Metafiktion*, I:262–67, for a typological discussion of the traditional norms that apply to the "classical" version of the genre, as compared to various contemporary developments of the historical novel.
10. Elizabeth Wesseling, *Writing History as a Prophet*, 49.
11. "Der historische Roman und wir" in *Aufsätze zur Literatur*, 169; my translation.
12. For a discussion of Parsons's terms, see Thomas G. Pavel, *Fictional Worlds*, 29–30.
13. *Possible Worlds in Literary Theory*, 143.
14. "Adapting History to the Novel."

fiction by their "inventory"—"identical" (to that of the real world) in the first, "expanded" in the second.[15]

Whereas Napoleon and Pierre perceive the same battle without actually perceiving one another, encounters between characters that belong to different ontological realms are not at all unusual in historical fiction and occur repeatedly at other moments of *War and Peace*. Thus Pierre briefly meets and converses with General Kutúzov, the real leader of the Russian army, on the eve of the Battle of Borodinó (854–55). And Napoleon, noticing the fictional Prince Andrew, lying wounded after the Battle of Austerlitz, addresses a few words to him; while the latter, "looking into Napoleon's eyes . . . thought of the insignificance of greatness" (314). Such close encounters dramatize the tendency of historical novels to assimilate their "immigrants," to treat them as inhabitants of the fictional world that no barrier separates from the natives.

But this tendency is even more strikingly configured by way of inside views of the kind that Tolstoy applies to Napoleon at Borodinó. In this scene, a historical figure is treated just like any other fictional figure, corresponding to Tolstoy's belief that artists and historians "have two quite different tasks before them" when it comes to presenting "heroes": whereas the historian's task is "to represent the [historical] person always in his historical significance," "for the artist treating of man's relation to all sides of life, there cannot and should not be heroes, but there should be men" (1368). It would be hard to imagine a less heroic, a more human moment in Napoleon's life—and one more removed from a historian's vista—than the nightmarish fantasy Tolstoy invents for him in the Borodinó scene. Clearly, when it comes to presenting the inner life of historical figures, the historian's and the novelist's narrative domains are most sharply and most noticeably contrasted.

In this respect, Tolstoy modified the tradition of Sir Walter Scott, in whose novels such immigrants from the real world as the Duke of Argyle, Cromwell, or Louis XI, though they appear in the cast of characters, remain at a distance. They are viewed only through the eyes of the protagonists, who are themselves invariably native to the fictional world. Georg Lukács's admiration for Scott's novels on this account is well known, as is his belief that historical figures should never hold center stage in a nov-

---

15. *Possible Worlds, Artificial Intelligence, and Narrative Theory*, 35. Ryan makes this contrast obligatory for the genre, forgetting that there are some historical novels—e.g., George Garrett's *The Death of the Fox* and Michel Tournier's *Jeanne et Giles*—where *all* the characters are historical figures, and others—like *A Tale of Two Cities*—that include no historical figures at all.

el. It is somewhat paradoxical that Lukács nonetheless—despite the scenes that foreground Napoleon and other historical personages—regarded *War and Peace* as the supreme "historical novel of the classical type." One reason (as he explains himself) is that Tolstoy reduced "the consciously acting 'heroes' of history" to "ludicrous and harmful puppets," while at the same time showing that it is "the living forces of popular life" that move history forward.[16] But in fact, Tolstoy's departure from Scott in this respect is an important pioneering move: his reduction of important men to fallible human beings by looking inside their heads anticipates the practice of modern novelists: Thomas Mann's ways with Goethe in *The Beloved Returns* (where he has him wake in his bed from an erotic dream) or Anthony Burgess's baring the dying thoughts of the French emperor in his *Napoleon Symphony*.

The grounding of the distinction of historical fiction in inside views is sometimes thought to have been muted by those philosophers of history—from Dilthey to Paul Veyne—who understood the historian's task primarily as the presentation and interpretation of past mental attitudes (individual and collective). In my view, however, such theorists rather confirm that the historian's relationship to his human subjects is different *in kind* from the novelist's. This may be illustrated by a look at the work of an influential proponent of this theory in the English-speaking world, R. G. Collingwood, whose ideas on this score are generally thought to make the history/fiction distinction "lose its force."[17]

Granted that Collingwood explicitly attributes to the historian the obligation to "re-enact past experience," to attain in particular a "knowledge of the mind" that allows him to emulate the "inner side" of participants in a historical event.[18] But that Collingwood does not thereby signify an endeavor rivaling the ways of a fictional narrator is plain from the very fact that the historian's "re-enactment" needs to be justified—and Collingwood justifies it at great length. At one point he analogizes it to the process one brings to bear on real persons in everyday life: "If it is by historical thinking that we rethink and so rediscover the thought of Hammurabi or Solon, it is in the same way that we discover the thought of a friend who writes us a letter."[19]

---

16. Georg Lukács, *Studies in European Realism,* selection reprinted in Norton Critical Edition, 1425–26.
17. Mark A. Weinstein, "The Creative Imagination in Fiction and History," 267.
18. R. G. Collingwood, *The Idea of History,* 215–17.
19. Ibid., 219.

The idea that documentation is essential for the discovery of the past thoughts of historical figures is even more strongly stressed when Collingwood draws on the analogy with autobiography—"using that name for a strictly historical account of my own past." An autobiographical account of this sort can only be achieved on the basis of "revealing" indications: "If I want to be sure that twenty years ago a certain thought was really in my mind, I must have evidence of it." The historian, likewise, "by using evidence of the same general kind, can discover the thoughts of others." But Collingwood is acutely aware of the limitations involved in such an attempt. "We shall never know how the flowers smelt in the garden of Epicurus or how Nietzsche felt the wind in his hair as he walked on the mountains; we cannot relive the triumph of Archimedes or the bitterness of Marius. . . . The immediate as such cannot be re-enacted."[20]

Contrary to its reputation, then, the practice of "re-enactment" recommended by Collingwood in no sense makes historical figures transparent in the manner of fiction; rather, it displays the historian's effort to find ways of overcoming their constitutional opacity. As Brian McHale has shown, the classical historical novelist, by contrast, thrives on such opacity: it is precisely within such "dark areas" of history that he can freely use his imagination to "introspect his historical characters."[21]

This freedom applies with particular force to the hidden motivations that lie behind manifest actions. An astute formulation of the history/fiction contrast in this regard may be found in the aesthetic writings of the philosopher Alain: "In short, there is no room for intimacy in history; at best it can bring men to life as we see them in life, always making us move backwards from their actions to their motives. The peculiarity of the novel is its intimacy, an intimacy that cannot be attested, that needs no proof, and that, in reverse of the historical method, makes actions real."[22] What Alain recognizes in this passage is that, where the knowledge of the inner motives of a historical figure is concerned, there is a difference in kind, not just in degree, between historiography and fiction. One could, in such cases, speak of the nescience of the historian as compared the the omniscience of the novelist, keeping in mind that the latter is of course no "science" at all, but free invention. Paradoxical as it may seem that the psychological realism of Tolstoy's Borodinó scenes should be out of reach for a historian bent on recounting reality "as it really was," the fact is that the

20. Ibid., 295–97.
21. *Postmodernist Fiction*, 87.
22. Alain, "Système des Beaux Arts," in *Les Arts et les dieux*, 450–51; my translation.

vision into inner reality depends on the magically unreal optics of fiction.[23]

This is not to say, however, that no historian ever (advertently or inadvertently) adopts this optic, but only that, when he does, a critical reader will notice it and call it to notice. For a standard example, see a review of Joseph E. Persico's *Nuremberg: Infamy on Trial* (1994) by the Holocaust historian James E. Young, subtitled "This account of the Nuremberg trials takes imaginative license." Persico, we are told, produces "novelized history-telling" of a sort that is "neither purely history nor fiction": "Not only does he imagine himself in the hearts and minds of the defendants, but he insinuates himself into the complex relations between prosecutors and judges." At one point this author even "imagines himself into Hans Frank's prison bed in order to bring us the Nazi's wet dreams." No doubt the reviewer would have been less — or at any rate differently — critical if this work had paratextually (by subtitle or preface) presented itself as fiction.

Well-known historians, even when they explicitly announce their transgressive games, do not escape negative criticism altogether. The reception of Simon Schama's *Dead Certainties* (1991) is a case in point. Though his Afterword designates the two pieces it contains as "historical novellas," his critics severely objected to his use of such techniques as interior monologue to present the thoughts of real persons. Gordon S. Wood, for one, found this book highly confusing on this score, reproaching Schama for wanting to "have it both ways" and leaving it unclear "just what his experiment in narration is trying to accomplish."

Returning to the classical historical novel, we have yet to face an important question raised by the treatment of historical events as the experiences of fictional characters: to what degree do these events thereby lose their historical reality?

Theorists who emphasize — as I do myself — the essential separation of the historical novel from historical narrative often insist that their fictional treatment results in a total de-realization of historical events. Paul Ricoeur, for example, writes: "From the mere fact that the narrator and the leading characters are fictional, all references to historical events are di-

23. Though the serious practicing historian's adherence to these constraints has not been widely studied, Philippe Carrard has demonstrated that French New Historians — widely known for their interest in the "history of mentalities" — never "rely on internal focalization to communicate the experiences of the people they are considering"; see *Poetics of the New History*, 111.

vested of their function of standing for the historical past and are set on a par with the unreal status of the other events."[24] Peter Demetz believes that even the inclusion of documentary evidence does not counteract this effect, but rather compounds it: "The ontological result of such interpolations is unexpected: the interpolated document, far from transforming fiction into history, is itself readily transformed into 'fiction' by its fictional surroundings."[25] Käte Hamburger goes so far as to maintain that a specific date inscribed in a historical novel "plays a role no different from that of any other characterization of a day in a novel"; it is "a fictive Now, a Today even, in the life of a [fictional] figure."[26] Applied to *War and Peace,* these theoretical views would signify that the verifiable facts of Russian history that span from July 1805 (the date of Anna Schérer's party, inscribed on the novel's first page) to spring 1813 (the immediate aftermath of the frequently and precisely dated events of Napoleon's 1812 invasion) become part and parcel of the fictional world: that they are transformed into experiential moments in the lives of Natasha, Prince Andrew, Nicholas, and Pierre and wholly detached from history as we know it from other sources.

Such a view of the historical novel seems to me to lose sight of the peculiarity of this genre as compared to other novelistic genres—to lose sight, more precisely, of the peculiar response of a reader who identifies a work *as* a historical novel. In this respect, I agree with Joseph W. Turner, who calls attention to the reader's particularly keen "historical expectations" when reading novels that deal with past events of which he or she has prior knowledge, and especially novels that include characters taken from history.[27] *War and Peace* on the whole conforms to such expectations, adhering in this respect to a general norm of the classical historical novel.[28] It is, in fact, the normalcy of this norm that charges works that *don't* adhere to it with their shock value—most notoriously those postmodern novels Brian McHale calls "apocryphal history."[29]

It is not always easy to decide whether such alternative versions of official history are sociopolitically or aesthetically inspired, whether they are

24. *Time and Narrative,* III:129.
25. *Formen des Realismus: Theodor Fontane,* 21; my translation.
26. *The Logic of Literature,* 110.
27. "The Kinds of Historical Fiction," 343–44.
28. Tolstoy's generally accurate use of his historical sources, as well as his occasional departure from these sources (in the Borodinó section and elsewhere) is examined in R. F. Christian, *Tolstoy's War and Peace,* 59–94.
29. *Postmodernist Fiction,* 90.

to be interpreted as ideological strategies or as artistic games. What is certain is that an individual reader's reaction to them is conditioned by the degree to which the historical material concerned touches on his or her values and sensitivities. When I recently learned certain biographical facts about the desert explorer Laszlo Almasy, for example, my initial admiration for Michael Ondaatje's novel *The English Patient* (in which Almasy figures as the titular character) dropped down a few notches. There is, it seems, documentation to show that Almasy was an opportunistic and highly nefarious Nazi collaborator, not (as the novel shows him) a semi-innocent victim of the ruthless German army. By contrast, my high estimation of Coetzee's *The Master of Petersburg* was not in the least dislodged when I found out that Dostoevsky's stepson Pavel, whose death Coetzee's Dostoevsky mourns throughout the novel, in fact survived him by several years. All this goes to show that, though distortions of known facts in a historical novel may only occasionally detract from our value judgment, we do tend to approach this genre differently from other novelistic genres.

This difference is considerably compounded when a historical novel includes a narrator who sounds—and means to sound—like a historian or a philosopher of history. The pronouncements of Tolstoy's (in)famously loquacious narrator are especially prominent in the Borodinó section where (as I have not mentioned to this point) he supplements the perspectives of Pierre and Napoleon with some chapters presenting his own *backward* look at the events of 1812.[30] Having read the numerous historical accounts that discover a profound meaning in this battle, he declares them to be "all quite wrong" (842). "Why was the battle of Borodinó fought? There was not the least sense in it for either the French or the Russians" (840); "[it] did not take place at all as . . . it has been described" (844). In reality, the troops followed the strategies of neither the French nor the Russian commanders, but "acted according to the mood of the moment. . . . these men were floundering about. . . . Under the influence of fear of death they lost their discipline and rushed about according to the chance promptings of the throng" (893).

In the Borodinó section of *War and Peace,* then, we at times get an emphatically retrospective point of view. It is, however, provided in chapters

---

30. This occurs in five chapters (19, 27, 28, 33, and 39) of the twenty-one that deal with the Battle of Borodinó in book 10. Four chapters of this section focus on Napoleon (26, 29, 34, and 38) and seven on Pierre (20–23 and 30–32). Of the remaining chapters (to which I don't refer in what precedes or follows), three focus on Prince Andrew (24, 36, and 37), one on Kutúzov, and one presents a conversation between Prince Andrew and Pierre (25).

from which all the characters of the novel are conspicuously absent. Here the discourse of the narrator rules supreme, rejecting the historians' false reports and providing his own views on the battle. Largely cast in nescient terms, these views ultimately refer to "some incomprehensible, mysterious power" (912) that controlled all the participants. This temporally distanced essayistic commentary of a narrator cast in the role of (anti)historical spokesman thus remains sharply separated from the fictional experiences of the characters, even as his insistence on the impossibility of knowing and telling the historical truth is clearly reflected in Pierre's and Napoleon's perplexities.

The dichotomy of narrative modes in the latter half of Tolstoy's novel is quite typical of the genre: to one side, the historiographically oriented authorial discourse of a "contemporary" narrator concerned with past events; to the other, the psychologically oriented rendering of the thoughts and feelings of characters involved in experiencing these same events. Though less extensive and less numerous than in *War and Peace,* essayistic disquisitions are often featured in historical novels of the nineteenth century and early twentieth century (notably in those of Scott and Hugo).[31] But if these authorial digressions in themselves sound at times every bit like historiographic texts, they in no sense detract from the specific modes and devices of fiction that reign supreme in the sections of the text with which they alternate.

A corollary to the conception that only fiction-specific *formal* markers essentially distinguish the historical novel from historiography is the conception that only *thematic* differences distinguish between historical novels and all other types of novels. Accordingly, since most novels deal with complex (or complexes of) thematic material, it is not at all easy to decide what is, and what is not, a historical novel. Should we therefore agree with Lukács that there are no grounds at all for differentiating this genre from other novelistic genres?[32] Not, I think, if we bring to thematic differen-

---

31. Hans Vilmar Geppert, in particular, has studied this structural pattern in detail, exemplifying it in such works as Scott's *Waverly,* Hugo's *Quatrevingt-Treize,* Alfred Döblin's *Wallenstein,* and Heinrich Mann's *Henri Quatre* novels (see *Der "andere" historische Roman,* 76–85, 129–35, 139–44). In view of this tradition, Morson seems to me in error when he declares the essayistic language of *War and Peace* to be "deliberately violating" novelistic conventions (*Hidden in Plain View,* 13).

32. This view is held, among others, by Lukács: "Which facts of life underlie the historical novel and how do they differ from those that give rise to the genre of the novel in general? . . . there can only be one answer—none" (*The Historical Novel,* 242). See also Geppert, *Der "andere" historische Roman,* 45.

tiation an awareness of its variability, and particularly of its dependence on the individual reader's relative focus.[33]

This possibility of orienting the reading of a novel toward different thematic emphases applies also to *War and Peace,* the prominence of its war-related scenes notwithstanding. One can, for example, make a case for its being a family novel, dealing essentially with the fortunes of two generations of Rostovs and Bolkónskis. There are equally strong reasons for classifying it as a Bildungsroman: Pierre's development to mature manhood—by way of searching for a father figure, a profession, a suitable wife—is clearly a central theme, as is Natasha's similarly arduous development to mature womanhood. Such readings would take in certain moments of the work that are left out when it is read as a historical novel: the famous hunting sequence in book 7, for example, or the conclusively peaceful lives sampled in the First Epilogue. It is important to realize that, when literary genres are understood in a properly flexible manner, differing classifications are by no means mutually exclusive. In this perspective, there is no contradiction between the classification of *War and Peace* as a historical novel, a family novel, or a (multiple) Bildungsroman, since it is all of these things at once.

To detach it from rigid definitions, to conceive of it in terms of thematic emphasis, is not, however, to deny that, in the wake of Scott, the historical novel became a consolidated genre. Numerous writers, including Tolstoy, created works that more or less conformed to the tradition known by this generic name; while others, like Henry James, quite overtly refused to do so.[34] Late twentieth-century novelists, moreover, variously play with its conventional norms: John Fowles in *The French Lieutenant's Woman,* for example, ironizes the hindsighted narrator; whereas Dieter Kühn in *N* deliberately alters the known historical facts of the Napoleonic era.[35] But whether taken up seriously (in a "classical" vein) or playfully (in a postmodern vein) the historical themes of this thematically determined genre can always be disregarded in favor of other thematic concerns.

By the same token, I would propose that it is on principle possible to read *any* novel as a historical novel. An approach of this sort is tantamount

33. For the idea that—among the several extremely heterogenous criteria used for defining literary genres—numerous designations rely primarily on thematic differences, see Jean-Marie Schaeffer, *Qu'est-ce qu'un genre littéraire?* 108.

34. See James's letter (dated October 5, 1901), where he wrote: "The 'historical novel' is, for me, condemned . . . to a fatal *cheapness;* . . . the real thing is almost impossible to do."

35. For surveys of these developments, see McHale, *Postmodernist Fiction,* 84–96; Linda Hutcheon, "'The Pastime of Past Time,'" 54–74; Nünning, *Von historischer Fiktion zu historiographischer Metafiktion,* Vol. 2.

to bypassing all narrowly arbitrary definitions of this fictional genre: one, for example, that would insist on a temporal distance of at least two (or one) generation between the date of the fictional action and the date of writing, and that would exclude such novels as *The Possessed* or *The Counterfeiters*; or one that would insist on the presence of historical figures, and that would exclude such novels as *A Sentimental Education*. Even novels that don't overtly refer to verifiable public events, such as *Malte Laurids Brigge* or *Notes from Underground,* contain themes that tie them to their specific spatio-temporal settings. And even fictional works that create such apparently unfamiliar orders of reality as *The Castle* can be (have been) understood as allegories of familiar historical situations.

This way of coming to terms with the term *historical novel* actually takes it quite literally: its noun indicates (to use Döblin's words) that it "is, in the first place, a novel"; its adjective points to the fact that, although "it isn't history," the historical dimension is (may be considered to be) more importantly involved in certain novels than in others. What is more, conceiving the genre in this broad and elastic way ties the works one assigns to it more solidly to the fiction side of the great divide—the divide I have been highlighting throughout this volume.

10

Optics and Power in the Novel

Optical imagery has traditionally pervaded the language of critics and the-orists of fiction: window and mirror, microscope and telescope, lens and X ray, perspective and focalization, reflection and transparency. Recently, in the wake of Michel Foucault, a further trope has been added to this se-ries: the panopticon and its derivatives: panopticism, panoptic vision, panoptical narration. However, unlike the more standard ocular images that are as a rule used descriptively and neutrally to characterize norms and types of novelistic representation, the panoptic conceit is powerfully charged with negative meaning and is invariably contextualized in ideo-logical interpretations that cast a peculiarly hostile light on the novel as a genre and/or on its practitioners.

Before exemplifying this critical optics, we need a brief reminder of the significance that Foucault himself attributes to the panopticon in the sec-tion of *Discipline and Punish* entitled "Panopticism." At its origin stands, of course, the innovative design proposed by Jeremy Bentham for prison architecture in 1791: the inmates are confined to lighted cells that surround a tower from which a guard observes them while remaining himself in-visible. Foucault explains that this spatial arrangement functions as "a ma-chine for dissociating the see/being seen dyad: in the peripheric ring, one is totally seen, without ever seeing; in the central tower, one sees every-thing without ever being seen."[1] He stresses, moreover, that the "state of conscious and permanent visibility" thereby induced in the prisoner "as-sures the automatic functioning of power." According to Foucault, all in-stitutions of what he calls "the disciplinary society"—schools, hospitals, factories, the family—are modeled on this panoptic schema; all are en-dowed with "the instrument of permanent, exhaustive, omnipresent sur-veillance, capable of making all visible, as long as it could itself remain in-visible"; all are "like a faceless gaze that transformed the whole social body into a field of perception: thousands of eyes posted everywhere, mobile attentions ever on the alert."[2]

1. Michel Foucault, *Discipline and Punish*, 202.
2. Ibid., 214.

As dispassionate readers of these pages have no doubt noted, Foucault rather obsessively overstates the absolute power of the one-way gaze that he derives from Bentham's penitentiary design.[3] Modern institutions that supposedly transfix their charges in this manner are not, after all, known to produce uniformly and perfectly obedient and submissive prisoners, students, workers, or sons/daughters. But I shall leave this critique to social scientists. More relevant for introducing the concerns of the present chapter is to acknowledge the power Foucault himself has exerted, largely by way of his panoptic thesis, on ideological approaches to the novel; to note that this thesis has, for the most part, been accepted quite uncritically; to speculate that its appeal may have depth-psychological grounds related to the invisibly all-seeing parental eye abidingly lodged in our unconscious and that each and all of us secretly wish to find and blind; and to anticipate my argument by suggesting that, even if one grants that panopticism may apply to the power relations represented within fictional worlds no less than to those enacted in the real world, serious problems are raised by its application to the formal relations that pertain between novelistic narrators and fictional characters.

FOUCAULT-DERIVED APPROACHES TO FICTION

These problems first arrested me in a study in which formal concerns are clearly subordinated to thematic concerns: D. A. Miller's *The Novel and the Police*. In this explicitly "Foucaldian reading of the Novel,"[4] the analogy between narrative technique and panoptic vision only briefly and quite locally enters what is in other respects a provocatively cogent argument concerning the fiction of the Victorian canon. Even so, the moment in question—a couple of pages of the introductory chapter[5]—deserves close scrutiny because it features a number of ideas we will meet again in the work of other Foucault-influenced critics.

Miller arrives at the problematic analogy by way of the uncanny and impenetrable visionary power with which Balzac endows his fictional police agents in *Une ténébreuse Affaire*. At this point the argument begins to move from impressionistic parallels between the police and the novelist— "Not unlike the novel, the new police has charge of a 'world' and a 'plot'"; "They [Balzac's *agents*] thus resemble the novelist whose activity is also conceived as a penetration of social surfaces"—to their full-fledged iden-

---

3. As I will note below, Foucault qualifies the unidirectionality of power relations far more strongly at other moments of his oeuvre.
4. *The Novel and the Police*, viii, n. 1.
5. Ibid., 23–25.

tification: "Balzac's omniscient narration assumes a fully panoptic view of the world it places under surveillance. Nothing worth knowing escapes its notation, and its complete knowledge includes the knowledge that it is always right" (230). Continuing to model his discourse on Foucault's, Miller further describes the Balzacian narrator's "infallible supervision" as follows: "This panoptic vision constitutes its own immunity from being seen in turn. For it intrinsically deprives us of the outside position from which it might be 'placed.' . . . We are always situated inside the narrator's viewpoint, and even to speak of a 'narrator' at all is to misunderstand a technique that . . . institutes a faceless and multilateral regard" (24). It soon becomes clear that what is described here applies not only to the Balzacian narrative,[6] but quite generally to so-called omniscient narration. The masters of Realism—the pages that immediately follow refer to Flaubert, George Eliot, Trollope, and Zola—all police their fictional worlds by means of "panoptical narration."

In sum: novel writing equals policing. What enables the positing of the identity is quite simply a huge rhetorical leap—from matter to manner, mimetic theme to narrative technique. Incomparable differences are left yawning below: between the nature of political and artistic power, real and fictional worlds, and ocular vision enhanced by empirical observation and the uniquely privileged and entirely unreal vision that generic convention grants to "omniscient" novelistic narrators. Reserving a closer look at these disregarded differentials for a later context, I will first follow Miller's corollary comments regarding novelistic form, then move on to other critics who have proposed a similar thesis.

Foucault is not the only theorist on whom Miller draws for his panoptic vision of the novel. He also calls on a witness whose testimony is rarely missing from critical cases these days: Mikhail Bakhtin. After acknowledging the narrator's absolute control over his discourse, Miller tells us: "The panopticism of the novel thus coincides with what Mikhail Bakhtin has called its 'monologism': the working of an implied master-voice whose accents have already unified the world in a single interpretive center." It hardly needs pointing out that the only way Bakhtin can be made to support this view of "the novel" is by turning him on his head. He viewed this genre—excluding only the monologic Tolstoy—as the dialogic literary form par excellence, as constitutionally polyphonic or het-

---

6. Even if one were willing to share Miller's view for this particular author, one would surely have to defend it against certain readers of Balzac who are by no means "deprived of an outside position": for example, Roland Barthes, who characterizes Balzac's authorial voice as "nauseating" (*S/Z: An Essay*, 206).

eroglossic; and he wrote hundreds of pages detailing the techniques that enforce its plural vision, among them narratorial irony and free indirect style.

Miller's brief remarks on this latter device, though he assumes them to confirm his Bakhtinian affiliation, in fact fly in the face not only of the Russian theorist but also of the numerous narratologists who have analyzed this notoriously ambiguous and complex narrative device. Since free indirect style is the means by which a narrator, far from imposing his own voice on his characters, allows them to impose *their* voices *on him,* Miller takes it to be an instance of what he calls "shamming." Even as free indirect style masterfully camouflages the abiding power of the "master-voice," it "simultaneously subverts their [the characters'] authority and secures its own." Thanks to Foucault, Miller here easily recognizes "the basic move of a familiar power play, in which the name of power is given over to one agency in order that the function of power may be less visibly retained by another" (25).

Following this aperçu on free indirect style, Miller's introductory chapter modulates back to thematic matters, to the "story of social discipline" that his subsequent readings of nineteenth-century novels will exemplify thematically.[7] Indeed, the ideas on narrative form outlined above remain largely extraneous to the principal development of *The Novel and the Police*.[8] Even so, they begin to delineate the astonishing picture that emerges when the novel is viewed in light of the panopticon.

Enlarged, and with more details filled in, the same picture is found in the work of other critics who have been inspired by the same Foucaldian image. They all tend to present the novel, particularly in its realist guise, as a genre whose form replicates the malevolent power structures of a society that both produces and consumes it, a genre that—though Machiavellian tactics may at times hide its target—exists largely in order to wield absolute cognitive control over the lives of the characters it incarcerates and whose psyches it maliciously invades and inspects.

My attention will focus on two critical studies that feature these more extensive versions of the novel-panopticon equation, Mark Seltzer's *Henry James and the Art of Power* (1984) and John Bender's *Imagining the Penitentiary: Fiction and the Architecture of Mind in Eighteenth-Century En-*

---

7. Miller, *The Novel and the Police,* 27.
8. Miller only briefly returns to these ideas when he mentions free indirect style in the Trollope chapter (ibid., 137 and 139). This is hardly surprising in view of the fact that Miller's other chapters are almost exclusively concerned with first-person novels.

gland (1987). As their titles indicate, they differ widely in both subject matter and scope. We will see, however, that their vision is parallel and their design at times overlapping.[9]

Though Seltzer's book takes the form of a single-author monograph, he makes it clear from the start that for him James is the supreme (and most extreme) representative of fictional realism. His ideological approach is thus directed at the novel as a genre even as it focuses on the oeuvre of a paradigmatic practitioner. He also emphasizes early on that what he calls "the politics of the novel" determines the genre's manner no less than its matter, so that his critique will of necessity target both at once: "Power and authority are not external interventions in the novel but are already immanent in the novelist's policies of representation. In fact, the techniques of representation that James invents to defer, dissimulate, and disavow the technologies of power that pressure his texts reinvent these very technologies." And: "The Jamesian techniques of narrative seeing and point of view reproduce social modes of surveillance and supervision . . . the realist project operates through a comprehensive surveillance and policing of the real."[10]

Though Foucault will only be called on to support this view further on, it is evident that the panopticon already looms over the rhetoric of this introductory outline of Seltzer's thesis. When it makes its explicit appearance, the context is predictable: "Perhaps the most powerful tactic of supervision achieved by the traditional realist novel inheres in its dominant technique of narration—the style of 'omniscient narration' that grants the narrative voice an unlimited authority over the novel's 'world,' a world thoroughly known and thoroughly mastered *by the panoptic 'eye' of the narration*. The technique of omniscient narration . . . [results from] the fantasy of such *an absolute panopticism*."[11] Here again, then, as in Miller's work, realist fiction is conceived as a prison whose character-subjects are governed by omniscient supervision from the malevolent central tower.

Seltzer has to concede, of course, that James's fiction does not, on the face of it, conform to this panoptic schema. As everyone knows, in his major works "omniscient narration" consistently gives way to the focalized

---

9. Miller's book (1988) actually postdates the books by Seltzer and Bender; however, its initial chapter, which contains the Panoptic analogy, was originally published in *Glyph* 8 (1981) and was known to Seltzer (who refers to it in a note). Since Bender, so far as I can see, refers to neither Miller nor Seltzer, I must assume that his ideas were developed independently—which only makes the triple coincidence more significant.

10. Mark Seltzer, *Henry James and the Art of the Novel*, 15–16 and 18.

11. Ibid., 54; my emphases.

vision of a fictional figure—the figure James himself alternately tagged "central consciousness" and "central intelligence." How can "limited omniscience," as this narrative mode is often (and paradoxically) termed, still qualify for the "unlimited authority" that rules its subjects by "absolute panopticism"? Not surprisingly, Seltzer—who brings up this question in his discussion of James's most overtly political novel, *The Princess Casamassima*—is ready with an answer that further reinforces his thesis: in order to disengage himself from "the spy mania that the novel [by way of its plot] everywhere engages," from the "compelling resemblance between his haunting and perpetual prowling and the surveillance and policing," he "disavows any direct interpretive authority over the action" and offers "the alibi of a 'powerless' imagination."[12] (Note how close the terms of this explanation—"disavows," "alibi"—come to Miller's conception of free indirect style as "shamming.")

Though Seltzer does not adhere to his early focus on fictional form in the later chapters of his work—least of all in his reading of *The Golden Bowl* where, as he maintains, "policing has achieved a discretion that allows for neither overt recognitions nor protests"[13]—we can assume that the evil design he attributes to James's modified version of conventional realist techniques is at least partially responsible for the virulence of his ultimate condemnation of Jamesian ambiguity: he calls it "absurd confusion," charging that it "at once names and screens the criminal [!] continuities of the Jamesian work."[14]

Even as Bender's *Imagining the Penitentiary* rivals Seltzer's book in the negative light it casts on realist fiction, its historical focus is on the mid-eighteenth-century beginnings rather than the late-ninteenth-century culmination of this tradition. Its principal analogic thesis concerning novelistic form, moreover, is not the *intra*textual parallel between theme and technique posited by Seltzer's reading of James novels but the *inter*-textual parallel between innovative architectural designs for penitentiaries and innovative verbal devices for presenting characters in contem-

---

12. Ibid., 55–56.
13. Ibid., 64.
14. Ibid., 156–57. Henry James, incidentally, had a far more direct (and far more critical) connection to the panopticon than the one Seltzer attributes to his novelistic technique. Having read Charles Dickens's "Philadelphia, and Its Solitary Prisons"—where a fellow realist novelist recounted his visit to the panoptic Eastern Penitentiary—James went to see this institution for himself, talked to its inmates, and reported on it in *The American Scene*. (I owe this information to the anonymous reader of my book for the Johns Hopkins University Press.)

poraneous novels.[15] In this respect, Bender's study is more overtly allied to new historicism or cultural poetics than either Miller's or Seltzer's,[16] though in my view it all too readily exemplifies the weak points of this critical movement—which have been called its "facile associationism" and its "arbitrary connectedness."[17]

Bender's analogic thesis is most explicitly and insistently stated in the following passage:

> In the realist novel, fictional consciousness is experienced as actuality through the convention of transparency, epitomized by the device of free indirect discourse, which presents thought as if it were directly accessible. . . . *Correlatively,* the penitentiary [i.e., the prison built on the model of Bentham's Panopticon] stages impersonal, third-person presence . . . so as to represent an actual character and conscience as fictions capable of alteration. The penitentiary habilitates, in its own technical practices, devices *parallel* to those of free indirect discourse. The mode of literary production and the social institution present *collateral* images of one another.[18]

Here and elsewhere, Bender teases out the presumed likeness between novel and prison by using concepts with (at least) double meanings. I count no less than four such lexical ambiguities in the quoted passage: "transparency," "character," "technical practices" (as well as its synonym "devices"), and "fiction." I will return in a later context to the first of these terms, transparency, which most crucially enables Bender's simile-creating argument throughout his book. Here I will merely note what semantic analysis could readily demonstrate: that each of these words denotes a different, entirely distinctive meaning when it is employed in literary-critical discourse as compared to its application to physical, social, or psychological reality.[19]

---

15. By taking this central thesis as my exclusive concern, I am not able to do justice to the richness and variety of Bender's book. *Imagining the Penitentiary* does not, in fact, follow a single line of argument; and many of its analyses—among others, the discussion of Defoe's prison narratives, of the interrelation between Fielding's juridical and novelistic careers, of Adam Smith's concept of sympathy—add valuable insights to the history of the eighteenth-century novel.

16. See Bender's self-characterization of his book as representative of new historicism in Stephen Greenblatt and Giles Gunn, eds., *Redrawing the Boundaries,* 81.

17. Dominick LaCapra's and Walter Cohen's phrases, quoted in *Redrawing the Boundaries,* 400.

18. Bender, *Imagining the Penitentiary,* 203; my emphases.

19. The confusion between the meaning of "fiction" as literary, nonreferential narrative and its meaning (often, as here, in its plural form) as theoretical construct is pervasive in modern literary criticism (see Chapter 1 above). In Bender's book (see esp. 213) this confusion is both

As the above quote makes clear, the axial device of realist narrative that orients Bender's panoptic vision of the novel is free indirect style—unlike Miller and Seltzer, who, as we have seen, consider this technique as something of an embarrassment (to be explained away, as sham or alibi).[20] But although many conventions of realism did actually become established during the decades that gave birth to panoptic prison designs, this is not the case for free indirect discourse (whose vogue was launched by Flaubert in the 1850s). This technique for rendering a character's consciousness was only quite sporadically used by eighteenth-century novelists, and barely at all by the English masters who partake in *Imagining the Penitentiary*.[21] Historically speaking, at any rate, the case for a "correlative," "parallel," "collateral" relationship between these two cultural phenomena seems to me entirely spurious. As I have already indicated, I view this relationship as highly misleading in a theoretical perspective as well, for reasons I will now explain in greater detail.

FOUCAULT AND THE NOVEL

Before stepping onto narratological grounds for a critical evaluation of the panopticon as an analogue for fictional form, a brief excursion onto Foucaldian grounds is in order. Without pretending to expertise in this domain, I am struck by at least two essential misunderstandings on Miller's, Seltzer's, and Bender's part in their critical applications of the French theorist's ideas to the poetics of the novel.

The first concerns the functioning of power in Foucault's theory. As he repeatedly spells out—most clearly in an essay entitled "The Subject and Power"—the exercise of power is "always a way of acting upon an acting subject or acting subjects by virtue of their acting or being capable of action. A set of actions upon other actions" (789). Power relations, in oth-

---

stimulated and compounded by the fact that Bentham points up at some length the obscurities of "fiction" (clearly in the sense of theoretical construct), which he tries to expel from legal language; see Ross Harrison, *Bentham,* a work to which Bender refers (213ff.), but without noticing his own semantic quid pro quo.

20. Bender too refers to Bakhtin in his discussion of free indirect style (ibid., 211–13 and 305–6, n. 25). Unlike Miller, however, he forthrightly faces his differences from the Russian theorist in this respect, maintaining that "Bakhtin romanticizes the novel" and as a result "neglects the containment of heterodoxy effected within the realist mode, where narration itself invisibly controls, contains, and becomes authoritative" (213). Strangely, however, he believes that "Bakhtin's treatment of the novel lays comparatively little stress on the issue of narrative structure," so that he can nonetheless rely on Bakhtin's "theory of ideology as communicative practice" (304).

21. No one familiar with this device would recognize it in the single quote from *Tom Jones* that Bender provides (ibid., 178) to show that "Fielding figures in the early history of free indirect discourse" (177).

er words, can only exist between entities that coexist, ontological equals that share the same space and the same time. Foucault further specifies that this relationship cannot be conceived without assuming the freedom of *both* participants: "Power is exercised only over free subjects, and only insofar as they are free" (790). He even insists—and this is especially relevant to the panoptic situation—that "there is no relationship of power without the means of escape or possible flight," and that such relations imply "at least *in potentia*, a strategy of struggle" that "may become a confrontation between two adversaries" (794).

Clearly then, such terms as "surveillance," "discourse of power," or "panoptic vision" make sense only when they are applied to relationships that are potentially reversible: master/slave (cf. Hegel), police/criminal, prison-guard/prisoner, parent/child, teacher/pupil, man/woman, and many more. They make no sense at all—no Foucaldian sense, at any rate—when they are applied to an author's (or heterodiegetic narrator's) relationship to his fictional characters. The latter do not exist on the same ontological plane as the former; they are not free subjects who can potentially escape their graphic prisons and make fictional subjects of—or even talk back to—their author or narrator (except of course in certain self-destructing novels like Unamuno's *Mist*). This is not to say that fiction has no truck with power. It goes without saying that its content can, and often does (as in the novels discussed by Miller, Seltzer, and Bender), represent disciplinary spaces where the powerful rule over the powerless, by faceless gaze or otherwise. But no matter how unequal their power status, fictional characters are all equally inhabitants of the same conflicted fictional world.

Another fiction-related connection between ontological equals, the one between authors and readers, is more controversial in respect to its virtual power play. Whereas for Lennard Davis "the author is like an all-powerful parent," and readers willingly allow novelists to "dominate and master them,"[22] Philippe Hamon follows Bakhtin in regarding the novel as a normative "patchwork" or ideological "polyphony," constitutionally incapable of indoctrinating the reader.[23]

The divergent conclusions of these two theorists open to a second blind spot in the panoptic critique of fiction: it disregards Foucault's own stance toward literature. Both his early critical writings and his rare later allusions to the novel genre suggest that he would have disavowed this di-

---

22. *Resisting Novels: Ideology and Fiction*, 140 and 144.
23. *Texte et idéologie: valeurs, hiérarchies et évaluations dans l'oeuvre littéraire*, 221.

rect transfer of his master trope from the sociohistorical to the aesthetic realm.[24] Davis, his Foucault-derived ideology notwithstanding, faces this problematic transfer more squarely than Miller, Seltzer, and Bender.[25] He comments on this matter briefly as follows: "[Foucault] avoids getting entangled in the stickier web of literature whose relation to power is more ambiguous than subjects like incarceration. Certainly a literary work is not governed by the law . . . or housed in a panopticon of incarceration. *Whose* power is asserted is a far more complex question."[26]

This "far more complex question" is given a duly complex answer in Simon During's study *Foucault and Literature: Toward a Genealogy of Writing*. During believes that a correctly understood Foucault would lead to a literary history that recognized the connection of past works with "the problematizations and 'undecidabilities' in which they were both written and continue to be read" (238). He arrives at this conclusion by way of close readings of a number of realist and naturalist novels in which the narrator's discourse, far from articulating (or camouflaging) the victimizing power with which Miller, Seltzer, and Bender charge it, is characterized by "its ideological emptiness and unflinchingness, . . . its refusal to offer any commentary based on belief" (60). During understands that this narratorial vacuity is the precondition for the reach of novelistic texts into what he calls "deep subjectivity," the presentation of the inner life of

24. See Simon During, *Foucault and Literature,* 68–91, on Foucault's early articles about a number of modern literary figures (Roussel, Bataille, Robbe-Grillet, and others). The single brief remark on the novel in Foucault's *Discipline and Punish* (193–94)—where the eighteenth-century "passage from the epic to the novel" (from highborn heroes to lowborn antiheros) is related to the newly awakened "scientifico-disciplinary" curiosity about the psyche—concerns the genre's typical subject matter, not its standard form. This idea is further developed in the introduction to *The Life of Infamous Men* in Meaghan Morris and Paul Patton, eds., *Michel Foucault,* 89–91, where we also find a direct (and cautiously complex) statement about the relation of literature to societal power: "Literature forms part of that great system of constraint by which the West compelled the everyday to bring itself into discourse; *but it occupied a special space there* . . . . [It tends] *to place itself outside the law* or at all events to take upon itself the charge of scandal, of transgression or of rebellion. More than any other form of language, it remains the discourse of 'infamy': it remains its task to say the most unsayable—the worst, the most intolerable, the shameless" (91; my emphases). Significantly, the first clause of this passage is quoted by Seltzer to support his thesis (*Henry James and the Art of the Novel,* 50), but he stops short of quoting the essential but-clause and the sentence that follows it.
25. In a general sense (but without specific reference to the panopticon analogy), all three of these critics do acknowledge that their application of Foucault to literature represents something of a departure from the letter of their master, but all three also assert that they nonetheless follow his spirit. See Miller, *The Novel and the Police,* viii, n. 1; Bender, *Imagining the Penitentiary,* xv; and Seltzer's lengthy "Postscript: Reading Foucault: Cells, Corridors, Novels," in *Henry James and the Art of the Novel,* 171–95, where he argues his case against Foucaldian critics who "project an essential autonomy of the literary and an intrinsic opposition of literary resistance and social practices of regulation" (174).
26. Davis, *Resisting Novels,* 44.

characters that induces the reader to understand (and share) the predicaments of social victims like Clyde Griffiths of *An American Tragedy*.

Though During's book so manifestly reorients its vision of the realist-naturalist novel's structure away from critics who view it in the light of Foucault's panopticism, his passing comments on these critics (197–98) are, to my mind, all too mild and restrained.[27] His timidity may not be unrelated to his rather loosely empirical approach to matters of fictional form, seemingly quite uninformed by work in the field of narrative poetics—the ground on which I draw for the critical comments that follow.

NARRATOLOGICAL CONSIDERATIONS

I will group these remarks under three headings: transparency, omniscience, and focalization.

Transparency

Like all concepts designating physical properties, *transparency*, the concept that denotes the quality "of transmitting light so that objects beyond are entirely visible" (Webster's), can be used metaphorically. Certain linguists, for example, speak of the transparency of language when it becomes unnoticeable (effaced) in constative (referential) statements.[28] A comparable tropological meaning attends the word in the discourse of aesthetics. According to Arthur Danto, when the viewer of an artwork seeks an illusion of reality, pretending that the graphic medium is invisible, he holds to the "transparency theory."[29] Its antonym, which Danto labels "opaque theory," would apply to a formalist artist or art critic who maintained that "the artwork is only the material it is made from."[30] Similarly, Nelson Goodman believes that literary texts are characterized by the nontransparency (or opacity) of their language; in a fictional narrative, "what counts is not the story told, but how it is told."[31]

The assumption of transparency that Danto attributes to the naive museum goer, of course, has a highly respectable ancestry in the paratextual discourse of novelists with a realist orientation, where it inspires such im-

---

27. During merely suggests that the work of Foucaldian critics "passes too confidently from history to writing," that it "starts from a historical epoch and moves mimetically to examine its products." Both Miller's and Bender's books receive positive mention in this context (242, n. 7).
28. See François Récanati, *La Transparence et l'énonciation*, 84–87, for a critical analysis of this term, which is associated with "representationalism" in linguistic discourse.
29. *The Transfiguration of the Commonplace*, 157.
30. Ibid., 159.
31. *Of Mind and Other Matters*, 137.

ages as house of glass (Zola), windows (James), and glass pane (Sartre). Conversely, for modernists and postmodernists "transparency" figures as a crucially denigrating term in their critique of realist fiction, signifying the benighted ignorance of the impact of presentational conventions on presented content (discourse on story), the illusion that the linguistic sign immediately and invisibly gives access to the world as it is.[32]

An altogether different metaphoric use is made of transparency in the title and thesis of my book *Transparent Minds*. Whereas in all the above theories transparency symbolizes a disregard of the medium for the message, in my own study this same term imagistically foregrounds the medium itself: the set of devices that allows a fictional text to penetrate to the silent thoughts and feelings of its characters, artifactually traversing a visual barrier that remains forever closed to real eyes in real life (and narratives concerned with real life). Stressing the tropological divergence, one might say that what is "transparent" in Cohn's sense is "opaque" in Danto's and Goodman's sense—a paradox that arises solely from different figurative applications of an optical term. This paradox suggests, however, that realist fiction may not be as simplistically "transparent" as it is reputed to be in certain critical quarters.

If we now ask whether either of these metaphoric transparencies has anything to do with Bentham's glass-celled panopticon—or, by extension, with Foucault's panopticism—the answer must be a decisive *no*. My principal objection to Bender's *Imagining the Penitentiary* is that its thesis is essentially built on the deceptive analogy between the architectural optics of the panopticon and the metaphoric optics of Cohn, which Bender in turn confuses with the meaning attributed to transparency by Danto and contemporary critics of realism.[33] I detect this flawed conceptual basis at several moments of the Bender book, notably in the following generalizations that introduce the chapter culminating his analogic argument: "The representation of reflective consciousness in fiction [cf. Cohn], the juridical definition of character and conscience, and the conception of reformative confinement under the penitentiary regime [cf. Foucault] are interlocking developments. . . . Transparency is the convention that both author and beholder are absent from the representation [cf. Danto], the objects of which are rendered as if their externals were en-

32. See Christopher Nash, *World-Games: The Tradition of Anti-Realist Revolt,* 20, for assent to this description of realism; Christopher Prendergast, *The Order of Mimesis,* 59–60, for a more qualified assessment.

33. For Bender's explicit references to Cohn, see *Imagining the Penitentiary,* 253, n. 2; 295, n. 34; 303, n. 19. For mention of Danto's work, see 303, n. 17; this note also includes references to several contemporary critics of realism, one of which is also quoted in the main text (210–11).

tirely visible and their internality fully accessible [cf. Cohn]."[34] Though other critics with panopticon-inspired views on fictional form display their framing presuppositions less explicitly, they seem to me no less confusingly inspired by the plural semantics of the transparency concept.

Omniscience

As Gérard Genette has pointed out, *omniscience,* a standard term routinely applied by anglophone critical discourse to the third-person (or heterodiegetic) novel, is nothing short of absurd: "The author has nothing to 'know' since he invents everything."[35] Proposing to replace it with the phrase "complete information," Genette goes on to show that novelists in fact persistently tend to *restrict* the information they provide. They restrict it most systematically when they apply the technique Genette calls "(internal) focalization": when the fictional world is presented by way of the perception of one of the characters that inhabit it (e.g., Stephen Dedalus or Joseph K.). Since this technique involves the fiction-specific privilege of mind-reading, the narrator who restricts information in this fashion in fact reveals matters that would never be available to a real-world observer or narrator (which explains the even more absurd tag of "limited omniscience" sometimes affixed to this narrative mode).

Qualified and modified in this fashion, "omniscience" can now be seen to refer to an artifactual phenomenon constitutionally unrelated to the panopticon. Two incomparable processes are involved: to one side, a revelatory vision that provides imagined beings with an imagined inner life; to the other, a spatial arrangement designed to lead to empowering knowledge—the knowledge that, for Foucault, *is* power—for the guardian in the tower observing his prisoners in their translucent cells.[36] The guardian (and this holds true as well for his analogues: the teacher, the psychiatrist, the parent) can only perceive his subjects' manifest behavior, which he can punish or reward. He can *not* perceive their minds or see the world through their eyes—though he may, of course, adhere to the illusory belief that a show of obedience reflects psychic conformity.

34. Ibid., 201.
35. *Narrative Discourse Revisited,* 74.
36. Despite my belief (expressed earlier) that Foucault would have disavowed the similitude of carcereal surveillance and novelistic omniscience, it must be conceded that his formulations in *Discipline and Punish* are misleading on occasion. At one point, for example, he talks of an "omnipresent and omniscient power" (197). Elsewhere he writes: "The perfect disciplinary apparatus would make it possible for a single gaze to see everything constantly. A central point would be . . . the source of light illuminating everything . . . a perfect eye that nothing would escape" (173).

Its invalidity notwithstanding, it would appear that the comparison of "omnisciently" presented subjects in fiction and panoptically supervised prisoners has made considerable inroads into critical consciousness. I judge this from a recent article by Richard Hull entitled "Critique of Characterization." Overtly hoping to rescue the novel from the bad reputation it has acquired from critics like Miller, Seltzer, and Bender, Hull proposes ways in which the genre can "escape the policing function of the prevailing narrative discourse" (42). What he means by this latter phrase, as well as by his titular term "characterization," is essentially the "omniscient" presentation of inside views: the "invasive" devices that heterodiegetic narrators employ to enter the minds of their characters. The "non-characterizing techniques" that Hull points up with a view to rehabilitating the genre turn out to be nothing more nor less than those employed in first-person (or homodiegetic) novels. Attributing Hawthorne's choice of this novel-form in *The Blithedale Romance* to his "horror of panoptic exposure," he explains that "Coverdale's [the narrator's] refusal to characterize Priscilla is given as a loving respect for her privacy" (42).[37] But the fact is, of course, that loving respect or not, a homodiegetic narrator—whose voice belongs to a character incarnated in the fictional world—is by nature incapable of seeing into the minds of his or her fellow characters.[38] In this sense, first-person novels may be said to adhere to fundamentally different norms from those followed by third-person novels. But what Hull seems to forget is that there is one figure in Hawthorne's novel (as in all self-narrated novels) that *is* fully "characterized," namely Coverdale, the narrator, himself; his mind, no less fictional than that of other characters, stands fully exposed in (and by way of) his narration. First-person fiction, far from offering the escape-hatch sought by Hull, must clearly be regarded as merely a different tactic available for the novelist to communicate his "omniscient" knowledge of the figures he creatively imagines, inner life and all.

37. In point of fact, Coverdale is not nearly as discreet as Hull makes him out to be. He alternates between confused speculations about the mental state of his friends and acquaintances (including Priscilla) and awareness of his limited knowledge. What is more, Hawthorne seems to have had no trouble whatever in overcoming his "horror for panoptic exposure" in such third-person novels as *The Marble Faun* and *The Scarlet Letter*.
38. To be sure, this realistic norm, like all norms, can be transgressed: by more or less inadvertent lapse (tagged "paralepsis" in Genette, *Narrative Discourse*, 195) or (more spectacularly) by providing a flesh-and-blood narrator with magic instruments (as in E. T. A. Hoffmann's *Meister Floh*) or supernatural mental powers (as in George Eliot's *The Lifted Veil*).

Focalization

Under this heading several controversial matters must be taken up. I will begin by recapitulating what I take to be a set of well-established narratological views.

Narrative theorists distinguish between two types of presentation (or modes) in the third-person novel. In the first type—labeled "zero focalization" by Genette, "authorial narration" by Stanzel—the narrator maintains his own vantage point on the fictional world and its inhabitants, often telling us in no uncertain terms what he thinks of it and of them. In the second type—labeled "internal focalization" by Genette, "figural narration" by Stanzel—the fictional happenings are filtered through the experience of a character, with the narrator reduced to a merely functional presence. Though this distinction can be demonstrated by contrasting specific works (say, *Tom Jones* versus *What Maisie Knew*), the narrative text of most third-person novels weaves back and forth between these abstract types. One can nonetheless readily discern an overall historical change in the course of the nineteenth century, with Flaubert and James credited for an influential role in moving the novel from the first type to the second. In terms of novelistic technique, this change is associated with the increasing doses of free indirect style injected into novelistic discourse.

So far—differences in conceptual formulation notwithstanding—we are on firm consensual ground. But the more controversial region lies just a step away, a step that classical narratology usually stops short of taking—for good reasons, I think, since it leads beyond strictly descriptive poetics. We take this step as soon as we ask whether the two different narrative types correspond to two different ideological orientations.[39]

Critics who give a positive answer to this question have tended to believe that novels of the first type, especially when they are told by a loudly audible, moralistically judgmental narrator, are designed to propagate clear and absolute values, beliefs authoritatively held and didactically targeted. Conversely, they associate novels of the second type with a liberal stance that believes in normative flexibility and allows for multiple and ambiguous meaning. These associations of modal types with ideological positions are articulated quite as readily by critics who value the first type over the second (Wayne Booth) as by those—far more numerous in our

---

39. I deliberately omit from this discussion matters concerning focalization in first-person novels, where this concept applies as well but determines types with less distinct ideological implications. It should be noted, however, that critics often attribute to first-person narration as a whole (regardless of its focalization) the same meanings as to figural focalization in third-person novels.

own time—who value the second type over the first (Jean-Paul Sartre, Roland Barthes). It is no doubt their sense of how firmly this correspondence is entrenched that induces Miller's, Seltzer's, and Bender's defensive rhetoric when they insist on the panopticism of writers known to favor figural focalization (Flaubert, James), whereas they take this power-practice pretty much for granted when they discuss novelists who favor authorial focalization (Fielding, Balzac).

Miller's, Seltzer's, and Bender's particular insistence on the hidden power play involved in free indirect style also has a reason: this device has been the linchpin for understanding figural focalization as a (positively valued) liberal or (negatively valued) unstable fictional form, a form that counteracts all virtual claims the novel might make (and actual claims it has made) to communicating absolute truth.[40]

The most cogent development of this thesis in my purview is found in Dominick LaCapra's *Madame Bovary on Trial*. LaCapra concludes from a close examination of the documents that one of the principal concerns at this famous trial was whether Flaubert's novel presented "a reliable center of value and judgment which integrated various aspects of experience in an intelligible and secure manner" (56). He then proposes (like Hans Robert Jauss before him) that the centrality of this question—and perhaps the trial itself—was due to the prominence of free indirect style in Flaubert's novel. Understanding the Bovary trial as a particularly vivid illustration of his belief that "the question of 'style' and of narrative practice cannot be separated from the larger sociocultural and political issues" (127), LaCapra ultimately suggests the following origin and meaning for the style in question: "The larger cultural context that induces or facilitates the widespread use of free indirect style . . . is one wherein the writer is fairly definite about what he rejects in the larger society . . . but relatively uncertain and clearly undogmatic about viable alternatives. In this sense, the free indirect style might be seen (in an extension of Bakhtin's analysis) as a complex, exploratory, and often muted form of satire with carnivalesque features" (140). The Bakhtinian reference in this passage— with the "carnivalesque" (as well as "dialogic") meaning he attributes to the device even more strongly stressed in earlier and later passages[41] —is only one indication of the diametric opposition between LaCapra's so-

---

40. For two instances of this view (which stems from such authoritative scholars as Erich Auerbach and Wolfgang Kayser), see Roy Pascal, *The Dual Voice: Free Indirect Speech and Its Functioning in the Nineteenth-Century European Novel*, 49; and Philippe Hamon, *Texte et idéologie*, 223–24.

41. See esp. 148–49.

ciopolitical evaluation of free indirect style and that of Miller, Seltzer, and Bender.

There are at least two reasons why I find LaCapra's understanding of free indirect style in *Madame Bovary* far more plausible and convincing than the one prompted by the panoptic perspective on the realist novel. For one thing, he bolsters it by considerably closer attention to Flaubert's text than most other contextual critics—a group that includes not only Miller, Seltzer, and Bender, but the many cultural historians who, like La-Capra himself, adopt the more established perspective on free indirect style. For another thing, his discussion of Flaubert's narrative technique is solidly—though by no means uncritically—grounded in narratological work.[42]

But persuasive as I find LaCapra on free indirect style in the Flaubert novel, his "speculation" (as he himself calls the passage quoted above) becomes shaky to the extent that he intends for it to apply to the global meaning of this device, across the fictional board. For in my view, free indirect discourse can no more be understood as bearing a single, fixed ideological-cultural meaning, than can the figurally focalized type of fiction in which it is most often found and than can the contrastive, authorially focalized fictional type.

This brings me to a few final remarks to convey my skeptical assessment of all manners of simple and stable correspondence of modal type and moral stance. First, the traditional link between authorially focalized novels and clear normative values begins to fall apart as soon as one becomes aware that such novels open to a different reading option: one in which the judgmental narrator is not understood as a spokesman for the author but as a fictional voice whose normative comments on characters and events may not be reliable. A reading option of this kind has been increasingly adopted by critical readers of this type of novel in the last two decades, resulting in a series of new interpretations of canonical works.[43]

The traditional link between figurally focused novels and normative liberalism can be (and has been) loosened as well, on both theoretical and empirical grounds. I don't mean its ideologically motivated rupture, in the manner of Miller, Seltzer, and Bender, which merely reassigns figurally focalized novels (together with the novel genre in toto) to the oth-

42. See LaCapra's extensive comments on Ullmann, Cohn, Pascal, and other students of free indirect style (129–46).

43. See, for example, Eric A. Blackall's chapter on Goethe's *Elective Affinities* in *Goethe and the Novel* and Wolfgang Iser's chapter on *Vanity Fair* in *The Implied Reader*. See also my reading of *Death in Venice* in Chapter 8 above. A theoretical basis for these interpretations is provided in Félix Martínez-Bonati, *Fictive Discourse and the Structures of Literature*.

er, the conservative-autocratic pole. What I mean is a reassessment that opens our eyes to the fact that novels with a strongly propagandistic agenda can be focalized by one or more of their characters. What is more, this can be worked in two very different ways, depending on the positive or negative personality traits that are assigned to the focalizer. As Susan Lanser has shown, recent novels by African-American women writers use figural narration, including free indirect style, extensively to advance the cause of their race and gender.[44] Conversely, Sartre in the novella "L'Enfance d'un chef" ("The Childhood of a Leader") draws on these same techniques to present the portrait of a nefarious anti-Semite. In both of these cases, the authors have an unambiguous political-ethical agenda, with the African-American writers drawing on the potential of free indirect style to create sympathy for their protagonists, and Sartre drawing on its ironic-satirical potential to create antipathy.[45]

In sum, a novel bent on transmitting the most decisive values may rely on figural focalization, just as a novel intended to present normative ambiguities may be focalized by an eloquent narrator. I would maintain that this potential reversal of the mode-meaning correspondence vastly complicates the interpretive task. It sounds a cautionary note for ideologically oriented critics who, if they glance at fictional form at all, tend to preconceive it on rudimentary lines, passing far too rapidly from technique to interpretation, as well as from text to context.

Such cavalier imposition of univalently predetermined meaning on narrative form is even more disturbing when it is practiced on a larger scale, in the manner of Miller's, Seltzer's, and Bender's imposition of the panopticon on the novelistic genre as a whole. Though all three refer to narratological concepts—notably free indirect style—they show no awareness of the complexities involved. These moments in their works tend to make one despair about the potential use narratology—admittedly not a user-friendly discipline—could have for sociopolitical theories of literature. Still, there have been a few rarely felicitous meetings between narrative poetics and ideology, some of which I have mentioned above.[46] So perhaps there is hope for more to come. But first we had better close down the panopticon.

---

44. *Fictions of Authority*, 200.
45. On this dual virtuality of free indirect style, see Cohn, *Transparent Minds*, 116–26.
46. LaCapra, *Madame Bovary on Trial*; Lanser, *Fictions of Authority*; Hamon, *Texte et idéologie*. See also Susan Rubin Suleiman, *Authoritarian Fictions*.

References

Abbott, H. Porter. "Autobiography, Autography, Fiction: Groundwork for a Taxonomy of Textual Categories." *New Literary History* 19 (1988), 597–615.

Alain. *Les Arts et les dieux*. Paris, 1958.

Allemand, André. *L'Oeuvre romanesque de Nathalie Sarraute*. Neuchatel, 1980.

Arendt, Hannah. *Eichmann in Jerusalem: A Report on the Banality of Evil*. New York, 1963.

Atwood, Margaret. *The Handmaid's Tale*. New York, 1985.

Bal, Mieke. *Narratology: Introduction to the Theory of Narrative*. Trans. Christine von Boheemen. Toronto, 1985.

Banfield, Ann. *Unspeakable Sentences: Narration and Representation in the Language of Fiction*. London, 1982.

Barthes, Roland. "Historical Discourse." In *Introduction to Structuralism*, ed. Michael Lane. New York, 1970.

———. *Image—Music—Text*. Trans. Stephen Heath. New York, 1974.

———. *The Rustle of Language*. Trans. Richard Howard. New York, 1986.

———. *S/Z: An Essay*. Trans. Richard Miller. New York, 1974.

Beck, Hans-Joachim. *Der Selbstmord als eine schöne Kunst begangen: Prolegomena zu Wolfgang Hildesheimers psychoanalytischem Roman "Marbot. Eine Biographie."* Frankfurt am Main, 1986.

Bellos, Daniel M. "The Narrative Absolute Tense." *Language and Style* 13 (1980), 77–84.

Bender, John. *Imagining the Penitentiary: Fiction and the Architecture of the Mind in Eighteenth-Century England*. Chicago, 1987.

Benveniste, Emile. *Problems in General Linguistics*. Trans. Mary Elizabeth Meek. Coral Gables, Fla., 1971.

Berkhofer, Robert. "The Challenge of Poetics to (Normal) Historical Practice." *Poetics Today* 9 (1988), 435–52.

Berlin, Isaiah. *The Hedgehog and the Fox: An Essay on Tolstoy's View of History*. New York, 1970.

Bertin, Celia. *Marie Bonaparte: A Life*. New York, 1982.

Blackall, Eric A. *Goethe and the Novel*. Ithaca, N.Y., 1976.

Booth, Wayne. *The Rhetoric of Fiction*. Chicago, 1961.

Bowie, Malcolm. *Freud, Proust, and Lacan: Theory as Fiction*. Cambridge, 1987.

Brée, Germaine. *Marcel Proust and the Deliverance of Time*. Trans. C. J. Richards and A. D. Truitt. New Brunswick, N.J., 1955.

Brooke-Rose, Christine. "The Readerhood of Man." In *The Reader in the Text*, ed. Susan Suleiman and Inge Crosman. Princeton, N.J., 1980.

Brooks, Peter. *Reading for the Plot: Design and Intention in Narrative*. New York, 1984.

Bruss, Elizabeth. *Autobiographical Acts: The Changing Situation of a Literary Genre*. Baltimore, 1976.

Campion, Pierre. "Le 'Je' proustien: Invention et exploitation de la formule." *Poétique* 89 (1992), 3–29.

Carrard, Philippe. *Poetics of the New History: French Historical Discourse from Braudel to Chartier*. Baltimore, 1992.

———. "Récit historique et fonction testimoniale." *Poétique* 65 (1986), 47–61.

Casparis, Christian. *Tense without Time: The Present Tense in Narration*. Bern, 1975.

Certeau, Michel de. *L'Ecriture de l'histoire*. Paris, 1975.

———. "The Freudian Novel: History and Literature." *Humanities and Society* 4 (1981), 121–44.

Chatman, Seymour. *Story and Discourse: Narrative Structure in Fiction and Film*. Ithaca, N.Y., 1978.

Christian, R. F. *Tolstoy's War and Peace*. Oxford, 1962.

Coetzee, J. M. "Time, Tense and Aspect in Kafka's 'The Burrow.'" *MLN* 96 (1981), 556–79.

———. *Waiting for the Barbarians*. New York, 1982.

Cohn, Dorrit. *Transparent Minds: Narrative Modes for Presenting Consciousness in Fiction*. Princeton, N.J., 1978.

Collingwood, R. G. *The Idea of History*. Oxford, 1946.

Corngold, Stanley. *The Fate of the Self: German Writers and French Theory*. New York, 1986.

Culler, Jonathan. "Fabula and Sjuzhet in the Analysis of Narrative." *Poetics Today* 1 (1980), 27–37.

Danto, Arthur. *The Transfiguration of the Commonplace*. Cambridge, Mass., 1981.

———. "Philosophy as/and/of Literature." In *Literature and the Question of Philosophy*, ed. Anthony J. Cascardi. Baltimore, 1987.

Davis, Lennard J. *Factual Fictions: The Origins of the English Novel*. New York, 1983.

———. *Resisting Novels: Ideology and Fiction*. New York, 1987.

Day, Geoffrey. *From Fiction to Novel*. London, 1987.

Delay, Jean. *The Youth of André Gide*. Trans. June Guicharnaud. Chicago, 1963.

Deleuze, Giles. *Proust and Signs*. Trans. Richard Howard. New York, 1972.

De Man, Paul. *Allegories of Reading*. New Haven, Conn., 1979.

———. "Autobiography as Defacement." *Modern Language Notes* 94 (1979), 919–30.

———. *Blindness and Insight*. Oxford, 1971.

Demetz, Peter. *Formen des Realismus: Theodor Fontane*. Munich, 1964.

Derrida, Jacques. "The Purveyor of Truth." *Yale French Studies* 52 (1975), 31–113.

Descombes, Vincent. *Proust: Philosophy of the Novel*. Trans. Catherine Chance Macksey. Stanford, Calif., 1992.

Döblin, Alfred. *Aufsätze zur Literatur*. Olten und Freiburg im Breisgau, 1963.

Doležel, Lubomír. "Truth and Authenticity in Narrative." *Poetics Today* 1 (1980), 7–25.

Doubrovsky, Serge. *Writing and Fantasy in Proust: La Place de la Madeleine*. Trans. Carol Mastrangelo Bové. Lincoln, Neb., 1992.

During, Simon. *Foucault and Literature: Toward a Genealogy of Writing*. London, 1992.

Eakin, Paul John. *Fictions in Autobiography: Studies in the Art of Self-Invention*. Princeton, N.J., 1985.

———. *Touching the World: Reference in Autobiography*. Princeton, N.J., 1992.

Eickhenbaum, Boris. *Tolstoy in the Sixties*. Trans. Duffield White. Ann Arbor, Mich., 1982.

Ellison, David. *The Reading of Proust*. Baltimore, 1984.

Ellmann, Richard. *James Joyce*. Oxford, 1959.

Emerson, Caryl. "The Tolstoy Connection in Bakhtin." *PMLA* 100 (1985), 68–80.

Flaubert, Gustave. *A Sentimental Education*. Trans. Douglas Parmée. Oxford, 1989.

Fleischman, Suzanne. *Tense and Narrative: From Medieval Performance to Modern Fiction*. Austin, Tex., 1990.

Fludernik, Monika. *Toward a "Natural" Narratology*. London, 1996.

Foley, Barbara. *Telling the Truth: The Theory and Practice of Documentary Fiction*. Ithaca, N.Y., 1986.

Foucault, Michel. *Discipline and Punish: The Birth of the Prison*. Trans. Alan Sheridan. New York, 1979.

———. "The Subject and Power." *Critical Inquiry* 8 (1982), 777–95.

Freud, Sigmund. *Gesammelte Werke*. 18 vols. London, 1952.

——. *The Standard Edition of the Complete Psychological Works*. Trans. James Strachey. 24 vols. London, 1953–74.

Gay, Peter. *Freud: A Life for Our Time*. New York, 1988.

Gearhart, Suzanne. *The Open Boundary of History and Fiction*. Princeton, N.J., 1984.

Genette, Gérard. *Fiction and Diction*. Trans. Catherine Porter. Ithaca, N.Y., 1993.

——. *Fiction et diction*. Paris, 1991.

——. *Figures III*. Paris, 1972.

——. *Figures of Literary Discourse*. Trans. Alan Sheridan. New York, 1988.

——. *Narrative Discourse: An Essay in Method*. Trans. Jane E. Lewin. Ithaca, N.Y., 1980.

——. *Narrative Discourse Revisited*. Trans. Jane E. Lewin. Ithaca, N.Y., 1988.

——. *Palimpsestes*. Paris, 1982.

——. *Seuils*. Paris, 1987.

Geppert, Hans Vilmar. *Der "andere" historische Roman*. Tübingen, 1976.

Gill, Christopher, and T. P. Wiseman. *Lies and Fiction in the Ancient World*. Exeter, 1993.

Glowínski, Michál. "On the First-Person Novel." *New Literary History* 9 (1977), 103–14.

Goffman, Erving. *Frame Analysis*. New York, 1974.

Goodman, Nelson. *Of Mind and Other Matters*. Cambridge, Mass., 1984.

Grass, Günter. *Cat and Mouse*. Trans. Ralph Manheim. New York, 1963.

Greenblatt, Stephen, and Giles Gunn, eds. *Redrawing the Boundaries*. New York, 1992.

Grésillon, A., J. L. Lebrave, and C. Viollet. *Proust à la lettre: les intermittences de l'écriture*. Tussin, 1990.

Guerard, Albert. *André Gide*. Cambridge, Mass., 1951.

Habermas, Jürgen. *Erkenntnis und Interesse*. Frankfurt am Main, 1973.

Hamburger, Käte. "Authenticity as a Mask: Wolfgang Hildesheimer's *Marbot*." In *Neverending Stories: Toward a Critical Narratology,* ed. Ann Fehn, Ingeborg Hoesterey, and Maria Tatar, 87–97. Princeton, N.J., 1992.

——. *The Logic of Literature*. Trans. Marilynn Rose. Bloomington, Ind., 1973.

Hamon, Philippe. *Texte et idéologie: valeurs, hiérarchies et évaluations dans l'oeuvre littéraire*. Paris, 1984.

Harrison, Ross. *Bentham*. London, 1983.

Harshaw, Benjamin. "Fictionality and Fields of Reference." *Poetics Today* 5 (1984), 227–51.

Heissenbüttel, Helmut. "Die Puppe in der Puppe oder der Hildesheimer im Marbot." *Süddeutsche Zeitung* (November 1981), 21–22.

Heller, Erich. *The Ironic German: A Study of Thomas Mann*. Boston, 1958.

Hernadi, Paul. "Clio's Cousins: Historiography as Translation, Fiction, and Criticism." *New Literary History* 7 (1976), 247–57.

Hildesheimer, Wolfgang. "Arbeitsprotokolle des Verfahrens 'Marbot.'" *Jahrbuch der deutschen Akademie für Sprache und Dichtung*, 1982.

――. "The End of Fiction." *Merkur* 30 (1976), 57–70.

――. "Gespräch mit Wolfgang Hildesheimer." *Deutsche Bücher* 9 (1979), 187–91.

――. *Marbot. A Biography*. Trans. Patricia Crampton. New York, 1983.

――. *Marbot. Eine Biographie*. Frankfurt am Main, 1981.

――. *Mary Stuart: Eine historische Szene*. Frankfurt am Main, 1977.

――. *Mozart*. Frankfurt am Main, 1977.

――. *Mozart*. Trans. Marion Faber. New York, 1982.

Hull, Richard. "Critique of Characterization: It Was In Not Knowing That He Loved Her." *Style* 26 (1992), 33–49.

Hutcheon, Linda. "Metafictional Implications for Novelistic Reference." In *On Referring in Literature*, ed. Anna Whiteside and Michael Issacharoff. Bloomington, Ind., 1987.

――. "'The Pastime of Past Time': Fiction, History, Historiographic Metafiction." In *Postmodern Genres*, ed. Marjorie Perloff. Norman, Okla., 1989.

Imbs, Paul. *L'Emploi des temps verbaux en français moderne*. Paris, 1960.

Iser, Wolfgang. "Feigning in Fiction." In *Identity of the Literary Text*, ed. Mario J. Valdes and Owen Miller. Toronto, 1985.

――. *The Fictive and the Imaginary: Charting Literary Anthropology*. Baltimore, 1993.

――. *The Implied Reader*. Baltimore, 1974.

James, Henry. *The Art of the Novel: Critical Prefaces*. New York, 1962.

Kafka, Franz. *The Castle*. Trans. Willa and Edwin Muir. New York, 1969.

Kawin, Bruce H. *The Mind of the Novel*. Princeton, N.J., 1982.

Kayser, Wolfgang. "Wer erzählt den Roman?" In *Die Vortragsreise*. Bern, 1958.

Keller, Ulrich. *Fiktionalität als literaturwissenschaftliche Kategorie*. Heidelberg, 1980.

Kermode, Frank. *The Sense of an Ending: Studies in the Theory of Fiction*. Oxford, 1968.

Kesting, Hanjo. *Dichter ohne Vaterland: Gespräche und Aufsätze zur Literatur*. Berlin, 1982.

Kittler, Friedrich. *Aufschreibsysteme 1800/1900*. Munich, 1987.

Kosinski, Jerzy. *The Painted Bird*. New York, 1978.

Kracauer, Siegfried. *Das Ornament der Masse*. Frankfurt am Main, 1963.

Kristeva, Julia. *Time and Sense: Proust and the Experience of Literature*. Trans. Ross Guberman. New York, 1996.

LaCapra, Dominick. *Madame Bovary on Trial*. Ithaca, N.Y., 1982.

Lamarque, Peter, and Stein Haugom Olsen. *Truth, Fiction and Literature: A Philosophical Perspective*. Oxford, 1994.

Lang, Berel. *The Anatomy of Philosophical Style*. Oxford, 1990.

Lanser, Susan. *Fictions of Authority*. Ithaca, N.Y., 1992.

Lejeune, Philippe. *Moi aussi*. Paris, 1980.

———. *On Autobiography*. Trans. Katherine Leary. Minneapolis, 1989.

Ludwig, Emil. *Napoleon*. Trans. Eden and Cedar Paul. London, 1927.

Lukács, Georg. *The Historical Novel*. London, 1962.

MacDonald, Margaret. "The Language of Fiction." *Proceedings of the Aristotelian Society,* Suppl. 28 (1954), 165–84.

Mahony, Patrick. *Cries of the Wolf Man*. New York, 1984.

———. *Freud and the Rat Man*. New Haven, Conn., 1986.

Malcolm, Janet. "Reflections: J'appelle un chat un chat." *New Yorker,* 20 April 1987, 84–102.

Mann, Thomas. *Death in Venice and Other Stories*. Trans. David Luke. London, 1990.

———. *Dichter über ihre Dichtungen,* Teil I. Munich, 1975.

———. *Gesammelte Werke in zwölf Bänden*. Frankfurt am Main, 1960.

Mannoni, Maud. *La Théorie comme fiction: Freud, Groddeck, Winnicott, Lacan*. Paris, 1979.

Marcus, Steven. *Freud and the Culture of Psychoanalysis: Studies in the Transition from Victorian Humanism to Modernity*. Boston, 1984.

———. *Representations: Essays on Literature and Society*. New York, 1975.

Margolin, Uri. "Reference, Coreference, Referring, and the Dual Structure of Literary Narrative." *Poetics Today* 12 (1991), 517–42.

Marquand, Odo. "Kunst als Antifiktion." In *Funktionen des Fiktiven,* ed. Dieter Henrich and Wolfgang Iser. Munich, 1983.

Martin-Chauffier, Louis. "Proust et le double 'Je' de quatre personnages." In *Les Critiques de notre temps,* ed. Jacques Bersani, 54–66. Paris, 1971.

Martínez-Bonati, Félix. "The Act of Writing Fiction." *New Literary History* 11 (1980), 425–34.

——. *Fictive Discourse and the Structures of Literature: A Phenomenological Approach*. Trans. Philip W. Silver. Ithaca, N.Y., 1981.

Mason, Jeffrey Mousaieff, ed. and trans. *The Complete Letters of Sigmund Freud to Wilhelm Fliess, 1887–1904*. Cambridge, Mass., 1985.

May, Georges. *L'Autobiographie*. Paris, 1979.

McCormick, Peter. *Fictions, Philosophy, and Poetics*. Ithaca, N.Y., 1988.

McGuire, William, ed. *The Freud/Jung Letters: The Correspondence Between Sigmund Freud and C. G. Jung*. Trans. Ralph Manheim and R. F. C. Hill. Princeton, N.J., 1974.

McHale, Brian. *Postmodernist Fiction*. New York, 1987.

——. "Unspeakable Sentences, Unnatural Acts: Linguistics and Poetics Revisited." *Poetics Today* 4 (1983), 7–45.

Miller, D. A. *The Novel and the Police*. Berkeley, Calif., 1988.

Mink, Louis. "Narrative Form as a Cognitive Instrument." In *The Writing of History*, ed. Robert H. Canary and Henri Kozicki. Madison, Wisc., 1978.

Morris, Humphrey. "The Need to Connect: Representations of Freud's Psychical Apparatus." In *The Literary Freud: Mechanisms of Defense and the Poetic Will*, ed. Joseph H. Smith. New Haven, Conn., 1980.

Morris, Meaghan, and Paul Patton, eds. *Michel Foucault: Power, Truth, Strategy*. Sidney, 1979.

Morson, Gary Saul. *Hidden in Plain View: Narrative and Creative Potentials in "War and Peace."* Stanford, Calif., 1987.

Muller, Marcel. *Les Voix narratives dans La Recherche du temps perdu*. Paris, 1965.

Nägele, Rainer. *Reading after Freud*. New York, 1987.

Nash, Christopher. *World-Games: The Tradition of Anti-Realist Revolt*. London, 1987.

Neumann, Ann Waldron. "Escaping the 'Time of History'? Present Tense and the Occasion of Narration in J. M. Coetzee's *Waiting for the Barbarians*." *The Journal of Narrative Technique* 20 (1990), 65–89.

Nietzsche, Friedrich. *The Will to Power*. Trans. Walter Kaufmann and R. J. Hollingdale. New York, 1967.

Nünning, Ansgar. *Von historischer Fiktion zu historiographischer Metafiktion*. 2 vols. Trier, 1995.

Ogden, C. R., ed. *Bentham's Theory of Fiction*. New York, 1932.

Pascal, Roy. *The Dual Voice: Free Indirect Speech and Its Functioning in the Nineteenth-Century European Novel*. Manchester, 1977.

Pavel, Thomas G. "Between History and Fiction." In *Neverending Stories: To-*

ward a Critical Narratology, ed. Ann Fehn, Ingeborg Hoesterey, and Maria Tatar. Princeton, N.J., 1992.

———. *Fictional Worlds.* Cambridge, Mass., 1986.

———. *L'Art de l'éloignement: Essai sur l'imagination classique.* Paris, 1996.

———. *The Poetics of Plot: The Case of English Renaissance Drama.* Minneapolis, 1985.

Pawel, Ernst. *The Nightmare of Reason: A Life of Franz Kafka.* New York, 1984.

Pike, Burton. "Thomas Mann and the Problematic Self." *Publications of the English Goethe Society* 37 (1967), 120–41.

Potts, L. J. *Aristotle on the Art of Fiction.* Cambridge, 1953.

Prendergast, Christopher. *The Order of Mimesis.* Cambridge, 1980.

Prince, Gerald. *Narratology: The Form and Functioning of Narrative.* Amsterdam, 1982.

Proust, Marcel. *A la Recherche du temps perdu.* 4 vols. Paris, 1989.

———. *Remembrance of Things Past.* 3 vols. Trans. C. K. Scott Moncrieff and Terence Kilmartin. London, 1981.

Pugh, Anthony Cheal. "Claude Simon: Fiction and the Question of Autobiography." *Romance Studies* 8 (1986), 81–96.

Récanati, François. *La Transparence et l'énonciation: Pour introduire à la pragmatique.* Paris, 1979.

Reed, T. J. *Death in Venice: Making and Unmaking a Master.* New York, 1994.

———. *Thomas Mann: The Uses of Tradition.* Oxford, 1974.

Ricoeur, Paul. "Narrative Time." *Critical Inquiry* 7 (1980), 169–90.

———. "The Question of Proof in Psychoanalysis." *Journal of the American Psychoanalytic Association* 25 (1977), 835–71.

———. *Time and Narrative.* Trans. Kathleen McLaughlin and David Pellauer. Chicago, 1983–88.

Riffaterre, Michael. *Fictional Truth.* Baltimore, 1990.

Rigney, Ann. "Adapting History to the Novel." *New Comparison* 8 (1989), 127–43.

———. *The Rhetoric of Historical Representation: Three Narrative Histories of the French Revolution.* Cambridge, 1990.

Rimmon-Kenan, Shlomith. *Narrative Fiction: Contemporary Poetics.* London, 1983.

Roloff, Volker. "Die Entwicklung von 'A la Recherche du temps perdu.'" *Romanische Forschungen* 97 (1985), 165–96.

Ronen, Ruth. *Possible Worlds in Literary Theory.* Cambridge, 1994.

Rousseau, Jean-Jacques. *Les Confessions.* Paris, 1963.

Ryan, Marie-Laure. "Fiction as a Logical, Ontological, and Illocutionary Issue." *Style* 18 (1984), 121–39.

———. "The Modes of Narrativity and Their Visual Metaphors." *Style* 26 (1992), 368–87.

———. *Possible Worlds, Artificial Intelligence, and Narrative Theory*. Bloomington, Ind., 1991.

Sartre, Jean-Paul. *Nausea*. Trans. Lloyd Alexander. New York, 1964.

Schabert, Ina. "Fictional Biography, Factual Biography, and Their Contaminations." *Biography* 5 (1982), 1–16.

———. *In Quest of the Other Person: Fiction as Biography*. Tübingen, 1990.

Schaeffer, Jean-Marie. *Qu'est-ce qu'un genre littéraire?* Paris, 1989.

Schafer, Roy. "Narration in the Psychoanalytic Dialogue." *Critical Inquiry* 7 (1980), 29–53.

———. *Narrative Action in Psychoanalysis: Narratives of Space and Narratives of Time*. Worcester, Mass., 1981.

Schmidt, Siegfried J. "Toward a Pragmatic Interpretation of 'Fictionality.'" In *Pragmatics of Language and Literature*, ed. T. van Dijk. Amsterdam, 1976.

Scholes, Robert. "Language, Narrative and Anti-Narrative." *Critical Inquiry* 7 (1980), 204–12.

Searle, John. "The Logical Status of Fictional Discourse." *New Literary History* 6 (1975), 319–32.

Seltzer, Mark. *Henry James and the Art of the Novel*. Ithaca, N.Y., 1984.

Sherwood, Michael. *The Logic of Explanation in Psychoanalysis*. New York, 1969.

Sloan, James Park. "Kosinski's War." *New Yorker*, 10 October 1994, 46–53.

Smith, Barbara Herrnstein. *On the Margins of Discourse: Relations of Literature and Language*. Chicago, 1978.

———. "Narrative Versions, Narrative Theories." *Critical Inquiry* 7 (1980), 213–36.

Stael, Germaine de. *Zulmar et trois nouvelles*. London, 1813.

Stanley, Patricia H. *Wolfgang Hildesheimer and His Critics*. Columbia, S.C., 1993.

Stanzel, Franz K. *A Theory of Narrative*. Trans. Charlotte Goedsche. Cambridge, 1984.

Stern, J. P. "Sweet Sin." *London Review of Books*, 5–18 August 1982.

Sternberg, Meir. "Mimesis and Motivation: Two Faces of Fictional Coherence." In *Literary Criticism and Philosophy*, ed. Joseph P. Strelka. University Park, Pa., 1983.

Stewart, Philip. *Imitation and Illusion in the French Memoir Novel, 1700–1750*. New Haven, Conn., 1969.

Stierle, Karlheinz. "Erfahrung und narrative Form: Bemerkungen zu ihrem

Zusammenhang in Fiktion und Historiographie." In *Theorie und Erzählung in der Geschichte,* ed. J. Kocka and Th. Nipperdey. Munich, 1979.

———. "Geschehen, Geschichte, Text der Geschichte." In *Geschichte, Ereignis, Erzählung,* ed. Reinhart Koselleck and Wolf-Dietrich Stempel. Munich, 1973.

Strachey, Lytton. *Queen Victoria.* London, 1928.

Struve, Gleb. "Monologue intérieur: The Origin of the Formula and the First Statements of its Possibilities." *PMLA* 69 (1954), 1101–11.

Sturgess, Philip M. *Narrativity: Theory and Practice.* Oxford, 1992.

Suleiman, Susan Rubin. *Authoritarian Fictions: The Ideological Novel as a Literary Genre.* New York, 1983.

Swales, Martin. Review of Wolfgang Hildesheimer's *Marbot. Eine Biographie.* *Arbitrium* 3 (1983), 318–22.

Tadié, Jean-Ives. *Proust et le roman: Essai sur les formes et les techniques du roman dans "A la Recherche du temps perdu."* Paris, 1971.

Toliver, Harold. *Animate Illusions: Explorations of Narrative Structure.* Lincoln, Neb., 1974.

Tolstoy, Leo. *The Death of Ivan Ilyitch and Other Stories.* Trans. Aylmer Maude. New York, 1960.

———. *War and Peace.* Trans. Louise and Aylmer Maude. [The Norton Critical Edition]. New York, 1966.

Trimpi, Wesley. *Muses of One Mind.* Princeton, N.J., 1983.

Tuchman, Barbara. *The Guns of August.* New York, 1976.

Turner, Joseph W. "The Kinds of Historical Fiction: An Essay in Definition and Methodology." *Genre* 12 (1979), 333–55.

Uspensky, Boris. *A Poetics of Composition.* Berkeley, Calif., 1973.

Vaihinger, Hans. *Die Philosophie des Als Ob: System der theoretischen, praktischen und religiösen Fiktionen der Menschheit.* Leipzig, 1911.

———. *The Philosophy of "As if": A System of the Theoretical, Practical, and Religious Fictions of Mankind.* Trans. C. K. Ogden. London, 1924.

von Gronicka, André. "Myth Plus Psychology: A Stylistic Analysis of *Death in Venice.*" In *Thomas Mann: A Collection of Critical Essays,* ed. Henry Hatfield. Englewood Cliffs, N.J., 1964.

Wapnewski, Peter. Review of Wolfgang Hildesheimer, *Marbot. Eine Biographie.* *Der Spiegel,* 4 January 1982.

Warning, Rainer. "'Gefängnismusik': Feste des Bösen in Prousts *La Prisonnière.*" In *Das Fest,* ed. W. Haug and R. Warning. Munich, 1989.

———. "Romantische Tiefenperspektivik und moderner Perspektivismus: Chateaubriand, Flaubert, Proust." In *Romantik: Aufbruch zur Moderne,* ed. Karl Maurer and Winfried Wehle. Munich, 1991.

————. "Supplementäre Individualität: Prousts 'Albertine disparue.'" In *Individualität*, ed. M. Frank and A. Haverkamp. Munich, 1988.

————. "Vergessen, Verdrängen und Erinnern in Prousts *A la Recherche du temps perdu*." In *Memoria: Vergessen und Erinnern,* ed. Anselm Haverkamp. Munich, 1993.

Weinrich, Harald. *Tempus: Besprochene und erzählte Welt*. Stuttgart, 1964.

Weinstein, Mark A. "The Creative Imagination in Fiction and History." *Genre* 9 (1976), 263–77.

Weisstein, Ulrich. "Wolfgang Hildesheimer's *Marbot*: Fictional Biography and Treatise on Comparative Literature." *Yearbook of Comparative and General Literature* 32 (1983), 23–38.

Wesseling, Elizabeth. *Writing History as a Prophet: Postmodernist Innovation of the Historical Novel*. Amsterdam, 1991.

White, Hayden, *The Content of the Form*. Baltimore, 1987.

————. *Tropics of Discourse: Essays in Cultural Criticism*. Baltimore, 1978.

Williams, Raymond. *Key Words: A Vocabulary of Culture and Society*. Oxford, 1985.

Wilson, Edmund. *The Shores of Light*. New York, 1952.

Wilson, Jonathan. "Counterlives: On Autobiographical Fiction in the 1980s." *Literary Review* 31 (1988), 389–402.

Wolfe, Tom, and E. W. Johnson, eds. *The New Journalism*. New York, 1973.

Wolfson, Nessa. "Tense-Switching in Narrative." *Language and Style* 14 (1981), 226–31.

Wood, Gordon S. Review of Simon Schama, *Dead Certainties*. *New York Review of Books,* 27 June 1991.

Woolf, Virginia. *Collected Essays,* Vol. IV. London, 1966.

Wright, Susan. "Tense Meaning as Style in Fictional Narrative: Present Tense Use in J. M. Coetzee's *In The Heart of the Country*." *Poetics* 16 (1978), 53–73.

Yacobi, Tamar. "Fictional Reliability as a Communicative Problem." *Poetics Today* 2 (1981), 113–36.

Yehoshua, A. B. *The Lover*. Trans. Philip Simpson. New York, 1977.

Yerushalmi, Yosef Hayim. "Freud on the 'Historical Novel': From the Manuscript Draft (1934) of *Moses and Monotheism*." *International Journal of Psycho-Analysis* 70 (1989), 375–95.

Young, James E. Review of Joseph E. Persico, *Nuremberg: Infamy on Trial*. *New York Times Book Review,* 29 May 1994.

Zavarzadeh, Mas'ud. *The Mythopoetic Reality: The Postwar American Non-fiction Novel*. Urbana, Ill., 1976.

Index

Abbott, H. Porter, 31n
Alain, 156
Allemand, André, 106n
Almasy, Laszlo, 159
Arendt, Hannah, 31
Aristotle, 9, 10, 11
Atwood, Margaret: *The Handmaid's Tale*, 97; *Surfacing*, 97
Auerbach, Erich, 178n

Bacon, Francis, 4n
Bakhtin, Mikhail, 18, 26, 165–66, 170n, 171, 178
Bal, Mieke, 109n, 111n, 119n
Balzac, Honoré de, 123n, 138, 165n, 178; *Louis Lambert*, 29; *Une ténébreuse Affaire*, 164
Banfield, Ann, 25n
Barthes, Roland, 68, 71–72, 109, 111, 116, 118–19, 123, 138, 165n, 178
Bataille, Georges, 76, 172n
Beck, Hans-Joachim, 80n
Bellos, Daniel M., 106n
Bender, John, 5n, 168–74, 176, 178–80
Bentham, Jeremy, 3–5, 163–64, 170n, 174
Benveniste, Emile, 24, 99n, 103, 118
Berkhofer, Robert, 112, 113
Berlin, Isaiah, 152n
Bertin, Celia, 28n
Besant, Walter, 11
Blackall, Eric, 179n
Blanckenburg, Friedrich von, 86
Booth, Wayne, 33–35, 73, 125, 129n, 130, 133n, 177
Borges, Jorge Luis, 38
Bowie, Malcolm, 1, 7
Brée, Germaine, 67, 75

Brémond, Claude, 113
Broch, Hermann, *The Death of Virgil*, 22, 29, 85, 116
Brontë, Charlotte, *Jane Eyre*, 19
Brook-Rose, Christine, 146
Brooks, Cleanth, and Warren, R. P., 11
Brooks, Peter, 38, 40, 49n, 54–55
Bruss, Elizabeth, 30–31
Büchner, Georg, *Lenz*, 22, 85, 121
Bühler, Karl, 24
Burgess, Anthony: *Napoleon Symphony*, 155; *Nothing Like the Sun*, 22, 121
Butler, Samuel, *The Way of All Flesh*, 29

Campion, Pierre, 71n
Camus, Albert, 71
Carrard, Philippe, 115n, 121n, 157n
Casparis, Christian, 100n
Certeau, Michel de, 38, 44, 115
Cervantes, Miguel de, *Don Quixote*, 38
Charcot, Martin, 45
Chateaubriand, René de, 67
Chatman, Seymour, 109n, 111n, 119n, 129n
Chekhov, Anton, 97n
Christian, R. F., 158n
Clarendon, Edward Hyde, 20–21
Coetzee, J. M., 106n; *In the Heart of the Country*, 97; *The Master of Petersburg*, 15, 85, 159; *Waiting for the Barbarians*, viii, 97, 101–3, 105n
Cohen, Walter, 169n
Cohn, Dorrit, 16n, 25, 26n, 36n, 100n, 104n, 107n, 174–75, 179n, 180n
Collingwood, R. G., 27n, 155–56
Conrad, Joseph, 29, 38, 43; *Heart of Darkness*, 38

Corneille, Pierre, 7
Corngold, Stanley, 39n
Culler, Jonathan, 115n

Danto, Arthur, 86n, 173–74
Davis, Lennard J., 1, 3, 93n, 171–72
Day, Geoffrey, 3n
Defoe, Daniel, 169n; *Robinson Crusoe,* 3
Delacroix, Eugène, 79
Delay, Jean, 28n
Deleuze, Giles, 70
De Man, Paul, 7, 33, 68, 75–76, 78
Demetz, Peter, 158
Derrida, Jacques, 39n, 77, 123
Descombes, Vincent, 74
Dickens, Charles, 38, 41n, 168n; *David Copperfield,* 42, 98, 125; *A Tale of Two Cities,* 154n
Diderot, Denis de, 7
Dilthey, Wilhelm, 27, 155
Döblin, Alfred, 153, 162; *Wallenstein,* 160
Doctorow, E. L., 8
Doležel, Lubomír, 129n
Dostoevsky, Feodor, 26, 38, 41n, 159; *A Gentle Creature,* 36; *Notes from Underground,* 162; *The Possessed,* 162
Doubrovsky, Serge, 58; *Fils,* 32n, 94
Doyle, Conan, 38
Dujardink, Edouard, *Les Lauriers sont coupés,* 36, 104
Duras, Marguerite: *The Lover,* 34; *Moderato Cantabile,* 120
During, Simon, 172–73

Eakin, Paul John, 1, 2n, 32n
Eickenbaum, Boris, 153n
Eliot, George, 168; *The Lifted Veil,* 176n
Eliot, T. S., 8
Ellison, David, 67–68
Ellmann, Richard, 36n
Emerson, Caryl, 26n
Emerson, Ralph Waldo, 71
Exley, Frederick, *A Fan's Notes,* 94

Faulkner, William, 38; *Absalom, Absalom!* 38; *The Sound and the Fury,* 116

Feuchtwanger, Lion, 22
Fielding, Henry, 169n, 178; *Tom Jones,* 170n, 177
Fitzgerald, Scott, *The Great Gatsby,* 43
Flaubert, Gustave, 165, 177–79; *Madame Bovary,* 15; *A Sentimental Education,* 14, 162; *A Simple Heart,* 22
Fleischman, Suzanne, 102n
Fliess, Wilhelm, 56
Fludernik, Monika, 12n, 97n
Foley, Barbara, 20n
Foucault, Michel, 76, 123, 163–80
Fowles, John, *The French Lieutenant's Woman,* 63n, 161
Freud, Sigmund, viii, 4, 23, 38–57, 77, 91, 92
Friedländer, Saul, 61
Frisch, Max, *Gantenbein,* 83
Frye, Northrop, 31, 113
Fuentes, Carlos, *The Death of Artemio Cruz,* 22

Gallie, W. B., 113
Garrett, George, 154
Gay, Peter, 47
Gearhart, Suzanne, 7
Genette, Gérard, viii, 1, 10, 11n, 25, 61n, 65n, 67–69, 72n, 74, 76–78, 93, 99–100, 108–9, 111n, 116, 119–20, 122–25, 127, 175, 176n, 177
Geppert, Hans Vilmar, 160n
Ghose, Zulfikar, 1
Gide, André: *The Counterfeiters,* 162; *The Immoralist,* 33, 66
Gill, Christopher, and T. P. Wiseman, 10n
Glowínski, Michál, 30, 36, 98
Godzich, Wlad, 8
Goethe, Johann Wolfgang von, 4, 71, 80, 98
Goffman, Erving, 93
Goodman, Nelson, 4, 173–74
Grass, Günter, *Cat and Mouse,* 43, 122
Grésillon, A., J. L. Lebrave, and C. Violet, 72n
Guerard, Albert, 33, 66n

Habermas, Jürgen, 27n
Hamburger, Käte, viii, 6, 10, 15, 16n,
    23–26, 30, 32, 70n, 81n, 86, 97–98,
    100n, 127, 158
Hamon, Philippe, 171, 178n, 180n
Hamsun, Knut, *Hunger,* 34, 107n
Harrison, Ross, 5n, 170n
Harshaw, Benjamin, 13, 14n, 113n
Hauptmann, Gerhart, 105n
Hawthorne, Nathaniel: *The Blithedale
    Romance,* 176; *The Marble Faun,*
    176n; *The Scarlet Letter,* 176n
Hegel, Georg Wilhelm Friedrich, 8, 71,
    171
Heissenbüttel, Helmut, 83
Heller, Erich, 138n, 143n
Hemingway, Ernest, *The Killers,*
    120–21
Hernadi, Paul, 124–25
Hildesheimer, Wolfgang, *Marbot,* viii,
    29, 79–95
Hoffman, E. T. A.: *The Golden Flower-
    pot,* 63n; *Meister Floh,* 176n
Huet, Pierre Daniel, 10, 11n
Hugo, Victor, 160
Hull, Richard, 176
Hume, David, 3, 8
Hutcheon, Linda, 14n, 113n, 161n

Ibsen, Henrik, 41
Imbs, Paul, 99n
Iser, Wolfgang, 1, 4n, 5n, 6n, 12n,
    179n

James, Henry, 1, 11, 25, 38, 83, 107, 161,
    167–68, 174, 177–78; *The Golden Bowl,*
    168; *The Princess Casamassima,* 168;
    What Maisie Knew, 177
Janet, Pierre, 45
Jauss, Hans Robert, 178
Jens, Walter, 187
Jensen, Wilhelm, *Gradiva,* 45
Jones, Ernest, 23
Joyce, James, 36–38; *A Portrait of the
    Artist,* 25, 42, 128; *Ulysses,* 18, 36, 99,
    103–4, 116, 152
Jung, C. G., 48

Kafka, Franz, 27, 97n, 106n; *The Castle,*
    13–14, 128, 162
Kant, Immanuel, 4, 8, 71
Kawin, Bruce H., 30n
Kayser, Wolfgang, 124, 178n
Keller, Ulrich, 11n
Kermode, Frank, 5–6
Kesting, Hanjo, 83n
Kittler, Friedrich, 38, 52n
Kierkegaard, Søren, 71
Kosinski, Jerzy, *The Painted Bird,* 34–35
Kracauer, Siegfried, 28n
Kristeva, Julia, 58
Kühn, Dieter, *N,* 161

LaCapra, Dominick, 169n, 178–79, 180n
Lamarque, Peter, and Stein Haugom
    Olsen, 2n, 4n, 5n, 9n, 17n
Lang, Berel, 2n
Lanser, Susan, 180
Lejeune, Philippe, viii, 30–32, 34,
    59–60, 64, 67–68, 125
Levin, Harry, 36
Ludwig, Emil, 28
Lukács, Georg, 121, 154–55, 160n
Lytton, Bulwer, 22

MacDonald, Margaret, 13n
Mahoney, Patrick, 40n, 49n, 52n
Malcolm, Janet, 49n
Mann, Heinrich, 160n
Mann, Thomas, 16, 38, 144, 148–49;
    The Beloved Returns, 22, 85, 155; *Death
    in Venice,* ix, 22, 30n, 84–85, 128–30,
    132–49; *Doctor Faustus,* 15, 29, 43, 60,
    65n, 87–88, 130n, 149; *Felix Krull,*
    30n, 32, 71, 125; *The Magic Mountain,*
    9, 16, 96, 116; *Tonio Kröger,* 30n, 42,
    144
Mannoni, Maud, 1
Marcus, Steven, 38, 40–41, 44, 47, 49n,
    51
Margolin, Uri, 13n, 14n
Marquand, Odo, 12n
Martin-Chauffier, Louis, 67
Martínez-Bonati, Félix, 16n, 73n, 89n,
    126–27, 129, 130n, 133n, 179n

May, Georges, 33
McCarthy, Mary, 2
McCormick, Peter, 8
McHale, Brian, 25, 94, 120n, 127, 156, 158, 161n
Mereshkowski, Dmitri, 22
Miller, D. A., 164–66, 167n, 169–73, 176, 178–80
Miller, Henry, *The Tropic of Cancer*, 35
Mink, Louis, 113–14
Montaigne, Michel de, 71
Montesquieu, Charles Louis de, 7
Morris, Humphrey, 40n
Morson, Gary Saul, 151n, 152n, 160n
Muller, Marcel, 61n, 66n, 67n, 70n
Murdoch, Iris, *The Red and the Green*, 117
Musil, Robert, *The Man without Qualities*, 71n

Nabokov, Vladimir, 38, 61, 86, 98; *Lolita*, 86, 125; *Pale Fire*, 50n; *The Real Life of Sebastian Knight*, 30
Nägele, Rainer, 42n, 44n, 49n
Nash, Christopher, 174n
Nerval, Gérard de, *Aurélia*, 34
Neumann, Ann Waldron, 102n
Newton, Isaac, 4
Nietzsche, Friedrich, 4
Nünning, Ansgar, 153n, 161n

Ondaatje, Michael, *The English Patient*, 159
Ong, Walter, 1

Parsons, Terence, 153
Pascal, Roy, 178n, 179n
Pavel, Thomas G., 3, 7n, 110n, 113, 153n
Pawel, Ernst, 27n
Persico, Joseph E., 157
Pike, Burton, 133n, 140n, 144n
Pirsig, Robert, *Zen and the Art of Motorcycle Maintenance*, 97
Potts, L. J., 10n
Plato, 139, 143
Prendergast, Christopher, 174n
Prince, Gerald, 109n, 111n, 113

Proust, Marcel, 38, 58, 123; *A la Recherche du temps perdu*, viii, 9, 13, 15, 36, 58–78
Pugh, Anthony Cheal, 67n

Rayburn, Sir Henry, 79
Récanati, François, 173
Remarque, Erich Maria, 97n
Reed, T. J., 132n, 140, 146–48
Ricoeur, Paul, vii, 9, 19n, 42n, 57, 67, 96, 111, 113–14, 117n, 157
Riffaterre, Michael, 1, 3
Rigney, Ann, 121n, 153
Rilke, Rainer Maria, 8; *Malte Laurids Brigge*, 38, 162
Rimmon-Kenan, Shlomith, 96, 109n, 111n, 119n
Robbe-Grillet, Alain, 172n
Roberts, Thomas J., 1
Roloff, Volker, 72n
Ronen, Ruth, 153
Rousseau, Jean-Jacques, 4, 7, 19, 33, 67
Roussel, Raymond, 172n
Ryan, Marie-Laure, 12n, 13, 126n, 153, 154n

Sarraute, Nathalie: *Martereau*, 97; *Portrait of an Unknown Man*, 97
Sartre, Jean-Paul, 174, 178; *L'Enfance d'un chef*, 180; *Nausea*, 96
Schabert, Ina, 22n, 28n, 84n
Schaeffer, Jean-Marie, 161
Schafer, Roy, 42n, 50
Schama, Simon, 157
Schmidt, Siegfried J., 110n
Schnitzler, Arthur, 45; *Fräulein Else*, 99, 104; *Leutnant Gustl*, 104
Scholes, Robert, 16n, 96
Scott, Sir Walter, 121, 154, 160
Searle, John, 20n, 117, 126
Seltzer, Mark, 166–72, 176, 178–80
Sherwood, Michael, 42n
Simon, Claude, 67
Sloan, James Park, 34n
Smith, Adam, 169n
Smith, Barbara Herrnstein, 7, 20–21, 23, 30, 35n, 111n, 117n

Stael, Germaine de, 11
Stanley, Patricia H., 80n
Stanzel, Franz K., 22n, 100, 108, 119n, 177
Stendhal: *La Chartreuse de Parme,* 15, 151; *La Vie d'Henri Brulard,* 67
Stern, J. P., 79, 80, 92
Sternberg, Meir, 126n
Stevens, Wallace, 1, 6, 8
Stewart, Philip, 3
Stierle, Karheinz, 18n, 112n
Stone, Irving, 22–23, 29
Stratchey, Lytton, 19, 22, 27
Struve, Gleb, 152n
Sturgess, Philip M., 12n
Styron, William, *The Confessions of Nat Turner,* 32n
Sukenik, Ronald, 8; *Up,* 94
Suleiman, Susan Rubin, 180n
Swales, Martin, 92n

Tadié, Jean Ives, 61n, 67n
Todorov, Tzvetan, 109n, 113
Toliver, Harold, 6n
Tolstoy, Leo, 22; *Anna Karenina,* 13; *The Death of Ivan Ilyitch,* 20–21, 37; *War and Peace,* ix, 150–62
Tournier, Michel, 154n
Toynbee, Arnold, 8
Trimpi, Wesley, 10n
Trollope, Anthony, 165, 166n
Tuchmann, Barbara, 118
Turner, Joseph W., 121n, 158

Ullmann, Stephen, 179n
Unamuno, Miguel de, *Mist,* 63n, 171

Updike, John, 27
Uspensky, Boris, 134n

Vaihinger, Hans, 1, 2, 4–6, 40n
Veyne, Paul, 155
Vidal, Gore, *Lincoln,* 116
Voltaire, François Marie Arouet, 7
von Gronicka, André, 145n

Walker, Percy, *The Moviegoer,* 97
Wapnewski, Peter, 80n
Warning, Rainer, 76–78
Weinrich, Harald, 99n
Weinstein, Mark A., 155
Weisstein, Ulrich, 80n
Wesseling, Elizabeth, 153n
White, Hayden, 3, 8, 9n, 111n, 113–14
Williams, Raymond, 2n
Wilson, Edmund, 35
Wilson, Jonathan, 94n
Wolfe, Tom, 24n, 94n
Wolfson, Nessa, 99n
Wood, Gordon S., 157
Woolf, Virginia, 28, 38, 55; *Mrs. Dalloway,* 9, 18, 152
Wright, Susan, 107n

Yacobi, Tamar, 73n, 89n, 148
Yehoshua, A. B., *The Lover,* 37
Yerushalmi, Yosel Hayim, 44n, 47n
Young, James E., 157
Yourcenar, Marguerite, *Hadrian's Memoirs,* 32n, 116

Zavarzadeh, Mas'ud, 29n
Zola, Emile, 64, 165, 174

The Library of Congress has cataloged the hardcover edition of this book as follows:

Cohn, Dorrit.
The distinction of fiction / Dorrit Cohn.
p.   cm.
Expansion of material first delivered in a Christian Gauss Seminar
at Princeton University: many chapters are rev. versions of articles
previously published in various sources.
Includes bibliographical references and index.
ISBN 0-8018-5942-5 (alk. paper)
1. History in literature.   2. Narration (Rhetoric)   3. Mimesis in
literature.   4. Fiction—History and criticism.   I. Title.
PN50.C64   1998
809.3′9358—dc21   98-6733
CIP

ISBN 0-8018-6522-0